TO THE MOON

The Revolutionary Cryptocurrency Guide that Shocked America. How 937 American People with No-Experience Enter the Crypto World and Monetize from the First Day. Home-Based Business Tips and Tricks Included

By

Iruka Nakamoto

This document is geared towards providing exact and reliable information regarding the topic and issue covered. The publication is sold with the idea that the publisher is not required to render accounting, officially permitted, or otherwise, qualified services. Suppose advice is necessary, legal, or professional. In that case, a practiced individual in the profession should be ordered from a Declaration of Principles, which was accepted and approved equally by a Committee of the American Bar Association and a Committee of Publishers and Associations. In no way is it legal to reproduce, duplicate, or transmit any part of this document in either electronic means or printed format. Recording of this publication is strictly prohibited, and any storage of this document is not allowed unless with written permission from the publisher. All rights reserved.

The information provided herein is stated to be truthful and consistent. In terms of inattention or otherwise, any liability, by any usage or abuse of any policies, processes, or directions contained within is the recipient reader's solitary and utter responsibility. Under no circumstances will any legal responsibility or blame be held against the publisher for reparation, damages, or monetary loss due to the information herein, either directly or indirectly.

Table of Contents

Bubble or Revolution? The Basics of Bitcoin and Blockchain.

Chapter 1. What Is Bitcoin? 19

Chapter 2. What is Blockchain? 38

Chapter 3. Understanding the Crypto Market..............................70

Chapter 4. Investing in Crypto Market 82

Chapter 5. The Beginner's Guide 98

The Cryptocurrency Investing | Advanced Guide

Chapter 1. Understanding cryptocurrency 126

Chapter 2. Mining of Cryptocurrency 165

Chapter 3. Before You Begin 195

Chapter 4. Are cryptocurrencies a good investment? 238

Private Label Crash Course

Introduction 251

Chapter 1: Getting Started-Private Label................................258

1.1 What is Private Label?..259

1.2 Private Label Categories 259

1.3 Different types of Private Label as profitable strategies 260

1.4 White Label vs. Private Label Dropshipping? 262

1.5 Dropshipping Private Label..267

1.6 Deciding What to Private Label 269

Chapter 2: Profitable Strategies in Building Six-Figure Business .278

2.1 Private Label for Profitability 278

2.2 9+1 Pricing Strategies..284

2.3 Best Practices in Private Label Branding 291

2.4 Positives and Negatives of Private Label.............................294

2.5 Keys to Private Label Greatness 297

Chapter 3: Finding the Products & Starting Your Personal Brand

....304

3.1 How to Start Your Private Label Brand from Scratch?..........306

3.2 Understand the costs of private labeling 308

3.3 Choosing the Right Products 322

3.4 Building a Team and Starting your Personal Brand 327

Conclusion 334

<u>Short Stays Real Estate with No (or Low) Money Down</u>

Introduction 341

CHAPTER 1: Understand Income and Importance of Passive Income 345

1.1 Active Income 345

1.2 Portfolio Income 348

1.3 Passive Income 350

1.4 Taxing of passive income 354

1.5 Why Passive Income Beats Earned Income 355

1.6 Reasons Why Passive Income Is So Important 357

CHAPTER 2: Passive income ideas to help you make money in 2021 364

2.1 How many streams of income should you have? 365

2.2 Passive income ideas for building wealth 366

2.3 Selling information products 366

2.4 Rental income 367

2.5 Affiliate marketing 369

2.6 Flip retail products 371

2.7 Peer-to-peer lending 372

2.8 Dividend stocks 374

2.9 Create an app 375

2.10 REITs 376

2.11 A bond ladder 378

2.12 Invest in a high-yield CD or savings account 380

2.13 Buy Property...381

2.14 Rent out your home short-term through Airbnb 382

2.15 Air BnB Business as a Passive income Strategy 383

2.16 Advertise on your car 388

2.17 Invest in Stocks...389

2.18 Make Your Car Work for You.......................................390

2.19 Sell your Videos 391

2.20 Create YouTube Videos 392

2.21 Write an eBook 392

2.22 Sell Digital Products 393

2.23 CPC Ads (Cost Per Click) 394

2.24 Minimize your taxes on passive income............................395

CHAPTER 3:   Airbnb Offers The Best Passive Income Generation Strategy...397

3.1 Understand the Vacation Rental Industry...........................398

3.2 Create a Maintenance Management System 399

3.3 Put Together a Vacation Rental Marketing Strategy 400

3.4 Invest in Property Management Tools 401

3.5 Outline Your Guest Management Strategy 403

3.6 Set a Reasonable (But Competitive) Price..........................404

3.7 How an Airbnb Business Works 405

3.8 The Bottom Line..417

Conclusion 419

The 9+1 Best Home-Based Business Model of 2021

Introduction 425

CHAPTER 1: The Nirma Washing Powder's Success Story 429

1.1 Invention of Nirma detergent? 429

1.2 Karsanbhai Patel's sale policy for Nirma detergent...............432

1.3 Invest In Research and Development.......................................434

1.4 No Higher Costs...435

1.5 Be Proactive in your approach as it is beneficial for the business 437

1.6 Provide Customers with 'Value for Money' 437

1.7 Define Your Segment 438

1.8 Focus on Building a Brand 439

1.9 Astutely Manage the Brand Wars 440

1.10 Diversify the Portfolio...443

1.11 Conclusion 444

1.12 What Karsanbhai Patel and Nirma detergent did for the Indian Economy 445

1.13 Karsanbhai Patel's ventures other than the Nirma detergent 446

CHAPTER 2: Start a Profitable Soap Making Business 448

2.1 What will you name your business?...................................454

2.2 Form a legal entity 455

2.3 Small Business Taxes..456

2.4 Open a business bank account & credit card 456

2.5 Open a business bank account...456

2.6 Get a business credit card..457

2.7 Obtain necessary permits and licenses...............................457

2.8 State & Local Business Licensing Requirements 458

2.9 Labor safety requirements...458

2.10 Certificate of Occupancy 458

2.11 Trademark & Copyright Protection...................................459

2.12 Get business insurance...460

2.13 Learn more about General Liability Insurance 460

2.14 Define your brand...460

2.15 Soap Making Plan...462

2.16 Soap selling process...472

2.17 Soap making supplies...474

2.18 Marketing area for soap..474

2.19 Total investment..475

2.20 Selling price...476

2.21 Profit margin..476

2.22 Precaution...477

2.23 Risk..477

2.24 Conclusion..478

2.25 Advantage of starting a soap making business at home.....478

2.26 How Much Money Can You Make Making Soap?..............479

CHAPTER 3: Start a Profitable Candle Making Business.............480

3.1 Steps for starting a candle making business..........................480

3.2 How much can you charge customers? 485

3.3 Benefits of candle making business 497

Conclusion 499

Bookkeeping and QuickBooks Made Easy

Introduction..509

Chapter 1. Bookkeeping 515

1.1. What is Bookkeeping? 515

1.2. Who is A bookkeeper?...516

1.3. Importance of Bookkeeping....................................518

1.4. Type of Accounting Method....................................519

1.5. What do the bookkeepers do? 520

1.5.1. Record the Transactions Each Day.......................521

1.5.2. Sending Invoices to Clients 521

1.5.3. Keep Track of Payments 522

1.5.4. Being Responsible for the Payable Ledger 522

1.5.5. Responsible for Managing the Cash Flow 522

1.5.6. Compile All Accounts 523

1.6. How can a Bookkeeper be Beneficial for Business?.............523

1.6.1. Let you Focus on Your Business Strategy 524

1.6.2. The Accounting Cost can be Saved. 524

1.6.3. Double Check Your Cashflow...525

1.6.4. Be Informed of Current Financial Situation: 525

1.6.5. The Financial Data is Organized 525

Chapter 2. QuickBooks Explained 527

1.7. 2.1. What is QuickBooks? 527

2.1.1. QuickBooks 528

2.1.2. The History of QuickBooks 529

1.8. 2.2. QuickBooks Features 529

2.2.1. user Friendly 530

2.2.2. Data Migration 530

2.2.3 Smooth Navigation 530

2.2.4. Smooth Transactions 531

2.2.5. Invoices 531

2.2.6. Calculate Tax..531

2.2.7. Projections 532

1.9. 2.3. Set-up QuickBooks 532

2.3.1. Start 533

2.3.2. setup 533

2.3.3. Vendor Setup 534

2.3.4. Setup Employee Accounts.......................................534

2.3.5. Set Up Customer Account 535

2.3.6. Setup Report Generation 535

1.10.   2.4. Using QuickBooks 536

2.4.1. Chart of Accounts 536

2.4.2. Other Lists...537

2.4.3. The Reports 538

2.4.4. payroll 539

1.11.   2.5. QuickBooks Versions 539

Chapter 3. Choosing the Best Version of QuickBooks....................541

1.12.   3.1. QuickBooks for Self-Employed 545

3.1.1. QuickBooks Self Employed Package 546

3.1.2. QuickBooks for Self-Employed Tax Bundle 546

3.1.3. QuickBooks for Self-Employed Live Tax Bundle 547

3.1.4. Benefit 547

3.1.5. Drawback 547

1.13.   3.2. QuickBooks Online...548

3.2.1. Common Features...549

3.2.2. QuickBooks Online Simple Start 550

3.2.3. QuickBooks Online Essentials 550

3.2.4. QuickBooks Online Plus 550

3.2.5. QuickBooks Online Advanced.....................................551

3.2.6. Benefits..551

3.2.7. Drawbacks..551

1.14.   3.3. QuickBooks Desktop...552

3.3.1. QuickBooks Desktop Pro:..552

3.3.2. QuickBooks Desktop Premier:....................................553

3.3.3. QuickBooks Desktop Enterprise:................................553

3.3.4. QuickBooks Desktop Plus and QuickBooks Desktop Pro
....554

3.3.5. QuickBooks for Mac 554

1.15.   3.4. QuickBooks Apps 555

3.4.1. QuickBooks Payments...555

3.4.2. QuickBooks Point of Sale 555

3.4.3. QuickBooks Payroll 556

1.16.   3.5. Find the Best Version for You........................556

3.5.1. Read Reviews...557

3.5.2. Take an Online Survey 557

3.5.3. Talk to an Expert. 557

Chapter 4. The Best Way to Make Money In 2021 558

1.17.   4.1. Salary of Part-Time QuickBooks Bookkeepers 559

1.18.   4.2. The Top 10 Highest Paying Cities for Bookkeepers in the USA..562

1.19.   4.3. Best Paying QuickBooks Bookkeeping Jobs in the USA 565

4.3.1. CPA Firm Bookkeeper...566

4.3.2. QuickBooks Remote Bookkeeper 567

4.3.3. Telecommute Bookkeeper 567

4.3.4. At Home Bookkeeper 567

4.3.5. QuickBooks Consultant 568

Chapter 5. Becoming a QuickBooks Bookkeeper 568

1.20.   5.1. The Type of Investment Required for Certification...570

1.21. 5.2. The Different Courses Offered 571

1.22. 5.3. Information About QuickBooks Certification............571

1.23. 5.4. Why Should You Invest..573

1.24. 5.5. The Certification Fee 574

1.25. 5.6. The Length of Courses 575

Chapter 6. Hacks and Tricks for QuickBooks 578

1.26. 6.1. Cash Receipts Should be Created...................................579

1.27. 6.2. Use Attachments..580

1.28. 6.3. Use Keyboard Shortcuts 582

1.29. 6.4. Automate the emails. 583

1.30. 6.5. Use the QuickBooks Online to Track Time 583

1.31. 6.6. Always use the Bank Rules 584

Chapter 7. QuickBooks Usage in Small Businesses 585

1.32. 7.1. Make and Track Invoices...586

1.33. 7.2. Monitor Expenses and Other Bills 586

1.34. 7.3. Generate Business Financial Statements 587

1.35. 7.4. Manage Payroll 587

1.36. 7.5. Do the Inventory...588

1.37.   7.6. Simplify Taxes 588

1.38.   7.7. Online Payments 589

1.39.   7.8. Record Receipts 589

1.40.   7.9. Manage Mileage 589

Conclusion 590

Bubble or Revolution? The Basics of Bitcoin and Blockchain.

The Idiot-Proof Guide to Understand the Crypto Market and Become a Skilled Investor and Trader Starting from Scratch.

By

Iruka Nakamoto

Table of Contents

Chapter 1. What Is Bitcoin? 19

Chapter 2. What is Blockchain? 38

Chapter 3. Understanding the Crypto Market 70

Chapter 4. Investing in Crypto Market 82

Chapter 5. The Beginner's Guide 98

Chapter 1. What Is Bitcoin?

Bitcoin is advanced cash that was made in January 2009. It follows the thoughts set out in a white paper by the strange and pseudonymous Satoshi Nakamoto.The personality of the individual or people who made the innovation is as yet a secret. Bitcoin offers the guarantee of lower exchange charges than conventional online installment instruments, and, not at all like officially sanctioned monetary forms, it is worked by a decentralized position.

Bitcoin is a sort of cryptographic money. There are no physical bitcoins and just adjusts on a public record that everybody has straightforward admittance to. A monstrous measure of processing power checks all bitcoin exchanges. Bitcoins are not given or supported by any banks or governments, nor are individual bitcoins significant as a product. Notwithstanding it not being legitimate delicate, Bitcoin is well known and has set off many other digital forms of money, altogether alluded to as Altcoin. Bitcoin is normally condensed as "BTC."

Understanding Bitcoin

The bitcoin framework is an assortment of PCs (additionally alluded to as "hubs" or "diggers") that all run bitcoin's code and store its blockchain. Allegorically, a blockchain can be considered as an assortment of squares. In each square is an assortment of exchanges. Since every one of the PCs running the blockchain has similar rundown of squares and exchanges and can straightforwardly see these new squares being loaded up with new bitcoin exchanges, nobody can swindle the framework.

Regardless of whether they run a bitcoin "hub" or not, anybody can see these exchanges happening live. To accomplish a scandalous demonstration, a troublemaker would have to work 51% of the registering power that makes up bitcoin. Bitcoin has around 12,000 hubs as of January 2021, and this number is developing, making such an assault very unlikely.

In any case, if an assault were to occur, the bitcoin diggers, individuals who participate in the bitcoin network with their PC, would almost certainly fork to another blockchain putting forth the attempt the agitator set forth to accomplish the assault a waste.

Equilibriums of bitcoin tokens are kept utilizing public and hidden "keys," which are long series of numbers and letters connected through the numerical encryption calculation used to make them. The public key (similar to a financial balance number) fills in as the location distributed to the world and to which others may send bitcoins.

The private key (similar to an ATM PIN) is intended to be a watched secret and simply used to approve Bitcoin transmissions. Bitcoin keys ought not to be mistaken for a bitcoin wallet, a physical or computerized gadget that works with the exchanging of bitcoin and permits clients to follow responsibility for. The expression "wallet" is somewhat deceptive, as bitcoin's decentralized nature implies that it is rarely put away "in" a wallet but instead appropriately on a blockchain.

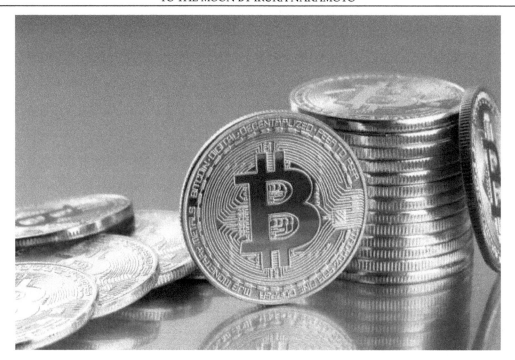

Peer-to-Peer Technology

Bitcoin is one of the main advanced monetary standards to utilize distributed innovation to work with moment installments. The autonomous people and organizations that own the overseeing figuring control and take an interest in the bitcoin network bitcoin "excavators" are accountable for handling the exchanges on the blockchain and are roused by remunerations (the arrival of new bitcoin) and exchange charges paid in bitcoin.

These excavators can be considered as the decentralized authority upholding the validity of the bitcoin network. New bitcoin is delivered to the diggers at a fixed yet intermittently declining rate. There is just 21 million bitcoin that can be mined altogether. As of January 30, 2021, there are around 18,614,806 bitcoin in presence and 2,385,193 bitcoin left to be mined.

Along these lines, bitcoin other digital forms of money work uniquely in contrast to fiat cash; in unified financial frameworks, the cash is delivered at a rate coordinating with the development in merchandise; this framework is proposed to keep up value steadiness. A decentralized framework, as bitcoin, sets the delivery rate early and as per a calculation.

Bitcoin Mining

Bitcoin mining is the interaction by which bitcoins are delivered into dissemination. By and large, mining requires settling computationally troublesome riddles to find another square, which is added to the blockchain.

Bitcoin mining adds and confirms exchange records across the organization. Excavators are compensated with a couple bitcoins; the prize is split each 210,000 squares. The square prize was 50 new bitcoins in 2009. On May 11, 2020, the third splitting happened, bringing the prize for each square revelation down to 6.25 bitcoins.

An assortment of equipment can be utilized to mine bitcoin. Nonetheless, some yield higher prizes than others. Certain CPUs, called Application-Specific Integrated Circuits (ASIC), and further developed handling units, similar to Graphic Processing Units (GPUs), can accomplish more rewards. These intricate mining processors are known as "mining rigs."

One bitcoin is detachable to eight decimal spots (100 millionths of one bitcoin), and this littlest unit is alluded to as a Satoshi if important. On the off chance that the taking interest diggers acknowledge the change, Bitcoin could at last be distinguishable to much more decimal spots.

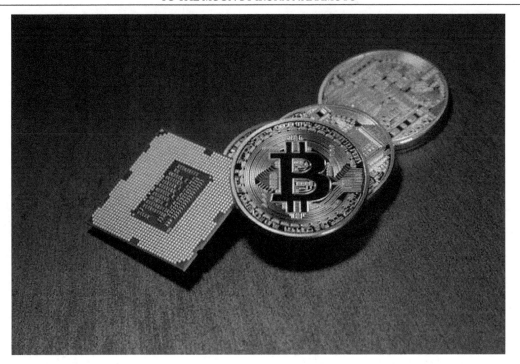

History of Bitcoin

August 18, 2008

The area name bitcoin.org is enrolled. Today, this space is "WhoisGuard Protected," which means the personality of the individual who enrolled it isn't public data.

October 31, 2008

An individual or gathering utilizing the name Satoshi Nakamoto makes a declaration on The Cryptography Mailing list at metzdowd.com: "I've been chipping away at another electronic money framework that is completely distributed, with no confided in outsider. This now-acclaimed whitepaper distributed on bitcoin.org, named "Bitcoin: A Peer-to-Peer Electronic Cash System," would turn into the Magna Carta for how Bitcoin works today.

January 3, 2009

The principal Bitcoin block is mined Block 0. This progression is otherwise called the "beginning square" and contains the content: "The Times 03/Jan/2009 Chancellor near the very edge of second bailout for banks," maybe as evidence that the square was mined on or after that date, and maybe likewise as significant political commentary.

Jan. 8, 2009

The principal variant of the bitcoin programming is reported on The Cryptography Mailing list.

January 9, 2009

Square 1 is mined, and bitcoin mining begins vigorously.

Who Is Satoshi Nakamoto?

No one understands who made bitcoin, or if nothing else not conclusively. Satoshi Nakamoto is the name related with the individual or social event of people who conveyed the main Bitcoin white paper in 2008 and worked on the primary Bitcoin programming conveyed in 2009. Since that time, various individuals have either declared to be or have been proposed as the certifiable people behind the nom de plume. Regardless, as of January 2021, the certified character (or characters) behind Satoshi stays blurred.

Despite the fact that it is enticing to accept the media's twist that Satoshi Nakamoto is a lone, impractical virtuoso who made Bitcoin out of nowhere, such advancements don't ordinarily occur in a vacuum. Regardless of how unique appearing, all major logical revelations were based on beforehand existing exploration.

There are forerunners to Bitcoin: Adam Back's Hashcash, imagined in 1997,8 and thusly Wei Dai's b-cash, Nick Szabo's touch gold, and Hal Finney's Reusable Proof of Work. The bitcoin whitepaper itself refers to Hashcash and b-cash and different works traversing a few examination fields. Maybe obviously, a considerable lot of the people behind different ventures named above have been estimated to have likewise had a section in making bitcoin.

There are a couple of potential inspirations for bitcoin's creators choosing to stay quiet. One is protection: As bitcoin has acquired in notoriety—turning out to be something of an overall wonder— Satoshi Nakamoto would almost certainly collect a ton of consideration from the media and governments...

Another explanation could be the potential for bitcoin to cause a significant interruption in the current banking and financial frameworks. On the off chance that bitcoin were to acquire mass selection, the framework could outperform countries' sovereign fiat monetary standards. This danger to existing cash could propel governments to need to make a lawful move against bitcoin's maker.

The other explanation is wellbeing. 32,489 squares were mined; at the award pace of 50 bitcoin per block, the absolute payout in 2009 was 1,624,500 bitcoin. One may reason that solitary Satoshi and maybe a couple of others were mining through 2009 and have a dominant part of that reserve of bitcoin.

Somebody possessing that much bitcoin could turn into an objective of crooks, particularly since bitcoins are less similar to stocks and more like money. The private keys expected to approve spending could be printed out and held under a sleeping pad. The designer of Bitcoin would avoid potential risk to make any blackmail prompted moves discernible; staying mysterious is a decent path for Satoshi to restrict openness.

Special Considerations
Bitcoin as a Form of Payment

Bitcoins can be acknowledged as methods for installment for items sold or benefits gave. Physical stores can show a sign saying "Bitcoin Accepted Here"; the exchanges can be taken care of with the imperative equipment terminal or wallet address through QR codes and contact screen applications. An online business can undoubtedly acknowledge bitcoins by adding this installment alternative to its other online installment choices: Mastercards, PayPal, and so on

Bitcoin Employment Opportunities

The individuals who are independently employed can find paid for a line of work identified with bitcoin. There are a few different ways to accomplish this, for example, making any web access and adding your bitcoin wallet address to the website as a type of installment. There are additionally a few sites and occupation sheets that are committed to computerized monetary standards:

- Cryptogrind unites work searchers and imminent managers through its site.
- Coinality highlights occupations—independent, low maintenance and full-time—that offer installment in bitcoins, just as other digital currencies like Dogecoin and Litecoin
- Jobs4Bitcoins, part of reddit.com
- BitGigs
- Bitwage offers an approach to pick a level of your work check to be changed over into bitcoin and shipped off your bitcoin address.

Putting resources into Bitcoins

Numerous Bitcoin allies accept that advanced cash is what's to come. Numerous people who underwrite bitcoin accept that it works with a lot quicker, low-expense installment framework for exchanges around the world. Albeit any administration or national bank doesn't back it, bitcoin can be traded for conventional monetary forms; truth be told, its conversion scale against the dollar draws in expected financial backers and brokers intrigued by cash plays. For sure, one of the essential purposes behind the development of computerized monetary standards like bitcoin is that they can go about as an option in contrast to public fiat cash and conventional wares like gold.

In March 2014, the IRS expressed that every virtual cash, including bitcoins, would be burdened as property instead of money. Gains or misfortunes from bitcoins held as capital will be acknowledged as capital increases or misfortunes, while bitcoins held as stock will cause normal additions or misfortunes. The offer of bitcoins that you mined or bought from another gathering, or the utilization of bitcoins to pay for merchandise or administrations, is instances of exchanges that can be burdened.

Like some other resource, the standard of purchasing low and selling high applies to bitcoins. The most famous method of storing up the money is through purchasing on a bitcoin trade, however there are numerous alternate approaches to procure and claim bitcoins.

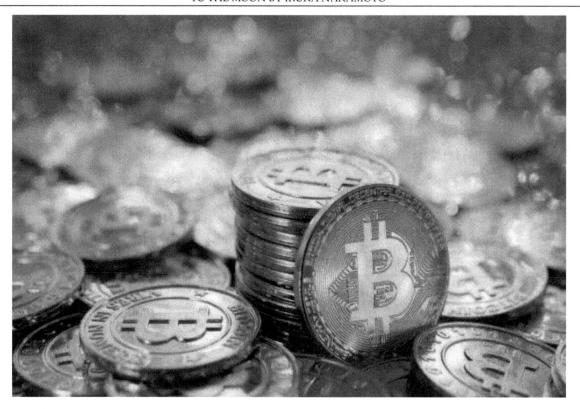

Types of Risks Associated With Bitcoin Investing

In spite of the fact that Bitcoin was not planned as an ordinary value venture (no offers have been given), some theoretical financial backers were attracted to the computerized cash after it appreciated quickly in May 2011 and again in November 2013. Subsequently, numerous individuals buy bitcoin for its speculation esteem as opposed to its capacity to go about as a mode of trade.

Nonetheless, the absence of ensured worth and its advanced nature implies the buy and utilization of bitcoins conveys a few inalienable dangers. Numerous financial backer cautions have been given by the Securities and Exchange Commission (SEC), the Financial Industry Regulatory Authority (FINRA), the Consumer Financial Protection Bureau (CFPB), and different organizations.

The idea of virtual cash is as yet novel and, contrasted with conventional speculations; bitcoin doesn't have a very remarkable longterm history or history of validity to back it. With their expanding prominence, bitcoins are turning out to be fewer tests each day; after just 10 years, all advanced monetary forms stay in an improvement stage. "It is essentially the most noteworthy danger, best yield venture that you can make," says Barry Silbert, CEO of Digital Currency Group, which fabricates and puts resources into Bitcoin and blockchain organizations.

Administrative Risk

Putting cash into bitcoin in any of its numerous pretenses isn't for the danger loath. Bitcoins are an adversary to government cash and might be utilized for underground market exchanges, illegal tax avoidance, criminal operations, or tax avoidance. Therefore, governments may look to manage, confine, or boycott the utilization and offer of bitcoins (and some as of now have). Others are thinking of different standards.

For instance, in 2015, the New York State Department of Financial Services settled guidelines that would require organizations managing the purchase, sell, move, or capacity of bitcoins to record the personality of clients, have a consistence official, and keep up capital stores. The exchanges worth $10,000 or more should be recorded and detailed.

The absence of uniform guidelines about bitcoins (and other virtual money) brings up issues over their life span, liquidity, and all-inclusiveness.

Security Risk

Most people who own and use bitcoin have not procured their tokens through mining activities. Maybe, they purchase and sell bitcoin and other computerized monetary standards on some famous online business sectors, known as bitcoin trades.

Bitcoin trades are completely computerized and, similarly as with any virtual framework, are in danger from programmers, malware, and operational glitches. In the event that a criminal accesses a Bitcoin proprietor's PC hard drive and takes their private encryption key, they could move the taken bitcoin to another record. (Clients can forestall this just if bitcoins are put away on a

PC that isn't associated with the Internet, or, more than likely by deciding to utilize a paper wallet printing out the bitcoin private keys and addresses and not keeping them on a PC by any means.)

Programmers can likewise target Bitcoin trades, accessing a great many records and advanced wallets where bitcoins are put away. One particularly famous hacking episode occurred in 2014, when Mt. Gox, a bitcoin trade in Japan, had to shut down after large number of dollars' worth of bitcoins was taken.

This is especially hazardous, given that all Bitcoin exchanges are lasting and irreversible. It resembles managing cash: Any exchange did with bitcoins must be turned around if the individual who has gotten them discounts them. There is no outsider or an installment processor, as on account of a charge or MasterCard — thus, no wellspring of assurance or allure if there is an issue.

Protection Risk

A few ventures are safeguarded through the Securities Investor Protection Corporation. Typical financial balances are guaranteed through the Federal Deposit Insurance Corporation (FDIC) up to a specific sum contingent upon the purview.

As a rule, bitcoin trades and bitcoin accounts are not protected by any bureaucratic or government program. In 2019, the great seller and exchanging stage SFOX reported it would furnish bitcoin financial backers with FDIC protection, however just for the part of exchanges including cash.13

Extortion Risk

While bitcoin utilizes private key encryption to check proprietors and register exchanges, fraudsters and tricksters may endeavor to sell bogus bitcoins. For example, in July 2013, the SEC brought lawful activity against an administrator of a bitcoin-related Ponzi conspire. There have likewise been recorded instances of bitcoin value control, another basic type of misrepresentation.

Market Risk

Like with any speculation, Bitcoin esteems can vary. Undoubtedly, the money's worth has seen wild swings in cost over its short presence. Subject to high volume purchasing and selling on trades, it has a high affectability to any newsworthy occasions. As per the CFPB, the cost of bitcoins fell by 61% in a solitary day in 2013, while the one-day value drop record in 2014 was just about as large as 80%.

In the event that fewer individuals start to acknowledge bitcoin as money, these computerized units may lose esteem and could get useless. Without a doubt, there was theory that the "bitcoin bubble" had blasted when the cost declined from its untouched high during the cryptographic money surge in late 2017 and mid-2018.

There is as of now a lot of rivalry. In spite of the fact that Bitcoin has a colossal lead over the many other advanced monetary standards that have jumped up on account of its image acknowledgment and investment cash, a mechanical leap forward as a superior virtual coin is consistently a danger.

Splits in the Cryptocurrency Community

In the years since Bitcoin dispatched, there have been various examples in which conflicts between groups of excavators and engineers incited huge scope parts of the digital currency local area. In a portion of these cases, gatherings of Bitcoin clients and diggers have changed the bitcoin network convention itself.

This cycle is known as "forking" and it as a rule brings about making another sort of bitcoin with another name. This split can be a "hard fork," in which another coin imparts exchange history to bitcoin until a definitive split point, so, all in all another token is made. Instances of cryptographic forms of money that have been made because of hard forks incorporate bitcoin cash (made in August 2017), bitcoin gold (made in October 2017), and Bitcoin SV (made in November 2017).

A "delicate fork" is a change to the convention that is as yet viable with the past framework rules. For instance, bitcoin delicate forks have expanded the complete size of squares.

Chapter 2. What is Blockchain?

Blockchain appears to be convoluted, and it unquestionably can be, yet its center idea is very basic. A blockchain is a sort of data set. Understanding blockchain assists first with understanding what an information base is.

A data set is an assortment of data that is put away electronically on a PC framework. In data sets, data or information is regularly organized in table arrangement to take into consideration simpler looking and separating of explicit data. What is the contrast between utilizing a bookkeeping page to store data instead of an information base?

Bookkeeping pages are intended for one individual, or a little gathering of individuals, to store and access restricted measures of data. Conversely, a data set is intended to house altogether bigger measures of data that can be gotten to, separated, and controlled rapidly and effectively by quite a few clients on the double.

Enormous data sets accomplish this by lodging information on workers made of amazing PCs. These workers can some of the time be constructed utilizing hundreds or thousands of PCs to have the computational force and capacity limit important for some clients to get to the information base at the same time. While a bookkeeping page or information base might be open to numerous individuals, it is regularly possessed by a business and overseen by a selected person who has unlimited oversight over how it functions and the information inside it.

Storage Structure

One key distinction between a normal data set and a blockchain is the manner by which the information is organized. A blockchain gathers data together in gatherings, otherwise called blocks that hold sets of data. Squares have certain capacity limits and, when filled, are affixed onto the recently filled square, framing a chain of information known as the "blockchain." All new data that follows that newly added block is arranged into a recently shaped square that will at that point likewise be added to the chain once filled.

A data set designs its information into tables, while a blockchain, similar to its name suggests, structures its information into pieces (blocks) affixed together. This makes it with the goal that all blockchains are data sets, however not all data sets are blockchains. This framework likewise naturally makes an irreversible timetable of information when executed in a decentralized nature. At the point when a square is filled, it is unchangeable and turns into a piece of this course of events. Each square in the chain is given a precise timestamp when added to the chain.

Decentralization

For comprehension blockchain, it is informative to see it with regards to how Bitcoin has carried out it. Like an information base, Bitcoin needs an assortment of PCs to store its blockchain. For Bitcoin, this blockchain is only a particular kind of information base that stores each Bitcoin exchange at any point made. For Bitcoin's situation, and not at all like most information bases, these PCs are not all under one rooftop. Every PC or gathering of PCs is worked by an exceptional individual or gathering of people.

Envision that an organization claims a worker included 10,000 PCs with a data set holding the entirety of its customer's record data. This organization has a stockroom containing these PCs under one rooftop and has full control of every one of these PCs and all the data contained inside them. Likewise, Bitcoin comprises of thousands of PCs. All things considered, every PC or gathering of PCs that hold its blockchain is in an alternate geographic area, and they are completely worked by independent people or gatherings of individuals. These PCs that make up Bitcoin's Network are called hubs.

In this model, Bitcoin's blockchain is utilized in a decentralized way. Nonetheless, private, concentrated blockchains, where the PCs that make up its organization are possessed and worked by a solitary substance, exist.

In a blockchain, every hub has a full record of the information that has been put away on the blockchain since its commencement. For Bitcoin, the information is the whole history of all Bitcoin exchanges. In the event that one hub has a mistake in its information, it can utilize the huge number of different hubs as a kind of perspective highlight right itself. Thusly, nobody hub inside the organization can adjust data held inside it. Along these lines, the historical backdrop of exchanges in each square that make up Bitcoin's blockchain is irreversible.

In the event that one client alters Bitcoin's record of exchanges, any remaining hubs would cross-reference one another and effectively pinpoint the hub with the mistaken data. This framework assists with setting up a definite and straightforward request of occasions. For Bitcoin, this data is a rundown of exchanges. In any case, it is likewise feasible for a blockchain to hold different data like lawful agreements, state distinguishing pieces of proof, or an organization's item stock.

To change how that framework functions or the data put away inside it, the vast majority of the decentralized organization's registering force would have to concur on said changes. This guarantees that whatever changes happen are in the greater part's wellbeing.

Transparency

On account of the decentralized idea of Bitcoin's blockchain, everything exchanges can be straightforwardly seen by either having an individual hub or by utilizing blockchain wayfarer that permits anybody to see exchanges happening live. Every hub has its duplicate of the chain that gets refreshed as new squares are affirmed and added. This implies that you could follow Bitcoin any place it goes in the event that you needed to.

For instance, trades have been hacked in the past were the individuals who held Bitcoin on the trade lost everything. While the programmer might be altogether unknown, the Bitcoins they separated are effectively detectable. On the off chance that the Bitcoins taken in a portion of these hacks were to be moved or spent some place, it would be known.

Is Blockchain Secure?

Blockchain innovation represents the issues of safety and trust severally. To start with, new squares are constantly put away directly and sequentially. They are constantly added to the "end" of the blockchain. In the event that you take a gander at Bitcoin's blockchain, you'll see that each square has a situation on the chain, called a "tallness." As of November 2020, the square's stature had arrived at 656,197 squares up until now.

After a square has been added to the furthest limit of the blockchain, it is hard to return and change the substance of the square except if the larger part arrived at an agreement to do as such. That is on the grounds that each square contains its hash, alongside the hash of the square before it, just as the recently referenced time stamp. Hash codes are made by a numerical capacity that transforms advanced data into a series of numbers and letters. On the off chance that that data is altered in any capacity, the hash code changes.

Here's the reason that is critical to security. Suppose a programmer needs to modify the blockchain and take Bitcoin from every other person. If they somehow happened to change their single duplicate, it would presently don't line up with every other person's duplicate. At the point when every other person cross-references their duplicates against one another, they would see this one duplicate stick out, and that programmer's rendition of the chain would be given away a role as ill-conceived.

Prevailing with such a hack would necessitate that the programmer at the same time control and change 51% of the duplicates of the blockchain so their new duplicate turns into the dominant part duplicate and, along these lines, the settled upon chain. Such an assault would likewise require a tremendous measure of cash and assets as they would have to re-try the entirety of the squares since they would now have distinctive timestamps and hash codes.

Because of the size of Bitcoin's Network and how quick it is developing, the expense to pull off such an accomplishment would most likely be inconceivable. In addition to the fact that this would be amazingly costly, yet it would likewise likely be vain. Doing something like this would not go undetected, as organization individuals would see such radical changes to the blockchain. The organization individuals would then fork off to another rendition of the chain that has not been influenced.

This would make the assaulted form of Bitcoin fall in esteem, making the assault at last trivial as the troublemaker controls a useless resource. The equivalent would happen if the agitator assaulted the new fork of Bitcoin. It is constructed this way so that participating in the organization is definitely more financially boosted than assaulting it.

Bitcoin vs. Blockchain

The objective of blockchain is to permit advanced data to be recorded and appropriated yet not altered. Blockchain innovation was first laid out in 1991 by Stuart Haber and W. Scott Stornetta, two analysts who needed to carry out a framework where archive timestamps couldn't be messed with. In any case, it wasn't until right around twenty years after the fact, with the dispatch of Bitcoin in January 2009, that blockchain had its first genuine application.

The Bitcoin convention is based on a blockchain. In an exploration paper presenting the computerized money, Bitcoin's pseudonymous maker, Satoshi Nakamoto, alluded to it as "another electronic money framework that is completely shared, with no confided in outsider."

The critical thing to comprehend here is that Bitcoin simply utilizes blockchain to record a record of installments straightforwardly. In any case, in principle, blockchain can be utilized to record quite a few information focuses changelessly. As talked about over, this could be as exchanges, votes in a political decision, item inventories, state IDs, deeds to homes, and considerably more.

There is a wide assortment of blockchain-based activities hoping to carry out blockchain in approaches to help society other than recording exchanges. One genuine model is that of blockchain being utilized to cast a ballot in just decisions. The idea of blockchain's changelessness implies that deceitful democratic would get undeniably harder to happen.

For instance, a democratic framework could work to such an extent that every resident of a nation would be given a solitary digital currency or token. Every competitor would then be given a particular wallet address, and the electors would send their token or crypto to whichever up-and-comer's location they wish to decide in favor of. The straightforward and recognizable nature of blockchain would take out the requirement for human vote checking and the capacity of agitators to mess with actual polling forms.

Blockchain versus Banks

Banks and decentralized blockchains are inconceivably extraordinary. To perceive how a bank contrasts from blockchain, we should contrast the financial framework with Bitcoin's blockchain execution.

How is Blockchain Used?

As we currently know, blocks on Bitcoin's blockchain store information about money related exchanges. Yet, incidentally, blockchain is a solid method of putting away information about different sorts of exchanges.

A few organizations that have effectively joined blockchain incorporate Wal-Mart, Pfizer, AIG, Siemens, Unilever, and a large group of others. For instance, IBM has made its Food Trust blockchain to follow the excursion that food items take to get to their areas.

For what reason do this? The food business has seen endless flare-ups of e Coli, salmonella, listeria, and unsafe materials being unintentionally acquainted with food varieties. It has required a long time to discover the wellspring of these episodes or the reason for infection from what individuals are eating before.

Utilizing blockchain enables brands to follow a food item's course from its root, through each stop it makes, lastly, it is conveyance. In the event that a food is discovered to be sullied, it very well may be followed back through each stop to its root. That, however these organizations can likewise now see all the other things they may have interacted with, permitting the recognizable proof of the issue to happen far sooner, conceivably saving lives. This is one illustration of blockchains practically speaking yet numerous other blockchain execution structures.

Banking and Finance

Maybe no industry stands to profit by coordinating blockchain into its business activities more than banking. Monetary foundations just work during business hours, five days every week. That implies in the event that you attempt to store a keep an eye on Friday at 6 p.m., you will probably need to stand by until Monday morning to see that cash hit your record. Regardless of whether you set aside your installment during business hours, the exchange can in any case take one to three days to check because of the sheer volume of exchanges that banks need to settle. Blockchain, then again, never dozes.

By coordinating blockchain into banks, shoppers can see their exchanges prepared in just 10 minutes. The time it takes to add a square to the blockchain, paying little heed to occasions or the hour of day or week. With blockchain, banks additionally can trade assets between establishments all the more rapidly and safely. For instance, in the stock exchanging business, the repayment and clearing cycle can require as long as three days (or more, if exchanging universally), implying that the cash and offers are frozen for that period.

Given the size of the whole in question, even the couple of days that the cash is on the way can convey significant expenses and dangers for banks. European bank Santander and its exploration accomplices put the possible investment funds at $15 billion to $20 billion per year. Cap Gemini, a French consultancy, appraises that buyers could set aside to $16 billion in banking and protection charges every year through blockchain-based applications.

Money

Blockchain structures the bedrock for digital currencies like Bitcoin. The Federal Reserve controls the US dollar. Under this focal power framework, a client's information and money are in fact at the impulse of their bank or government. In the event that a client's bank is hacked, the customer's private data is in danger. On the off chance that the customer's bank breakdowns or they live in a country with a precarious government, the worth of their money might be in danger. In 2008, a portion of the banks that ran out of cash were rescued in part utilizing citizen cash. These are the concerns out of which Bitcoin was first imagined and created.

By spreading its activities across an organization of PCs, blockchain permits Bitcoin and other digital currencies to work without the requirement for a focal power. This lessens hazard and disposes of a large number of the preparing and exchange expenses. It can likewise give those in nations with insecure monetary standards or monetary frameworks a more steady cash with more applications and a more extensive organization of people and establishments they can work with, both locally and universally.

Utilizing digital money wallets for investment accounts or as methods for installment is particularly significant for the individuals who have no state recognizable proof. A few nations might be war-torn or have governments that do not have any genuine foundation to give ID. Such nations might not approach reserve funds or money market funds and, hence, no real way to store abundance securely.

Medical care

Medical care suppliers can use blockchain to store their patients' clinical records safely. At the point when a clinical record is created and marked, it tends to be composed into the blockchain, which gives patients the evidence and certainty that the record can't be changed. These individual wellbeing records could be encoded and put away on the blockchain with a private key so they are just open by specific people, accordingly guaranteeing security.

Records of Property

On the off chance that you have at any point invested energy in your nearby Recorder's Office, you will realize that the way toward recording property rights is both difficult and wasteful. Today, an actual deed should be conveyed to an administration representative at the neighborhood recording office, where it is physically gone into the region's focal data set and general list. On account of a property debate, cases to the property should be accommodated with the overall file.

This interaction isn't simply expensive and tedious; it is additionally filled with human mistake, where every error makes following property proprietorship less productive. Blockchain can possibly kill the requirement for filtering archives and finding actual documents in a nearby account office. On the off chance that property proprietorship is put away and checked on the blockchain, proprietors can believe that their deed is precise and forever recorded.

In war-torn nations or zones with practically zero government or monetary foundation and absolutely no "Recorder's Office," it very well may be almost difficult to demonstrate responsibility for property. On the off chance that a gathering of individuals living in such a region can use blockchain, straightforward and clear timetables of land owners could be set up.

Shrewd Contract

A savvy contract is a PC code incorporated into the blockchain to work with, confirm, or arrange an agreement understanding. Savvy contracts work under a bunch of conditions that clients consent to. At the point when those conditions are met, the provisions of the understanding are naturally done.

Say, for instance, a potential occupant might want to rent a loft utilizing a keen agreement. The landowner consents to give the inhabitant the entryway code to the condo when the occupant pays the security store. Both the inhabitant and the property manager would send their particular bits of the arrangement to the savvy contract, which would clutch and naturally trade the entryway code for the security store on the date the rent starts. On the off chance that the property manager doesn't supply the entryway code by the rent date, the shrewd agreement discounts the security store. This would wipe out the expenses and cycles normally connected with utilizing a legal official, outsider arbiter, or lawyers.

Supply Chains

As in the IBM Food Trust model, providers can utilize blockchain to record the roots of their bought materials. This would permit organizations to confirm the credibility of their items, alongside such basic marks as "Natural," "Neighborhood," and "Reasonable Trade."

As revealed by Forbes, the food business is progressively receiving blockchain to follow the way and security of food all through the homestead to-client venture.

Casting a ballot

As referenced, blockchain could be utilized to work with a cutting edge casting a ballot framework. Casting a ballot with blockchain conveys the possibility to wipe out political race misrepresentation and lift elector turnout, as was tried in the November 2018 midterm decisions in West Virginia. Utilizing blockchain in this manner would make cast a ballot almost difficult to alter. The blockchain convention would likewise keep up straightforwardness in the appointive interaction, lessening the faculty expected to lead a political decision and giving authorities almost moment results. This would dispose of the requirement for describes or any genuine worry that misrepresentation may compromise the political race.

Advantages and Disadvantages of Blockchain

For the entirety of its intricacy, blockchain's potential as a decentralized type of record-keeping is practically limitless. From more prominent client protection and increased security to bring down preparing expenses and less mistakes, blockchain innovation may well see applications past those laid out above. However, there are additionally a few burdens.

Pros

- Improved exactness by eliminating human contribution in check
- Cost decreases by disposing of outsider check
- Decentralization makes it harder to mess with
- Transactions are secure, private, and effective
- Transparent innovation
- Provides a financial other option and approach to protect individual data for residents of nations with precarious or immature governments

Cons

- Significant innovation cost related with mining bitcoin
- Low exchanges each second
- History of utilization in unlawful exercises
- Regulation

Here are the selling points of blockchain for organizations available today in more detail.

S

Benefits of Blockchain

Exactness of the Chain

An organization endorses exchanges on the blockchain organization of thousands of PCs. This eliminates practically all human inclusion in the check cycle, bringing about less human blunder and an exact record of data. Regardless of whether a PC on the organization were to commit a computational error, the blunder would just be made to one duplicate of the blockchain. For that mistake to spread to the remainder of the blockchain, at any rate 51% of the organization's PCs would should be made—a close to difficulty for an enormous and developing organization the size of Bitcoin's.

Cost Reductions

Ordinarily, buyers pay a bank to confirm an exchange, a public accountant to sign a record, or a priest to play out a marriage. Blockchain wipes out the requirement for outsider confirmation and, with it, their related expenses. Entrepreneurs cause a little expense at whatever point they acknowledge installments utilizing Visas, for instance, since banks and installment preparing organizations need to deal with those exchanges. Then again, Bitcoin doesn't have a focal position and has restricted exchange charges.

Decentralization

Blockchain doesn't store any of its data in a focal area. All things being equal, the blockchain is replicated and spread across an organization of PCs. At whatever point another square is added to the blockchain, each PC on the organization refreshes its blockchain to mirror the change. By spreading that data across an organization, blockchain turns out to be harder to mess with as opposed to putting away it in one focal data set. In the event that a duplicate of the blockchain fell under the control of a programmer, just a solitary duplicate of the data, as opposed to the whole organization, would be undermined.

Productive Transactions

Exchanges put through a focal authority can take up to a couple of days to settle. On the off chance that you endeavor to store a mind Friday evening, for instance, you may not see assets in your record until Monday morning. While monetary establishments work during business hours, five days every week, blockchain is working 24 hours per day, seven days per week, and 365 days per year. Exchanges can be finished in just ten minutes and can be viewed as secure after only a couple hours. This is especially valuable for cross-line exchanges, which generally take any longer on account of time-region issues and that all gatherings should affirm installment preparing.

Private Transactions

Numerous blockchain networks work as open information bases, implying that anybody with a web association can see an organization's exchange history list. Despite the fact that clients can get to insights regarding exchanges, they can't get to recognizing data about the clients making those exchanges. It is a typical misperception that blockchain networks like bitcoin are unknown when they are just secret.

At the point when a client unveils exchanges, their special code called a public key is recorded on the blockchain as opposed to their own data. In the event that an individual has made a Bitcoin buy on a trade that requires recognizable proof, at that point the individual's character is as yet connected to their blockchain address. In any case, in any event, when attached to an individual's name, an exchange doesn't uncover any close to home data.

Secure Transactions

When an exchange is recorded, its credibility should be checked by the blockchain network. A great many PCs on the blockchain hurry to affirm that the buy subtleties are right. After a PC has approved the exchange, it is added to the blockchain block. Each square on the blockchain contains its exceptional hash, alongside the novel hash of the square before it. At the point when the data on a square is altered in any capacity, that square's hash code changes; nonetheless, the hash code on the square after it would not. This inconsistency makes it incredibly hard for data on the blockchain to be changed without notice.

Straightforwardness

Most blockchains are altogether open-source programming. This implies that anybody and everybody can see its code. This enables inspectors to audit digital forms of money like Bitcoin for security. This additionally implies no genuine expert on who controls Bitcoin's code or how it is altered. Along these lines, anybody can recommend changes or moves up to the framework. In the event that most organization clients concur that the new form of the code with the overhaul is sound and beneficial, at that point Bitcoin can be refreshed.

Banking the Unbanked

Maybe the most significant aspect of blockchain and Bitcoin is the capacity for anybody, paying little heed to nationality, sex, or social foundation, to utilize it. As indicated by the World Bank, almost 2 billion grown-ups don't have ledgers or any methods for putting away their cash or abundance. Virtually these people live in non-industrial nations where the economy is outset and totally reliant upon cash.

These individuals frequently bring in little cash that is paid in actual money. They at that point need to store this actual money in secret areas in their homes or places of living, leaving them subject to burglary or superfluous viciousness. Keys in a bitcoin wallet can be put away on a piece of paper, a modest cell, or even remembered whether essential. For a great many people likely, these alternatives are more effortlessly covered up than a little heap of money under a sleeping pad.

Blockchains of things to come are likewise searching for answers for be a unit of record for abundance stockpiling and store clinical records, property rights, and an assortment of other legitimate agreements.

Disadvantages of Blockchain

While there are huge potential gains to the blockchain, there are additionally critical difficulties to its appropriation. The barricades to the utilization of blockchain innovation today are not simply specialized. The genuine difficulties are political and administrative, generally, to avoid mentioning the great many hours (read: cash) of custom programming plan and back-end programming needed to coordinate blockchain into current business organizations. Here are a portion of the difficulties holding up traffic of far reaching blockchain appropriation.

Innovation Cost

Despite the fact that blockchain can get a good deal on exchange charges, the innovation is a long way from free. The "evidence of work" framework that bitcoin uses to approve exchanges, for instance, burns-through huge measures of computational force. In reality, the force from the large numbers of PCs on the bitcoin network is near what Denmark burns-through yearly. Accepting power expenses of $0.03~$0.05 each kilowatt-hour, mining costs elite of equipment costs are about $5,000~$7,000 per coin.

In spite of the expenses of mining bitcoin, clients keep on driving up their power bills to approve exchanges on the blockchain. That is on the grounds that when diggers add a square to the bitcoin blockchain, they are remunerated with enough bitcoin to make their time and energy advantageous. In any case, with regards to blockchains that don't utilize cryptographic money, excavators should be paid or in any case boosted to approve exchanges.

A few answers for these issues are starting to emerge. For instance, bitcoin mining ranches have been set up to utilize sun oriented force, overabundance petroleum gas from deep oil drilling destinations, or force from wind ranches.

Speed Inefficiency

Bitcoin is an ideal contextual analysis for the potential failures of blockchain. Bitcoin's "confirmation of work" framework requires around ten minutes to add another square to the blockchain. At that rate, it's assessed that the blockchain organization can just oversee around seven exchanges each second (TPS). Albeit other digital currencies, for example, Ethereum perform better compared to bitcoin, they are as yet restricted by blockchain. Inheritance brand Visa, for setting, can deal with 24,000 TPS.

Answers for this issue have been being developed for quite a long time. There are presently blockchains that are gloating more than 30,000 exchanges each second.

Criminal behavior

While classification on the blockchain network shields clients from hacks and jelly protection, it additionally takes into account illicit exchanging and movement on the blockchain network. The most referred to illustration of blockchain being utilized for illegal exchanges is likely the Silk Road, an online "dim web" drug commercial center working from February 2011 until October 2013, when the FBI shut it down.

The site permitted clients to peruse the site without being followed utilizing the Tor program and make illicit buys in Bitcoin or other cryptographic forms of money. Current U.S. guidelines require monetary specialist co-ops to acquire data about their clients when they open a record, check the character of every client, and affirm that clients don't show up on any rundown of known or suspected psychological militant associations. This framework can be viewed as both an expert and a con. It gives anybody admittance to monetary records and permits hoodlums to execute all the more without any problem. Many have contended that the great employments of crypto, such as banking the unbanked world, exceed the awful employments of cryptographic money, particularly when most criminal behavior is as yet achieved through untraceable money.

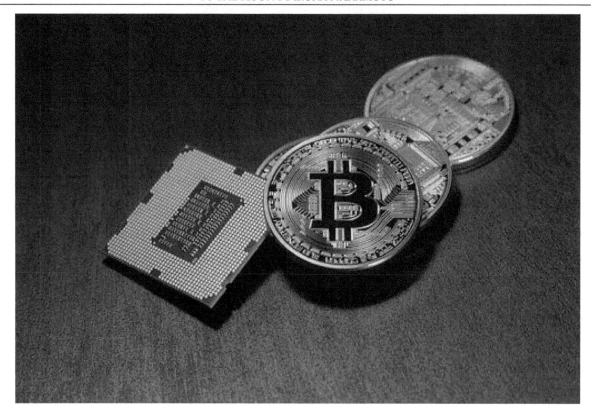

Guideline

Numerous in the crypto space have communicated worries about unofficial law over cryptographic forms of money. While it is getting progressively troublesome and close to difficult to end something like Bitcoin as its decentralized organization develops, governments could hypothetically make it illicit to claim digital currencies or partake in their organizations.

Over the long run this worry has developed more modest as enormous organizations like PayPal start to permit the possession and utilization of cryptographic forms of money on their foundation.

What's Next for Blockchain?

First proposed as an examination project in 1991, blockchain is serenely sinking into its late twenties. Like most recent college grads its age, blockchain has seen something reasonable of public examination in the course of the most recent twenty years, with organizations overall hypothesizing about what the innovation is able to do and where it's going in the years to come.

With numerous commonsense applications for the innovation previously being carried out and investigated, blockchain at long last becomes well known at age 27, in no little part in view of bitcoin and cryptographic money. As a popular expression on the tongue of each financial backer in the country, blockchain stands to make business and government activities more precise, productive, secure, and modest with fewer delegates.

As we get ready to head into the third decade of blockchain, it's not, at this point an issue of "if" heritage organizations will get on to the innovation; it's an issue of "when."

Chapter 3. Understanding the Crypto Market

There are a few things that each trying Bitcoin financial backer necessities. A digital currency trade account, individual ID reports on the off chance that you are utilizing a Know Your Customer (KYC) stage, a safe association with the Internet, and an installment strategy. It is additionally suggested that you have your wallet outside of the trade account. Legitimate techniques for installment utilizing this way incorporate ledgers, charge cards, and Mastercards. It is likewise conceivable to get Bitcoin at particular ATMs and by means of P2P trades. Notwithstanding, know that Bitcoin ATMs progressively required government provided IDs as of mid-2020.

Protection and security are significant issues for Bitcoin financial backers. Despite the fact that there are no actual Bitcoins, it is normally an impractical notion to gloat about enormous possessions. Any individual who acquires the private key to a public location on the Bitcoin blockchain can approve exchanges. Private keys ought to be kept mystery; hoodlums may endeavor to take them on the off chance that they learn huge possessions. Know that anybody can see the equilibrium of a public location you use. That makes it a smart thought to keep critical speculations at public tends to that are not straightforwardly associated with ones that are utilized for exchanges.

Anybody can see a past filled with exchanges made on the blockchain, even you. Yet, while exchanges are openly recorded on the blockchain, distinguishing client data isn't. Just a client's public key shows up close to an exchange on the Bitcoin blockchain, making exchanges secret yet not unknown. One might say, Bitcoin exchanges are more straightforward and detectable than cash; however the cryptographic money can likewise be utilized namelessly.

Following are a few stages you need to follow in the event that you need to put resources into digital currency:

1.   Choose an Exchange

Pursuing a digital money trade will permit you to purchase, sell, and hold digital money. It is by and large best practice to utilize a trade that permits clients to likewise pull out their crypto to their online wallet for more secure keeping. This element may not make any difference for those hoping to exchange Bitcoin or other digital forms of money.

There are numerous kinds of digital money trades. Since the Bitcoin ethos is about decentralization and individual sway, a few trades permit clients to stay unknown and don't expect clients to enter individual data. Such trades work self-governing and, commonly, are decentralized, which implies they don't have an essential issue of control.

While such frameworks can be utilized for odious exercises, they are additionally used to offer types of assistance for the world's unbanked populace. For specific classes of individuals – displaced people or those living in nations with practically no administration credit or banking framework – unknown trades can help carry them into the standard economy.

Be that as it may, the most mainstream trades are not decentralized and do require KYC. In the United States, these trades incorporate Coinbase, Kraken, Gemini, and Binance U.S., to give some examples. These trades have filled altogether in the quantity of highlights they offer.

Coinbase, Kraken, and Gemini offer Bitcoin and a developing number of altcoins. These three are presumably the simplest entrance to crypto in the whole business. Binance takes into account a further developed broker, offering more genuine exchanging usefulness and a superior assortment of altcoins to browse.

Something critical to note while making a digital currency trade account is to utilize safe web rehearses. This incorporates utilizing two-factor confirmation and utilizing an extraordinary and long secret phrase, including an assortment of lower-case letters, uppercase letters, exceptional characters, and numbers.

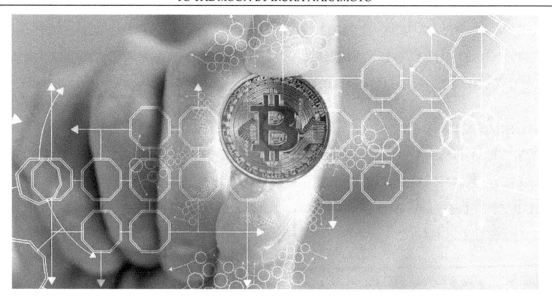

2.   Connect Your Exchange to a Payment Option

Whenever you have picked a trade, you presently need to accumulate your reports. Contingent upon the trade, these may incorporate photos of a driver's permit, government managed retirement number, just as data about your boss and wellspring of assets. The data you may need can rely upon the area you live in and its laws. The cycle is to a great extent equivalent to setting up an average investment fund.

After the trade has guaranteed your character and authenticity, you may now interface an installment alternative. At most trades, you can associate your ledger straightforwardly, or you can interface with a charge or Mastercard. While you can utilize a Visa to buy cryptographic money, it is by and large something that ought to be kept away from because of the instability that digital currencies can insight.

While Bitcoin is legitimate in the United States, a few banks don't take excessively benevolent to the thought and may address or even stop stores to crypto-related locales or trades. It is a smart thought to check to guarantee that your bank permits stores at your picked trade.

There are differing expenses for stores by means of a financial balance, charge, or Visa. Coinbase is a strong trade for fledglings and has a 1.49% expense for ledgers, with a 3.99% charge for charge and Mastercards. It is critical to investigate the charges related with every installment choice to help pick a trade or pick which installment alternative works best.

Trades additionally charge expenses per exchange. This charge can either be a level expense (if the exchanging sum is low) or a level of the exchanging sum. Visas cause a handling charge notwithstanding the exchange expenses.

3. Place an Order

Whenever you have picked trade and associated an installment alternative, you would now be able to purchase Bitcoin and other digital forms of money. Lately, cryptographic money trades have gradually become standard. They have filled altogether regarding liquidity and their broadness of highlights. The operational changes at cryptographic money trades equal the adjustment of impression of digital currencies. An industry that was once considered as a trick or one with problematic practices is gradually transforming into a genuine one that has attracted interest from every one of the enormous players the monetary administrations industry.

Presently, cryptographic money trades have arrived at a point where they have almost similar degree of highlights as their stock financier partners. Whenever you have discovered a trade and associated an installment strategy, you are all set.

Crypto trades today offer a few request types and approaches to contribute. Practically all crypto trades offer both market and breaking point requests, and some likewise offer stop-misfortune orders. Of the trades referenced above, Kraken offers the most request types. Kraken takes into account, as far as possible, stop-misfortune, stop-limit, take-benefit, and take-benefit limit orders.

Beside different request types, trades likewise offer approaches to set up repeating speculations permitting customers to dollar cost normal into their ventures of decision. Coinbase, for instance, allows clients to set repeating buys for consistently, week, or month.

4.   Safe Storage

Bitcoin and cryptographic money wallets are a spot to store computerized resources all the more safely. Having your crypto outside of the trade and in your wallet guarantees that lone you have authority over the private key to your assets. It additionally enables you to store finances from a trade and keep away from the danger of your trade getting hacked and losing your assets.

A few wallets have a larger number of highlights than others. Some are Bitcoin just, and some offer the capacity to store various altcoins. A few wallets likewise offer the capacity to trade one token for another.

With regards to picking a Bitcoin wallet, you have a few choices. The main thing you should comprehend about crypto wallets is hot wallets (online wallets) and cold wallets (paper or equipment wallets).

5. Hot Wallets

Online wallets are otherwise called "hot" wallets. Hot wallets will be wallets that sudden spike in demand for web associated gadgets like PCs, telephones, or tablets. This can make weakness in light of the fact that these wallets produce the private keys to your coins on these web associated gadgets. While a hot wallet can be advantageous in the manner you can access and make exchanges with your resources rapidly, putting away your private key on a web associated gadget makes it more helpless to a hack.

This may sound unrealistic; however individuals who are not utilizing sufficient security when utilizing these hot wallets can have their assets taken. This is certainly not an inconsistent event, and it can happen by one way or another. For instance, gloating on a public discussion like Reddit about the amount Bitcoin you hold while you are utilizing almost no security and putting away it in a hot wallet would not be savvy. All things considered, these wallets can be made to be secure insofar as insurances are taken. Solid passwords, two-factor verification, and safe web perusing ought to be viewed as least prerequisites.

These wallets are best utilized for modest quantities of digital currency or cryptographic money that you are effectively exchanging on a trade. You could compare a hot wallet to a financial records. Ordinary monetary shrewdness would say to hold just going through cash in a financial records while the heft of your cash is in bank accounts or other speculation accounts. The equivalent could be said for hot wallets. Hot wallets incorporate versatile, work area, web, and trade account guardianship wallets.

As referenced beforehand, trade wallets are custodial records given by the trade. The client of this wallet type isn't the private key holder to the digital currency held in this wallet. On the off chance that an occasion was to happen where the trade is hacked, or your record becomes bargained, your assets would be lost. The expression "not your key, not your coin" is intensely rehashed inside digital money gatherings and networks.

6. Cold Wallets

The easiest portrayal of a cool wallet is a wallet that isn't associated with the Internet and stands at a far lesser danger of being undermined. These wallets can likewise be alluded to as disconnected wallets or equipment wallets.

These wallets store a client's private key on something that isn't associated with the Internet and can accompany programming that works in equal so the client can see their portfolio without putting their private key in danger.

Maybe the most secure approach to store cryptographic money disconnected is by means of a paper wallet. A paper wallet is a wallet that you can create off specific sites. It at that point produces both public and private keys that you print out on a piece of paper. Getting to digital money in these locations is just conceivable in the event that you have that piece of paper with the private key. Numerous individuals cover these paper wallets and store them in wellbeing store boxes at their bank or even protected in their homes. These wallets are intended for high security and long haul ventures since you can't rapidly sell or exchange Bitcoin put away thusly.

An all the more generally utilized kind of chilly wallet is an equipment wallet. An equipment wallet is normally a USB drive gadget that stores a client's private keys safely disconnected. Such wallets have genuine benefits over hot wallets as they are unaffected by infections on one's PC. Private keys never interact with your organization associated PC or possibly weak programming with equipment wallets. These gadgets are likewise normally open-source, permitting the local area to decide its wellbeing through code reviews as opposed to an organization announcing that it is protected to utilize.

Cold wallets are the most secure approach to store your Bitcoin or other cryptographic forms of money. Generally, be that as it may, they require somewhat more information to set up.

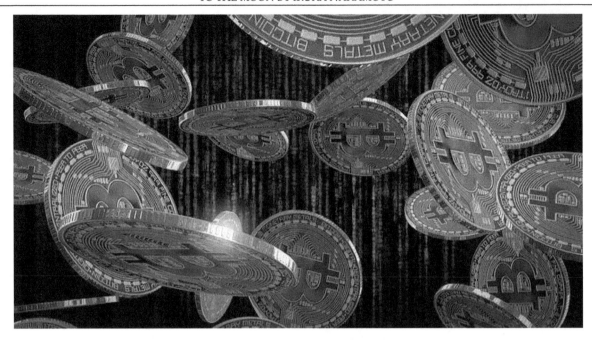

Chapter 4. Investing in Crypto Market

Putting resources into cryptographic money has advanced a ton since the pinnacle of 2017, when anybody could rapidly bounce in, get some Bitcoin on their nearby trade, and make a benefit. What the market has instructed us is actually similar to the financial exchange, a more key and thoroughly examined approach should be taken. This eBook contains the nuts and bolts of beginning in this market for the individuals who have no past experience putting resources into cryptographic forms of money. The part that follows, "The One Strategy," that anybody can apply to take their crypto contributing to the following level.

1.   Safety First

Before you jump online to begin constructing your pinnacle of crypto power, we should ensure your establishment is strong. This implies that before you start exchanging, your PC, apparatuses, and association should all be just about as free from any and all harm as could really be expected. In the crypto world, there is no bank to run crying to in the event that somebody takes your charge card and purchases 1000 dollars of treats. On the off chance that you get hacked, and your coins are taken, they are GONE. So offer yourself a tremendous kindness and find the accompanying ways to get your venture cash.

Secure Device

A simple spot to begin is to ensure you are utilizing a PC that is tidy and has forward-thinking security programming introduced. Preferably, it's likewise acceptable to exchange from a gadget exclusively utilized for crypto and not one that you additionally use to ride every one of the dull corners of the Internet. Secure organization As hip as it very well may be to purchase Ethereum from your smooth PC in your nearby coffeehouse with an almond milk latte in your grasp, don't exchange utilizing a public organization. No libraries, no eateries, and no malevolent companions' homes. Utilize your organization that is set up to be scrambled and secure.

Great Password Habits

An apparatus we firmly suggest is a secret key supervisor. You've likely caught wind of how significant a solid secret phrase is for limiting your danger of getting hacked (at least fifteen characters, including upper and lower-case letters, numbers, distinctive accentuation marks, and so forth) however, you actually use "timmy123" for the entirety of your records. We get it- - how are you going to recall each one of those diverse convoluted passwords? A secret key director is a piece of programming you can download that allows you to deal with every one of your passwords effectively and successfully, and you can get a beautiful darn great one free of charge

2. Fiat to Crypto

You've currently done, at any rate, what we've requested that you do to put resources into crypto with some degree of safety (perhaps somewhat more since you're that committed to the wellbeing of your future resources.) Now you're prepared to get rolling...

Register at an Exchange

To begin transforming your money into Bitcoin or some other coin (otherwise known as Altcoin), you need to set up a record on a trade. CoinBase is presumably the most notable, yet there are a couple of others, all of which offer fluctuated charge designs and coin contributions. Joining incorporates making a record with various layers of safety and interfacing an installment strategy, which are all clarified bit by bit in the trade's arrangement cycle. Whenever you are done, you are allowed to buy Bitcoin and a few other "fundamental" altcoins, including Ethereum, Bitcoin Cash, and Litecoin.

3.   Buying Different Coins

In the event that you will probably go farther than purchase and hold a portion of the principle coins, you'll need to get familiar with purchasing altcoins. Albeit new coins and organizations are promising incredible computerized arrangements springing up consistently, most won't ever proceed to become wildly successful. However, in case you're one of the first to contribute, easily, in another coin that succeeds, you could wind up winning the big stake. To purchase altcoins, you first need to discover which trades offer the Altcoin you might want to put resources into.

Enlisting at one of these trades will be basically the same as the enrollment cycle for your underlying trade. On the off chance that you did it the first occasion when, I have confidence that you can do it a second.

When set up, you should move crypto from your first trade to your new trade. This can be perhaps the most difficult advances in the event that you have never done anything identified with crypto. Basically, this is finished by reordering a location or code for the area you will send your assets to. For a nitty gritty model, we will utilize the guidelines for moving cash out of CoinBase.

Web

- Navigate to the "accounts" interface on the fundamental route bar.

- Select the "send" button for the computerized cash wallet that you'd prefer to send from.
- In the send discourse, select "wallet address" in case you're shipping off a computerized cash wallet outside to CoinBase or "email address" in case you're sending through email.
- Enter the measure of advanced money you'd prefer to send in the "sum" field.
- Alternatively, you can determine the sum you might want to send in your nearby money. Note that the finances will consistently be sent as advanced money, not your nearby cash.
- Click "proceed".
- Confirm the subtleties of the exchange and complete the send.

iOS (For CoinBase portable application)

- Tap the menu symbol close to the upper left of the screen to open the Navbar.
- Select the wallet you wish to send from, situated in the Navbar.
- Tap the paper plane symbol in the upper right hand of the screen.
- Enter the sum you wish to send
- Tap the up/down bolts to switch between monetary forms. • Press "send."
- Enter the email or wallet address and any notes you wish to incorporate.

- Review the subtleties of your exchange and select "send" in the upper right corner of the screen.
-

On the off chance that you have been given a QR code

- Tap the QR symbol in the upper right.
- Take an image of the QR code
- Enter the ideal sum and press "proceed."
- Review the subtleties of your exchange and select "send" in the upper right corner of the screen. Android (For the CoinBase versatile application)
- Tap the menu symbol close to the upper left of the screen to open the Navbar.
- Select the wallet you wish to send from, situated in the Navbar.
- Tap the "+" symbol close to the lower right hand of the screen.
- Select "send."
- Enter the sum you wish to send.
- Use the up/down bolts to switch between kinds of money.
- Enter the email or wallet address and any notes you wish to incorporate.
- Review the subtleties of your exchange and tap the "forward" bolt in the upper right corner of the screen.

Android (For the CoinBase portable application)

- Tap the menu symbol close to the upper left of the screen to open the Navbar
- Select the wallet you wish to send from, situated in the Navbar.

- Tap the "+" symbol close to the lower right hand of the screen
- Select "send."
- Enter the sum you wish to send.
- Use the up/down bolts to switch between sorts of money.
- Enter the email or wallet address and any notes you wish to incorporate.
- Review the subtleties of your exchange and tap the "forward" bolt in the upper right corner

Or then again in the event that you have been given a QR code

- Tap the QR symbol in the upper right.
- Take an image of the QR code
- Enter the ideal sum and press "proceed."
- Review the subtleties of your exchange and tap the "forward" bolt in the upper right corner of the screen. Since you've become a crypto reorder star, you are prepared to purchase altcoins and prepared to proceed onward to figuring out how to utilize a wallet for care.

4.   Using a Crypto Wallet

A crypto wallet isn't exactly similar to the ordinary wallet, which you push into your jeans pocket for putting away your fiat cash. Without getting a lot into the hidden innovation (in light of the fact that those of you who need to comprehend everything about everything can Google it for more data), a wallet is a product program that stores public and private "keys" so that individuals can send and get crypto and screen their equilibrium, which is recorded and scrambled on the blockchain.

At the point when somebody sends you cryptographic money, it's simply a trade of responsibility for cash to your wallet's location. To get this going, the private "key" put away in your wallet should relate to the public location the money is appointed to. In the event that people in general and private keys match, the exchange is finished, and you can give a major moan of alleviation that you didn't unintentionally glue in the URL of a dumb feline video on YouTube that you shipped off a companion an hour sooner. There are a few various types of wallets.

Portable

Wallet applications for your cell phone are helpful to get to and can even be utilized in certain stores however are generally not as refined and can't store as much information like different sorts because of a telephone's restricted stockpiling limit.

On the web

These wallets run on the cloud and are available from any gadget, anyplace. This makes it simple for you to get to your crypto. Lamentably, it additionally makes it simple for anybody hacking the outsider organization dealing with your wallet to take your crypto. Pick your wallet organization carefully in the event that you go this course.

Work area

These wallets are downloaded onto a solitary PC or PC and are just open from that point and no other gadget. This makes it less open, and somehow or another more secure, than an online wallet. In any case, if your gadget is hacked, gets an infection, or unintentionally drops off a bluff into the sea, you could wind up without something other than an unrepairable PC.

Paper

This is a technique for printing your public and private keys onto actual duplicate, which would then be able to be (and ought to be) securely put away. This is protected in light of the fact that it is put away disconnected however can at times be troublesome to get to.

Equipment

Regularly as a thumb-drive-type gadget, an equipment wallet gives an incredible harmony between disconnected wellbeing and simple access. With a speedy addition into a USB port, you can approach, send, and get digital currency.

Whichever structure you pick, it is critical to ensure that you duplicate your resources into a wallet when you are finished exchanging on a trade. On the off chance that your crypto is sitting in a trade and the site gets hacked, your coins are effectively available for the taking, and you'll most likely never get them back.

5. Basic Strategies

It's absolutely impossible we can make somebody with next to zero insight into a specialist crypto financial backer by perusing a couple of pages of text, however we can attempt to point you the correct way with the accompanying essential standards.

To be predictable with the general effortlessness of this guide, we'll give you three:

Purchase Low, Sell High

"Much obliged, Captain Obvious," you may be thinking, however in the event that this were so self-evident, for what reason do such countless individuals lose cash in contributing? It is the key law of contributing, yet to do this successfully, you should be straightforward with yourself about what sort of broker you are, just as what amount of cash, what amount hazard, and how long you can stand to contribute? The less you know your capacities, the less you will realize whose counsel to follow, which can eventually lead you to exchange a counterproductive way.

Examination, Research, Research

Simply doing what every other person is doing is a profoundly powerful method of getting messy seconds. Don't simply find out about market patterns. Become familiar with the organizations behind both new and existing coins. Who is an individual from their administration and specialized groups, and what is their central goal for what's to come? These basic advances can frequently remove a large number of the coins bound to come up short from the beginning.

Keep it Simple

From the start, simply contribute a limited quantity to get the hang of the "how to." Don't get extravagant. Get a portion of the top coins and sit on them. In the event that there is one thing that is steady about the unbelievably conflicting crypto market, genuine development requires years, not days. This way to sit and hold and don't get excessively combative and be a wild crypto pirate except if you realize that you understand what you're doing.

The One Strategy

Since you comprehend the fundamentals of putting resources into digital currency, it's an ideal opportunity to examine procedure. While a few specialists may trust it's beneficial to show many years' worth of contributing and exchanging mastery, we comprehend that this isn't commonsense for the vast majority. What number of us has the opportunity to learn everything about the unpredictable innovation of the blockchain world and how it means the organizations and tokens available? What numbers of us need to focus on turning into a specialist in the complexities of resource exchanging? What number of us can sit throughout the day before the PC watching the ongoing patterns on the lookout?

The appropriate response is, a great many people don't. Therefore, we need to discuss approaches to reasonably contribute, expand, and follow proficient techniques without taking up a great deal of your everyday life or turning into a full-time master dealer yourself.

Before most financial backers move into another market, there's a warm-up period that includes understanding a specific resource class and how it may find a way into your monetary picture. With digital forms of money and blockchain instruments, there are extra layers of intricacy, including the thought of cryptography, diggers, blockchains, tokens, hashing, and verifications. There's an extraordinary level of newness and intricacy related with digital forms of money for the unenlightened. However, the ordinary financial backer is relied upon to bounce onto a trade and begin exchanging, particularly in the event that exchanged nothing as long as they can remember.

Expansion is Key

Hand-picking digital currency ventures is a test. Cryptographic money markets are profoundly unpredictable, and surprisingly the most established are still truly in their outset stage. The choice cycle for token postings changes broadly among trades and is as of now not very much managed. Choosing champs from washouts or attempting to time the market has demonstrated to be amazingly troublesome. An investigation by Bitwise highlighted the worth of expansion on account of the limit changeability in the profits of even the best ten coins.

List Style Investing

In 2007, world-well known financial backer, Warren Buffett, bet 1,000,000 dollars that a record asset would outflank an assortment of multifaceted investments more than ten years. He won that bet and pointed out the viability of deliberately enhanced and sporadically rebalanced portfolios. There are numerous crypto portfolios available, however approaching one curated by a real expert, not a self-announced master on YouTube, is another story. These records are simply open to licensed financial backers (those with a total assets of in any event $1,000,000, barring the worth of one's main living place, or have a pay off at any rate $200,000 every year throughout the previous two years) however what numerous individuals don't know is that they all put their portfolio allotment online for people in general! Just by following the allotment rates of every token, you can take your venture and expand it very much like these selective and expertly oversaw reserves do.

Despite the fact that it will require some investment to do the exploration and choose which list reserve you might want to reflect, just as to figure and buy every token independently, fortunately these portfolios commonly just rebalance about once per month, so you will not need to do this regularly. Thus, the writing is on the wall, a manner by which, even with simply the most essential information, you can put resources into crypto with enhancement, adequacy, and expert ability.

Chapter 5. The Beginner's Guide

Exchanging cryptographic money can make a tremendous benefit. Notwithstanding, it's likewise profoundly hazardous. You can win and lose a lot of cash rapidly. This implies crypto exchanging is energizing, and it tends to be hard to hold significant serenity under hefty tension. There are numerous approaches to bring in cash in the digital currency markets, however not the entirety of the ways are viable and safe. I will investigate some demonstrated methods of putting resources into cryptographic money. Here are the main 10.

1. Trade digital money CFDs

Any item with value vacillations can be exchanged a Contract For Difference. CFD is a T+0 edge exchanging device, which permits you to exchange a bigger situation with a couple of capitals. For instance, you can exchange just 0.1 parcel bitcoin with a little store as an underlying edge.

The benefit of utilizing CFD is you can go long or go short regardless of the market moves; you will have the chances for dangerous gets back from business sectors fluctuating. Additionally, exchanging Bitcoin CFD is more adaptable, and you can exchange 24 hours and seven days.

It's likewise famous to utilize CFDs to support actual portfolios for financial backers, particularly in unstable business sectors.

As an ASIC-directed (AFSL398528) forex agent, Mitra de offers 100+ mainstream worldwide instruments, including forex, products, records, US stocks, and digital currencies. Mitra de offers you the chance to BUY (go long) or Sell (go short) on all Bitcoin exchanges, so you can utilize your favored methodology paying little mind to what direction the money is moving.

Pros:

- Speculate on crypto cost without possessing the crypto
- No compelling reason to manage crypto trades or open a crypto stockpiling wallet
- Low store, Higher influence
- The capacity to open long/short positions
- T+0 exchanging is more adaptable

Cons:

- The principle hazard related with CFD exchanging implies influence.
- Not reasonable for standing firm on a foothold in long haul

Presently, Mitrade gives advancements to new clients; You can apply for a 50USD free Trail Bonus to exchange any monetary resources with no dangers, which is useful for novices and amateurs.

2. Day Trading

Assume you are keen on bringing in cash with digital money in a quicker way. Around there, you can attempt crypto day exchanging, which is an exchanging methodology where financial backers purchase and sell orders on different occasions in a single day.

The high instability of Bitcoin and digital forms of money makes the crypto market like a thrill ride, which is ideal for day exchanging, as during the day, you will have enough good and bad times to get a decent benefit.

Preferably, you'll search for a low-evaluated freedom to purchase in and afterward sell it at a more exorbitant cost. In spite of the fact that this might be a little pay, this can acquire extensive benefits to financial backers the since a long time ago run.

Day exchanging is an expertise, very much like whatever else. On the off chance that you set aside more effort to see how it functions, it very well might be a full-time experience. Obviously, nobody will win in each exchanging, yet the objective of day exchanging is just to win more occasions.

So day exchanging requires financial backers more information and abilities. You can attempt to rehearse with a demo account on Mitrade, which gives a 50000 USD practice account. When you have a lot exchanging experience, you can choose to exchange a genuine record.

Pros:

- Relatively minimal effort
- Trading bitcoin on value changes

Cons:

- Need more abilities
- Much time and energy

3. Bitcoin Mining

Mining digital forms of money is not quite the same as the over two different ways of exchanging. Mining might be more troublesome than different ways, yet it very well might be more productive when you mine effectively. Albeit the mining cycle should be possible from a PC, you actually need essential programming, explicit equipment, crypto wallets, and much power. For the vast majority, mining is an exceptionally specific industry that isn't reasonable for singular financial backers. Most Bitcoin mining is done in an enormous distribution center with modest power.

In some cases, the equipment is additionally costly. For instance, during the positively trending market in 2017, the cost of GPU raised steeply, while as the market breakdowns, you can purchase great mining hardware with less expense.

In the early years, bitcoin excavators could acquire coins moderately rapidly. However, by 2019, cryptographic money mining is more convoluted. Numerous expert diggers have fabricated enormous exhibits to mine, making it harder for more modest excavators. Obviously, you can join a bitcoin mining pool to be more successful, however that accompanies a charge. I likewise discover some crypto excavator application in the crypto business professing to help you mine crypto coins. It's more similar to diversion mining. Try not to depend on the application to bring in extraordinary cash for you.

Pros:

- Earning possibilities is higher

Cons:

- High cost to begin

- relatively troublesome

4.   Long Term Investing

This is the simplest method to bring in cash with digital currency. Numerous individuals choose not to exchange cryptographic forms of money but rather purchase a specific number of coins and afterward put them in their wallets until the value ascends to make benefits. The reason of long haul contributing is that you have investigated and accept the digital currencies you put resources into will get more piece of the pie after some time.

In spite of the fact that there are a wide range of advanced coins, we suggest that you pick safe and profoundly fluid monetary forms, like BTC, LTC, and XRP. These coins have been famous available. In the event that you put resources into another crypto coin, it very well might be modest, however the coin is probably going to vanish after the market preliminary. Presently, numerous individuals acquire a major benefit from Bitcoin on the grounds that they purchased Bitcoin in the year 2011 or 2012, and they hold these computerized coins for quite a while regardless of whether the cost of bitcoin had ascended to 18,000 USD.

Pros:

- Easy to begin
- Beginner-accommodating

Cons:

- Take quite a while

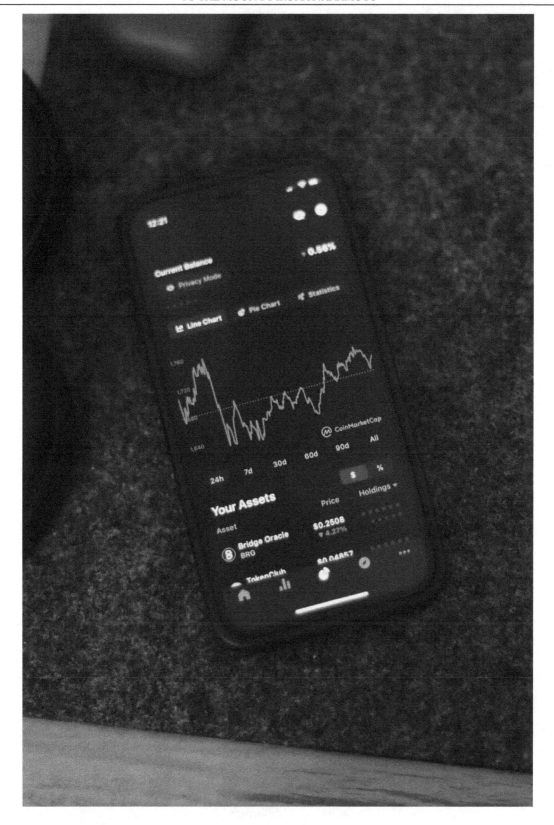

5.   Arbitrage

A few financial backers additionally utilize the method of exchange to bring in cash with digital forms of money. This implies when you purchase a computerized coin in crypto trade and afterward sell it on another crypto trade. Yet, truly, crypto exchange is uncommon that likely will not cause you to get rich rapidly.

Pros:

- Instant benefit
- Low prerequisites for section

Cons:

- Good openings are uncommon
- High hazard of losing benefits because of the great unpredictability in the digital currency markets

6.   Cryptocurrency spigot

In the event that you are tracking down a compelling method to benefit from modest quantities of digital forms of money, at that point a Crypto fixture might be one decision. A Crypto spigot resembles a trickling fixture. It is a site delivering very limited quantities of digital currencies, like Bitcoin, like clockwork. You need to do a few assignments as per the site necessities.

The crypto spigot site will bring in cash with publicizing and traffic. At the point when you're looking out for the page, there will be promotion arrangements.

Pros:

- Easy to utilize
- Easy to procure coins

Cons:

- Quite a limited quantity of coins
- Need to invest a lot of energy
- It can't cause you to get rich

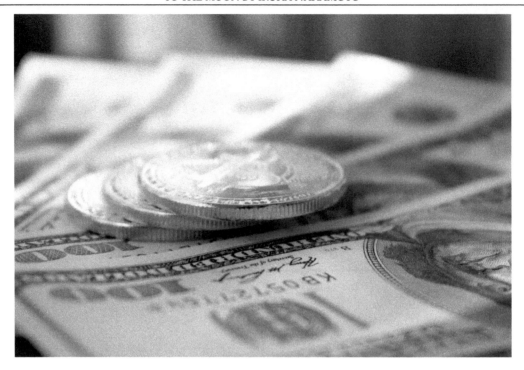

7. ICO

ICO implies Initial Coin Offerings, which are like crowd funding. ICO permits business visionaries to raise assets by making and selling their virtual money without hazard capital. It can make an enormous profit from your venture, however it likewise brings tremendous instability and dangers. ICO has a ton of traps. You must be cautious about picking the privilege ICO. In the event that the ICO coin isn't entirely significant, you may hazard losing cash. In this way, you would do well to contribute when you think the undertaking is sufficient and just put resources into what misfortunes you can bear.

Pros:

- Opportunity to put resources into point of view ventures at a beginning phase
- Low section limit

Cons:
- Many tricks
- Hacker assaults
- High chances

8. Crypto gaming

This is additionally a genuinely regular approach to acquire Bitcoin, messing around to get BTC; it is like joining the Bitcoin taps above. There will be new titles delivered, and they need to have more individuals download and mess around to make the game better known. These games will grant BTC prizes to clients. Your work is basically to have a telephone, download these games, and afterward sit and play. Subsequent to finishing the game, you will get a specific measure of BTC.

Pros:
- Easy to acquire Bitcoin

Cons:

- Have to invest a lot of energy
- Quite a modest quantity

9.   Be a blockchain engineer.

Blockchain improvement isn't very different from normal web advancement. Numerous designers have built up their own dispersed applications (DAPP) on certain stages, like Ethureum and NEO. At that point, you can bring in cash by showing advertisements, buys, memberships, and so forth, inside the application. Nonetheless, making and keeping a typical blockchain isn't simple. Above all else, the code is public and apparent to everybody. Anybody can see the code and check for blunders and weaknesses. This permits any software engineer to attack.

Pros:
- High pay
- Safe approach to acquire coins

Cons:

- You should think about coding

10. By advertising crypto with affiliate   marketing

In the event that you own a site or blog for crypto, this might be a decent method to acquire an optional pay. The cryptographic money industry, particularly Bitcoin, is developing, however the substance around Bitcoin on the Internet is still "scant." You can accept this open door to make a site work in posting news, tips, and directions for Bitcoin exchanging.

Pros:

- Low speculation costs
- Passive pay
- Flexible working timetable

Cons:

- You should have a site
- You don't control partner promoting programs
- Freelance occupations are not for everybody

What's preventing fledglings from making a steady pay from exchanging cryptographic money?

- **Make cash with digital currency will take a great deal of time and steady exertion.**

In contrast to proficient financial backers, most fledgling brokers figuring out how to exchange aren't full-time dealers to drench themselves in the business sectors.

That implies they need more an ideal opportunity to get themselves to the level where they can exchange like a star.

- **You have no unmistakable exchanging methodology.**

Ask yourself an inquiry: "What is my exchanging procedure?" If you replied: "System? Indeed, I just purchased and held up in trust, so was that viewed as a system? ". Presently we need to talk. On the off chance that you don't have a reasonable exchanging methodology, regardless of whether it depends on specialized pointers or essential information on crypto resources, or dependent on innovation (algorithmic exchanging), at that point surely there is very There are numerous potential issues that you may experience.

Notwithstanding, first, you need to get yourself and your exchanging style better. Advanced resources are quite possibly the most unpredictable resources nowadays, and yet, fundamental blockchain innovation sets out a freedom to get more extravagant later on.

- **You indiscriminately desire to recuperate.**

The visually impaired any expectation of a bounce back or Bull Run is something each broker has encountered in any event once. That is the reason you will see rehashed updates in speculation archives that, "What occurred in the past isn't a pointer of future value developments." Indeed, there is a contrast between specialized examination and gazing at the screen and reciting "Bitcoin will arrive at 21,000" until that occurs.

- **You are averaging your situation during the downtrend.**

Another difficult you may discover in the bear market is the normal of the downtrend, or all in all, to inundate you on the lookout. Some altcoins are viewed as promising or genuine prospects, however pause and wonder why you continue to stay nearby this coin and can't get out. Purchasing when the market is falling is a decent method to purchase low, however you likewise need to sell when it feels right, or perhaps you should see the cash's decrease significantly more profound before it shows any benefit.

You likely realize that a few group can purchase A for 100, the value tumbles to 80 and still doesn't cut misfortunes as recently suspected, and afterward to 60 individuals who trust that the market will return, go through cash, purchase in to trust you're not kidding "normal" position and diminish misfortunes. At that point it goes down once more, and you become terrified.

- ### You totally disregarded danger the board.

Without addressing why an altcoin (or even Bitcoin) is so unpredictable will lead us to the following justification responding to the inquiry, "for what reason are you losing cash in the bear market?" If you don't focus on hazard the board, you are putting yourself at a misfortune. Ask yourself your present normal danger level by resources and trades? Will I get an opportunity to recuperate on the off chance that one of the coins is delisted or the trade is hacked? In the event that you don't have clear responses to these inquiries - you might be strolling in a minefield.

- ### You don't gain from your own mix-ups.

The last explanation is presumably the most significant. Nearly everybody has begun a couple of times at the screen and asked for an expansion in venture. Or then again a few groups keep on purchasing a sinking crypto resource that is probably not going to recuperate. Yet, they have taken in a couple of things. In case you're committing an error from this bear market, focus on them. It is the expense of instruction, albeit the misfortune isn't fun; in the event that you don't make the most of that chance and gain from botches, particularly because of unnecessary expectation or restricted information, you will lose more expectation.

How to become a professional crypto trader?

The principal thing we will begin with is a clarification of who is a "proficient cryptographic money dealer" and what is "exchanging":
In basic words, exchanging implies trading or selling activities between two market members, where exchanging resources change hands.
Digital currency exchanging is a trade exchange between crypto-to-crypto or digital currencies to-fiat cash. Purchasing digital money like Bitcoin for US dollars is a trade activity, which implies you trade your money for crypto.
Being a merchant is something other than a diversion. It is a genuine energy or calling, which requires a ton of time and no less specialized information just; for this situation, exchanging will bring standard benefit.
A digital money merchant is a client of a cryptographic money stage or trade following up on its drive by exchanging advanced resources (cryptographic forms of money and fiat cash) to benefit from the exchanging interaction itself (purchasing and selling reserves). The motivation behind exchanging is to get cash for proficiently performed tasks (shut with benefit).
Cryptographic money exchanging is getting increasingly mainstream. Consistently an ever increasing number of individuals might want to attempt themselves as dealers. There are numerous fantasies around this calling, and most accept that to turn into a broker, you need higher monetary schooling or have an over-created instinct, over-reason, be an expert from God, and so forth Indeed, this would be a huge reward, yet in no way, shape or form an essential. What's more, today, we will demonstrate it!

Would i be able to see myself as a broker after a few effective exchanges?

The notable principle of "novice's karma" applies here too. You can benefit once or even a few times from opening exchanging positions indiscriminately, at the same time, tragically, it works in an unexpected way. For fruitful and successful digital money exchanging, you need to comprehend a few perspectives:

- Current market circumstance.
- How exchanging instruments work (what sorts of requests are accessible, and so forth);
- Understand how to understand graphs. For instance, you need to realize how to check the ethereum cost in pounds on the off chance that you are keen on exchanging this cash pair.
- Most critically, examine exchanging examples and developments on the outline to fabricate the correct exchanging procedure.

A broker's demonstrable skill lies he would say on the lookout, how he responds in upsetting circumstances, the amount he thinks out his exchanging steps, and "fallback alternatives."

Despite the exchanging system sought after, the primary exchanging objective remaining parts unaltered. To be specific, "Purchase less expensive – sell more costly" – the lone justification any exchanging activity is to benefit.

What information do I have to improve my exchanging abilities?

Market examination is the establishment of a fruitful exchanging methodology and makes a benefit. Not a solitary exchanging system, even Buy&HODL, is effective without seeing how market developments work and the primary exchanging candle designs.

Try not to BE SCARED

You don't need to be an expert to begin exchanging! Indeed, even a novice can bring in cash by purchasing/selling digital currencies with the privilege and insightful advances. Experience characterizes an expert, and experience is the thing that you need to procure. Hence, go through this way of turning out to be from an odd one out to a swan! For our situation, from amateur to proficient ;).

From the very beginning, it is critical to comprehend the kinds of orders gave on the stage utilized and what "pictures on the diagram" mean, how to put orders and what instruments are accessible on the stage. Interestingly, this will be all that anyone could need!

We can draw a similarity with power – to turn on a TV, forced air system, or night light – you don't really have to know how they work in the engine. It's sufficient to figure out how to work them. A similar rationale applies here!

Is there a simple success exchanging strategy to bring in cash on cryptographic forms of money?

Slight an interesting inquiry in light of the fact that the appropriate response is both "yes" and "no" all the while.

The truth of the matter is that the cryptographic money market is unstable; hence, it generally gives a chance to bring in cash for the individuals who follow the market "at the current second" and ability to utilize exchanging devices effectively.

"Purchase less expensive sell more costly" that is the proverb of any exchanging methodology.

The Buy&HODL system can be viewed as winning under specific conditions. Its substance is to purchase a resource and stand by till it develops. The primary concern isn't to miss the second and sell on schedule. Subsequently, when purchasing a specific exchanging resource for hold it, you need to make a primer investigation and get a few signs that the resources cost being referred to will probably flood. Something else, there is a danger of misfortunes.

How to pick a stage for crypto exchanging on the off chance that I am a novice?

Check the state's public assessment and notoriety. Security is critical! The stage should agree with the most elevated security norms to ensure your information and assets. Discover the rundown of the upheld nations: not all administrations cover clients' entrance all throughout the planet. Check if occupants of your nation can be the stage's clients. It is additionally critical to have client assistance nonstop. You need to ensure you can find support from the client care whenever you need it.

Benefits of the cryptographic money market:

Market instability no monetary market can contrast with the changes in digital money rates. Today, it is the most adaptable approach to bring in cash on exchanging; the cost of certain resources can make x100 in a real sense in a day. Despite the fact that note, they can likewise drop as quickly as they develop.

Cryptographic money accessibility advanced monetary forms are accessible whenever. The digital currency market works day in and day out, and you can exchange, store, or your crypto resources when you need. Namelessness regardless of whether the exchange can be followed – you'll see the wallet address, not the ID information of the proprietor. Unwavering quality cryptographic forms of money are protected. Be that as it may! Just on the off chance that you utilize a demonstrated and secure assistance. Slender discharge is useful for cryptographic money tokens. The less coins were given, the more interest for them.

Cryptographic money is decentralized cash; no single element or middle person controls the exchanges. Low exchange expenses the commission for moving assets is a lot of lower than the bank moves, for instance.

Why stopping? Go, pick the stage, make a record, and begin exchanging. Simply remember one principle consistently do your exploration first!

The Cryptocurrency Investing | Advanced Guide

Study, Anticipate the Crypto Market and Raise the first Million Dollar from Bitcoin, Ethereum, Cardano and other unknown Altcoins that costs less than 1$

By

Iruka Nakamoto

Table of Contents

Chapter 1. Understanding cryptocurrency 126

Chapter 2. Mining of Cryptocurrency...165

Chapter 3. Before You Begin..195

Chapter 4. Are cryptocurrencies a good investment? 238

Chapter 1. Understanding cryptocurrency

A cryptocurrency ("crypto") is a digital currency that may be used to shop for items and offerings but makes use of an online ledger with robust cryptography to relaxed online transactions. Much of the hobby in these unregulated currencies is to trade for profit, ith speculators at times driving prices skyward. A cryptocurrency is a form of payment that can be exchanged online for goods and offerings. Many organizations have issued their own currencies, often called tokens, and those can be traded especially for the best or provider that the employer gives. Think of them as you will arcade tokens or casino chips. You'll want to alternate real forex for the cryptocurrency to get entry to the best or carrier.

Why Cryptocurrency Is So Popular

Cryptocurrencies have gone from a difficult to understand part of finance to centre-level over the past 12 months. In the space of twelve months, bitcoin has exploded from buying and selling at $8,166 on 8 March 2020 to hit all-time highs of over $58,000 in February 2021 and now trading at $54,011 as of 9:31 am GMT on 9th March.

Their meteoric upward push has been observed by means of elevated institutional interest, consisting of big names like HSBC, Goldman Sachs, BNY Mellon and JPMorgan.

There are hundreds of cryptocurrencies around the sector but the core group of 20 coins constitutes around 99% of the marketplace through quantity, according to crypto internet site CoinDesk.

In the primary week of March — the quietest week for the reason that early January — inflows into digital asset investment products had been $108m, in step with James Butterfill, an investment strategist at CoinShares. Of these inflows, 90% had been bitcoin, with $4m invested in ethereum. Trading volumes for bitcoin, but, remained high, with each day average of $11.8bn for 2021 in comparison to $2.2bn in 2020.

As cryptocurrencies hold their rollercoaster rally into 2021 and hitting record highs in February and March, Financial News has compiled a list of the ten largest cryptocurrencies by using market capitalization.

Following are some reasons why cryptocurrency is popular for:

Low Fees

One of the reasons why cryptocurrency is famous around the world is that there are very few fees associated with using it. When you're using alternative options of online payment options, you're often going to incur massive costs. The very low charges that you have to deal with while the use of numerous cryptocurrencies will be a far higher deal for you. It makes the experience for many people to use cryptocurrencies to pay for items online and people also find it to be safe.

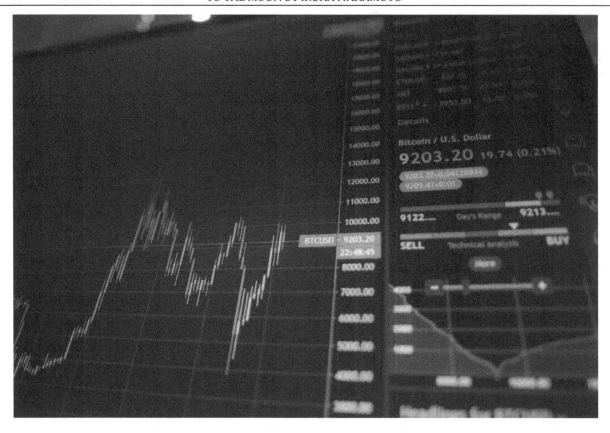

No Associatation of Cryptocurrencies with World Governments

Another reason why people have placed faith in cryptocurrencies is that those currencies aren't associated with world governments. This means that cryptocurrencies have the capacity to remain strong even if there is turmoil in a particular country. Some investors see cryptocurrencies as a terrific way to guard their wealth and that is one motive why cryptocurrency has persevered to upward push over time. The capacity that cryptocurrencies will be safer than some government currencies makes them extra appealing.

It's Getting Easier to Use Cryptocurrency

Using cryptocurrency is getting less complicated all of the time, thanks to greater online companies adopting it. You'll find that more web sites are beginning to accept cryptocurrencies as a fee and this could simplest emerge as more widely widespread in the future. It's also thrilling to notice that there are now things that include cryptocurrency debit cards popping up in certain locations.

This won't be widespread right now however it's far something that is very much occurring.

As cryptocurrency keeps turning out to be greater, not unusual, it's going to reach increasingly more people. This leads to a growth in consciousness and a common surge in popularity. More people remember the fact that that is an alternative now and some of the questions about what cryptocurrency is are being answered. Lots of people have at least a bit of understanding approximately what things such as Bitcoin are and this makes it extra ideal.

There Is Potential for Profit

Of course, the potential for profit is another huge reason why people get involved with cryptocurrencies. If you <u>buy Bitcoin</u> while it's at a low price, then you can potentially profit when that price rises. Lots of people who invested in cryptocurrencies before they got super hot wound up making huge profits. Investors are still making money from cryptocurrencies because the market has not cooled in recent years.

Overall Security Is Important

Protecting your identity and your money is important, and you know how hard cybersecurity has become in modern times. Using cryptocurrency to pay for things online is actually a lot safer than many other traditional payment options. If you're at all worried about cybersecurity issues, then deciding to use cryptocurrency might be a good idea. The security of cryptocurrency is one of the things that has helped it to become so popular over time.

It's Easy to Get

Getting cryptocurrency isn't some difficult thing that you're going to have to jump through a lot of hoops to do. It's actually possible to get the cryptocurrency that you want from reputable sources and the ease of getting cryptocurrency has helped it to grow in popularity. In the past, people might have thought of cryptocurrency as some type of shady and unknown entity but it's become a common thing in many circles now. If you have yet to purchase cryptocurrency, then you'll find that the process is decidedly simple and customer-friendly.

It's Seen as the Future

Finally, you could say that cryptocurrencies are seen as the future of money by many individuals. People who adopt cryptocurrency now are also adopting major technological innovations such as blockchain. This allows you to be on the cutting edge and it makes sense for many to get ahead of the curve. Blockchain technology is supposed to change the world in many ways and it's going to make trading a much more transparent process.

Types of Cryptocurrency

The first blockchain-based totally cryptocurrency became Bitcoin, which still remains the most popular and most valuable. Today, there are lots of alternate cryptocurrencies with diverse features and specs. Some of those are clones or forks of Bitcoin, while others are new currencies that were built from scratch.

Bitcoin was released in 2009 by an individual or group known by the pseudonym "Satoshi Nakamoto.1 As of March 2021, there had been over 18.6 million bitcoins in flow with a complete marketplace cap of around $927 billion.

Some of the competing cryptocurrencies spawned by means of Bitcoin's fulfilment, known as "altcoins," encompass Litecoin, Peercoin, and Namecoin, in addition to Ethereum, Cardano, and EOS. Today, the mixture price of all of the cryptocurrencies in life is round $1.5 trillion—Bitcoin currently represents more than 60% of the total value.

Advantages and Disadvantages of Cryptocurrency

Advantages

Cryptocurrencies preserve the promise of creating it less difficult to switch funds immediately among two parties, without the need for reliance on a third party like a financial institution or credit card enterprise. These transfers are alternatively secured through using public keys and private keys and distinctive kinds of incentive structures, like Proof of Work or Proof of Stake.

In modern cryptocurrency systems, a consumer's "wallet," or account address, has a public key, at the same time as the private key known only to the owner and is used to sign transactions. Fund transfers are finished with minimal processing expenses, allowing customers to keep away from the steep costs charged via banks and financial establishments for wire transfers.

Disadvantages

The semi-anonymous nature of cryptocurrency transactions makes them well-suited for a host of illegal activities, such as <u>money laundering</u> and <u>tax evasion</u>. However, cryptocurrency advocates often highly value their anonymity, citing benefits of privacy like protection for whistleblowers or activists living under repressive governments. Some cryptocurrencies are more private than others.

Bitcoin, for instance, is a relatively poor choice for conducting illegal business online, since the forensic analysis of the Bitcoin blockchain has helped authorities arrest and prosecute criminals. More privacy-oriented coins do exist, however, such as <u>Dash</u>, Monero, or <u>ZCash</u>, which are far more difficult to trace.

Special Considerations

Central to the appeal and functionality of Bitcoin and other cryptocurrencies is <u>blockchain</u> technology, which is used to keep an online ledger of all the transactions that have ever been conducted, thus providing a data structure for this ledger that is quite secure and is shared and agreed upon by the entire network of an individual node, or computer maintaining a copy of the ledger. Every new block generated must be verified by each node before being confirmed, making it almost impossible to forge transaction histories.

Many experts see blockchain technology as having serious potential for uses like online voting and crowdfunding, and major financial institutions such as JPMorgan Chase (JPM) see the potential to lower transaction costs by streamlining payment processing.4 However, because cryptocurrencies are virtual and are not stored on a central database, a digital cryptocurrency balance can be wiped out by the loss or destruction of a hard drive if a backup copy of the private key does not exist. At the same time, there is no central authority, government, or corporation that has access to your funds or your personal information.

Criticism of Cryptocurrency

Since market prices for cryptocurrencies are based on supply and demand, the rate at which a cryptocurrency can be exchanged for another currency can fluctuate widely, since the design of many cryptocurrencies ensures a high degree of scarcity.

Bitcoin has experienced some rapid surges and collapses in value, climbing as high as $19,000 per Bitcoin in Dec. of 2017 before dropping to around $7,000 in the following months.2 Cryptocurrencies are thus considered by some economists to be a short-lived fad or speculative bubble.

There is concern that cryptocurrencies like Bitcoin are not rooted in any material goods. Some research, however, has identified that the cost of producing a Bitcoin, which requires an increasingly large amount of energy, is directly related to its market price.

Cryptocurrency blockchains are highly secure, but other aspects of a cryptocurrency ecosystem, including exchanges and wallets, are not immune to the threat of hacking. In Bitcoin's 10-year history, <u>several online exchanges</u> have been the subject of hacking and theft, sometimes with millions of dollars' worth of "coins" stolen.

Nonetheless, many observers see potential advantages in cryptocurrencies, like the possibility of preserving value against inflation and facilitating exchange while being easier to transport and divide than precious metals and existing outside the influence of central banks and governments.

What Is Bitcoin?

Bitcoin is a digital currency that was created in January 2009. It follows the ideas set out in a white paper by the mysterious and pseudonymous Satoshi Nakamoto. The identity of the person or persons who created the technology is still a mystery. Bitcoin offers the promise of lower transaction fees than traditional online payment mechanisms and, unlike government-issued currencies, it is operated by a decentralized authority.

Bitcoin is a type of cryptocurrency. There are no physical bitcoins, only balances kept on a public ledger that everyone has transparent access to.

All bitcoin transactions are verified by a massive amount of computing power. Bitcoins are not issued or backed by any banks or governments, nor are individual bitcoins valuable as a commodity. Despite it not being legal tender Bitcoin is very popular and has triggered the launch of hundreds of other cryptocurrencies, collectively referred to as alcoin. Bitcoin is commonly abbreviated as "BTC."

Peer-to-Peer Technology

Bitcoin is one of the first digital currencies to use peer-to-peer technology to facilitate instant payments. The independent individuals and companies who own the governing computing power and participate in the bitcoin network—bitcoin "miners"—are in charge of processing the transactions on the blockchain and are motivated by rewards (the release of new bitcoin) and transaction fees paid in bitcoin.

These miners can be thought of as the decentralized authority enforcing the credibility of the bitcoin network. New bitcoin is released to the miners at a fixed, but periodically declining rate. There are only 21 million bitcoin that can be mined in total. As of January 30, 2021, there are approximately 18,614,806 bitcoin in existence and 2,385,193 bitcoin left to be mined.3

In this way, bitcoin other cryptocurrencies operate differently from fiat currency; in centralized banking systems, currency is released at a rate matching the growth in goods; this system is intended to maintain price stability. A decentralized system, like bitcoin, sets the release rate ahead of time and according to an algorithm.

What is Blockchain?

Blockchain seems complicated, and it definitely can be, but its core concept is really quite simple. A blockchain is a type of database. To be able to understand blockchain, it helps to first understand what a database actually is.

A database is a collection of information that is stored electronically on a computer system. Information, or data, in databases is typically structured in table format to allow for easier searching and filtering for specific information. What is the difference between someone using a spreadsheet to store information rather than a database?

Spreadsheets are designed for one person, or a small group of people, to store and access limited amounts of information. In contrast, a database is designed to house significantly larger amounts of information that can be accessed, filtered, and manipulated quickly and easily by any number of users at once.

Large databases achieve this by housing data on servers that are made of powerful computers. These servers can sometimes be built using hundreds or thousands of computers in order to have the computational power and storage capacity necessary for many users to access the database simultaneously. While a spreadsheet or database may be accessible to any number of people, it is often owned by a business and managed by an appointed individual that has complete control over how it works and the data within it.

So how does a blockchain differ from a database?

Storage Structure

One key difference between a typical database and a blockchain is the way the data is structured. A blockchain collects information together in groups, also known as blocks that hold sets of information. Blocks have certain storage capacities and, when filled, are chained onto the previously filled block, forming a chain of data known as the "blockchain." All new information that follows that freshly added block is compiled into a newly formed block that will then also be added to the chain once filled.

A database structures its data into tables whereas a blockchain, like its name implies, structures its data into chunks (blocks) that are chained together. This makes it so that all blockchains are databases but not all databases are blockchains. This system also inherently makes an irreversible timeline of data when implemented in a decentralized nature. When a block is filled it is set in stone and becomes a part of this timeline. Each block in the chain is given an exact timestamp when it is added to the chain.

Decentralization

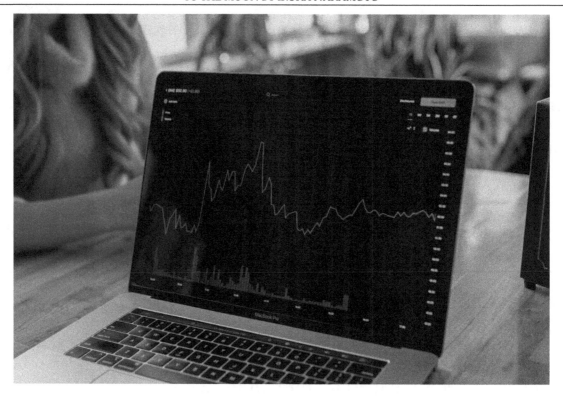

For the purpose of understanding blockchain, it is instructive to view it in the context of how it has been implemented by Bitcoin. Like a database, Bitcoin needs a collection of computers to store its blockchain. For Bitcoin, this blockchain is just a specific type of database that stores every Bitcoin transaction ever made. In Bitcoin's case, and unlike most databases, these computers are not all under one roof, and each computer or group of computers is operated by a unique individual or group of individuals.

Imagine that a company owns a server comprised of 10,000 computers with a database holding all of its client's account information. This company has a warehouse containing all of these computers under one roof and has full control of each of these computers and all the information contained within them. Similarly, Bitcoin consists of thousands of computers, but each computer or group of computers that hold its blockchain is in a different geographic location and they are all operated by separate individuals or groups of people. These computers that makeup Bitcoin's network are called nodes.

In this model, Bitcoin's blockchain is used in a decentralized way. However, private, centralized blockchains, where the computers that make up its network are owned and operated by a single entity, do exist.

In a blockchain, each node has a full record of the data that has been stored on the blockchain since its inception. For Bitcoin, the data is the entire history of all Bitcoin transactions. If one node has an error in its data it can use the thousands of other nodes as a reference point to correct itself. This way, no one node within the network can alter information held within it. Because of this, the history of transactions in each block that make up Bitcoin's blockchain is irreversible.

If one user tampers with Bitcoin's record of transactions, all other nodes would cross-reference each other and easily pinpoint the node with the incorrect information. This system helps to establish an exact and transparent order of events. For Bitcoin, this information is a list of transactions, but it also is possible for a blockchain to hold a variety of information like legal contracts, state identifications, or a company's product inventory.

In order to change how that system works, or the information stored within it, a majority of the decentralized network's computing power would need to agree on said changes. This ensures that whatever changes do occur are in the best interests of the majority.

Transparency

Because of the decentralized nature of Bitcoin's blockchain, all transactions can be transparently viewed by either having a personal node or by using blockchain explorer that allow anyone to see transactions occurring live. Each node has its own copy of the chain that gets updated as fresh blocks are confirmed and added. This means that if you wanted to, you could track Bitcoin wherever it goes.

For example, exchanges have been hacked in the past where those who held Bitcoin on the exchange lost everything. While the hacker may be entirely anonymous, the Bitcoins that they extracted are easily traceable. If the Bitcoins that were stolen in some of these hacks were to be moved or spent somewhere, it would be known.

Is Blockchain Secure?

Blockchain technology accounts for the issues of security and trust in several ways. First, new blocks are always stored linearly and chronologically. That is, they are always added to the "end" of the blockchain. If you take a look at Bitcoin's blockchain, you'll see that each block has a position on the chain, called a "height." As of November 2020, the block's height had reached 656,197 blocks so far.

After a block has been added to the end of the blockchain, it is very difficult to go back and alter the contents of the block unless the majority reached a consensus to do so. That's because each block contains its own hash, along with the hash of the block before it, as well as the previously mentioned time stamp. Hash codes are created by a math function that turns digital information into a string of numbers and letters. If that information is edited in any way, the hash code changes as well.

Here's why that's important to security. Let's say a hacker wants to alter the blockchain and steal Bitcoin from everyone else. If they were to alter their own single copy, it would no longer align with everyone else's copy. When everyone else cross-references their copies against each other, they would see this one copy stand out and that hacker's version of the chain would be cast away as illegitimate.

Succeeding with such a hack would require that the hacker simultaneously control and alter 51% of the copies of the blockchain so that their new copy becomes the majority copy and thus, the agreed-upon chain. Such an attack would also require an immense amount of money and resources as they would need to redo all of the blocks because they would now have different timestamps and hash codes.

Due to the size of Bitcoin's network and how fast it is growing, the cost to pull off such a feat would probably be insurmountable. Not only would this be extremely expensive, but it would also likely be fruitless. Doing such a thing would not go unnoticed, as network members would see such drastic alterations to the blockchain. The network members would then fork off to a new version of the chain that has not been affected.

This would cause the attacked version of Bitcoin to plummet in value, making the attack ultimately pointless as the bad actor has control of a worthless asset. The same would occur if the bad actor were to attack the new fork of Bitcoin. It is built this way so that taking part in the network is far more economically incentivized than attacking it.

How is Blockchain Used?

As we now know, blocks on Bitcoin's blockchain store data about monetary transactions. But it turns out that blockchain is actually a reliable way of storing data about other types of transactions, as well.

Some companies that have already incorporated blockchain include Walmart, Pfizer, AIG, Siemens, Unilever, and a host of others. For example, IBM has created its Food Trust blockchain1 to trace the journey that food products take to get to its locations.

Why do this? The food industry has seen countless outbreaks of e Coli, salmonella, listeria, as well as hazardous materials being accidentally introduced to foods. In the past, it has taken weeks to find the source of these outbreaks or the cause of sickness from what people are eating.

Using blockchain gives brands the ability to track a food product's route from its origin, through each stop it makes, and finally its delivery. If a food is found to be contaminated then it can be traced all the way back through each stop to its origin. Not only that, but these companies can also now see everything else it may have come in contact with, allowing the identification of the problem to occur far sooner, potentially saving lives. This is one example of blockchains in practice, but there are many other forms of blockchain implementation.

Banking and Finance

Perhaps no industry stands to benefit from integrating blockchain into its business operations more than banking. Financial institutions only operate during business hours, five days a week. That means if you try to deposit a check on Friday at 6 p.m., you will likely have to wait until Monday morning to see that money hit your account. Even if you do make your deposit during business hours, the transaction can still take one to three days to verify due to the sheer volume of transactions that banks need to settle. Blockchain, on the other hand, never sleeps.

By integrating blockchain into banks, consumers can see their transactions processed in as little as 10 minutes,2 basically the time it takes to add a block to the blockchain, regardless of holidays or the time of day or week. With blockchain, banks also have the opportunity to exchange funds between institutions more quickly and securely. In the stock trading business, for example, the settlement and clearing process can take up to three days (or longer, if trading internationally), meaning that the money and shares are frozen for that period of time.

Given the size of the sums involved, even the few days that the money is in transit can carry significant costs and risks for banks. European bank Santander and its research partners put the potential savings at $15 billion to $20 billion a year.3 Capgemini, a French consultancy, estimates that consumers could save up to $16 billion in banking and insurance fees each year4 through blockchain-based applications.

Currency

Blockchain forms the bedrock for cryptocurrencies like Bitcoin. The U.S. dollar is controlled by the Federal Reserve. Under this central authority system, a user's data and currency are technically at the whim of their bank or government. If a user's bank is hacked, the client's private information is at risk. If the client's bank collapses or they live in a country with an unstable government, the value of their currency may be at risk. In 2008, some of the banks that ran out of money were bailed out partially using taxpayer money. These are the worries out of which Bitcoin was first conceived and developed.

By spreading its operations across a network of computers, blockchain allows Bitcoin and other cryptocurrencies to operate without the need for a central authority. This not only reduces risk but also eliminates many of the processing and transaction fees. It can also give those in countries with unstable currencies or financial infrastructures a more stable currency with more applications and a wider network of individuals and institutions they can do business with, both domestically and internationally.

Using cryptocurrency wallets for savings accounts or as a means of payment is especially profound for those who have no state identification. Some countries may be war-torn or have governments that lack any real infrastructure to provide identification. Citizens of such countries may not have access to savings or brokerage accounts and therefore, no way to safely store wealth.

Healthcare

Health care providers can leverage blockchain to securely store their patients' medical records. When a medical record is generated and signed, it can be written into the blockchain, which provides patients with the proof and confidence that the record cannot be changed. These personal health records could be encoded and stored on the blockchain with a private key, so that they are only accessible by certain individuals, thereby ensuring privacy.

Records of Property

If you have ever spent time in your local Recorder's Office, you will know that the process of recording property rights is both burdensome and inefficient. Today, a physical deed must be delivered to a government employee at the local recording office, where it is manually entered into the county's central database and public index. In the case of a property dispute, claims to the property must be reconciled with the public index.

This process is not just costly and time-consuming it is also riddled with human error, where each inaccuracy makes tracking property ownership less efficient. Blockchain has the potential to eliminate the need for scanning documents and tracking down physical files in a local recording office. If property ownership is stored and verified on the blockchain, owners can trust that their deed is accurate and permanently recorded.

In war-torn countries or areas that have little to no government or financial infrastructure, and certainly no "Recorder's Office," it can be nearly impossible to prove ownership of a property. If a group of people living in such an area is able to leverage blockchain, transparent and clear timelines of property ownership could be established.

Smart Contracts

A <u>smart</u> contract is a computer code that can be built into the blockchain to facilitate, verify, or negotiate a contract agreement. Smart contracts operate under a set of conditions that users agree to. When those conditions are met, the terms of the agreement are automatically carried out.

Say, for example, a potential tenant would like to lease an apartment using a smart contract. The landlord agrees to give the tenant the door code to the apartment as soon as the tenant pays the security deposit. Both the tenant and the landlord would send their respective portions of the deal to the smart contract, which would hold onto and automatically exchange the door code for the security deposit on the date the lease begins. If the landlord doesn't supply the door code by the lease date, the smart contract refunds the security deposit. This would eliminate the fees and processes typically associated with the use of a notary, third-party mediator, or attornies.

Supply Chains

As in the IBM Food Trust example, suppliers can use blockchain to record the origins of materials that they have purchased. This would allow companies to verify the authenticity of their products, along with such common labels as "Organic," "Local," and "Fair Trade."

As reported by Forbes, the food industry is increasingly adopting the use of blockchain to track the path and safety of food throughout the farm-to-user journey.

Voting

As mentioned, blockchain could be used to facilitate a modern voting system. Voting with blockchain carries the potential to eliminate election fraud and boost voter turnout, as was tested in the November 2018 midterm elections in West Virginia. Using blockchain in this way would make votes nearly impossible to tamper with. The blockchain protocol would also maintain transparency in the electoral process, reducing the personnel needed to conduct an election and providing officials with nearly instant results. This would eliminate the need for recounts or any real concern that fraud might threaten the election.

Advantages and Disadvantages of Blockchain

For all of its complexity, blockchain's potential as a decentralized form of record-keeping is almost without limit. From greater user privacy and heightened security to lower processing fees and fewer errors, blockchain technology may very well see applications beyond those outlined above. But there are also some disadvantages.

Pros

· Improved accuracy by removing human involvement in verification

·Cost reductions by eliminating third-party verification

· Decentralization makes it harder to tamper with

· Transactions are secure, private, and efficient

· Transparent technology

· Provides a banking alternative and way to secure personal information for citizens of countries with unstable or underdeveloped governments

Cons

· Significant technology cost associated with mining bitcoin

· Low transactions per second

· History of use in illicit activities

· Regulation

Here are the selling points of blockchain for businesses on the market today in more detail.

Chapter 2. Mining of Cryptocurrency

Mining is how new units of cryptocurrency are released into the world, generally in exchange for validating transactions. While it's theoretically possible for the average person to mine cryptocurrency, it's increasingly difficult in proof of work systems, like Bitcoin.

"As the Bitcoin network grows, it gets more complicated, and more processing power is required," says Spencer Montgomery, founder of Uinta Crypto Consulting. "The average consumer used to be able to do this, but now it's just too expensive. There are too many people who have optimized their equipment and technology to outcompete."

And remember: Proof of work cryptocurrencies require huge amounts of energy to mine. It's estimated that 0.21% of all of the world's electricity goes to powering Bitcoin farms. That's roughly the same amount of power Switzerland uses in a year. It's estimated most Bitcoin miners end up using 60% to 80% of what they earn from mining to cover electricity costs.

While it's impractical for the average person to earn crypto by mining in a proof of work system, the proof of stake model requires less in the way of high-powered computing as validators are chosen at random based on the amount they stake. It does, however, require that you already own a cryptocurrency to participate. (If you have no crypto, you have nothing to stake.)

History of Cryptocurrency

In 1983, the American developed a cryptographic system referred to as eCash. Twelve years later, they developed every system DigiCash, that used cryptography to make economic transactions personal.

However, the first time the concept or time period "cryptocurrency" turned into coined changed into in 1998. That year, Wei Dai began to consider developing a brand new payment method that used a cryptographic system and whose important feature was decentralization. In 2008, a funding crisis affecting everybody, together with America's superpower, changed into booming. The effects of such a large economic disaster were dormant and the coins were losing value faster and faster.

In 2009, the so-called Satoshi Nakamoto someone whose identity still remains secret, no person knows who invented bitcoin, or at the least no longer conclusively. Satoshi Nakamoto is the call associated with the person or organization of people who released the authentic bitcoin white paper in 2008 and worked at the authentic bitcoin software program that was launched in 2009. As you have already read, he was not the first person who came up with the idea to create it. In the years since that time, many individuals have either claimed to be or have been suggested as the real-life people behind the pseudonym, but as of January 2021, the authentic identity (or identities) in the back of Satoshi remains obscured. Although it's far tempting to agree with the media's spin that Satoshi Nakamoto is a solitary, quixotic genius who created

Bitcoin out of thin air, such improvements do now not normally appear in a vacuum. All foremost medical discoveries, no matter how original-seeming, have been constructed on previously present research.

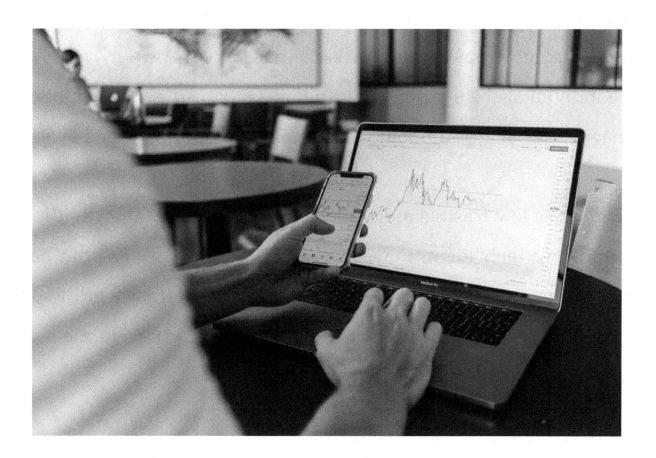

There are precursors to bitcoin: Adam Back's Hashcash, invented in 1997, and finally Wei Dai's b-money, Nick Szabo's bit gold, and Hal Finney's Reusable Proof of Work. The bitcoin whitepaper itself cites Hashcash and b-cash, as well as diverse different works spanning numerous studies fields. Perhaps unsurprisingly, most of the individuals behind the other initiatives named above had been imagined to have additionally had a component in creating bitcoin.

There are a few feasible motivations for bitcoin's inventor deciding to preserve their identity mystery. One is privacy: As bitcoin has gained in recognition—becoming some thing of a worldwide phenomenon—Satoshi Nakamoto would likely garner a number of attention from the media and from governments.

Another motive will be the ability for bitcoin to purpose a major disruption inside the contemporary banking and financial systems. If bitcoin have been to advantage mass adoption, the device should surpass nations' sovereign fiat currencies. This chance to existing forex should inspire governments to need to take legal movement in opposition to bitcoin's creator.

The different motive is safety. Looking at 2009 by myself, 32,489 blocks were mined; at the praise fee of 50 bitcoin according to block, the total payout in 2009 become 1,624,500 bitcoin. One may additionally finish that best Satoshi and perhaps a few different human beings had been mining via 2009 and that they possess a majority of that stash of bitcoin.

Someone in ownership of that lots bitcoin should turn out to be a target of criminals, especially since bitcoins are much less like shares and more like coins, in which the personal keys needed to authorize spending may be published out and actually kept underneath a mattress. While it is likely the inventor of bitcoin could take precautions to make any extortion-brought on transfers traceable, closing anonymous is a superb way for Satoshi to restrict publicity.

Why you should consider investing in Cryptocurrency?

Investing in currencies such as Bitcoin and Ethereum is considered a "high-risk" investment. The price of cryptocurrencies is generally volatile; some can go wrong, others could turn out to be scams, while others may increase in value and produce a great return for the investors. If you are considering investing in Cryptocurrency, you need to find a trusted and reliable trading platform such as Bitfinex. You can read about the <u>trusted Bitfinex review</u>.

To some people, Cryptocurrency could remain niche or vanish just like that. But Cryptocurrency should be considered a high-risk investment just like any other investment. With more and more businesses accepting crypto, it is now evident that Cryptocurrency is here to stay and it will not disappear any time soon.

Some of the big brands that have accepted crypto include Starbucks, Tesla, and other top casinos. This proves that crypto will soon find its way into so many big brands, making it a worthy investment. But just like any other investment, before you invest in crypto, you need to do extensive diligence and don't pin your hopes on one Cryptocurrency or one company. The best decision is to spread your money across so that you can spread the risk. Again, remember to invest only what you can afford to lose.

Types of Risks Associated with Cryptocurrency Investing

Although Bitcoin was not designed as a normal equity investment (no shares have been issued), some speculative investors were drawn to the digital currency after it appreciated rapidly in May 2011 and again in November 2013. Thus, many people purchase bitcoin for its investment value rather than its ability to act as a medium of exchange.

However, the lack of guaranteed value and its digital nature means the purchase and use of bitcoins carries several inherent risks. Many investor alerts have been issued by the Securities and Exchange Commission (SEC), the Financia Industry Regulatory Authority (FINRA), the Consumer Financial Protection Bureau (CFPB), and other agencies.

The concept of a virtual currency is still novel and, compared to traditional investments; bitcoin doesn't have much of a long-term track record or history of credibility to back it. With their increasing popularity, bitcoins are becoming less experimental every day; still, after only a decade, all digital currencies still remain in a development phase. "It is pretty much the highest-risk, highest-return investment that you can possibly make," says Barry Silbert, CEO of Digital Currency Group, which builds and invests in Bitcoin and blockchain companies.10

Regulatory Risk

Investing money into bitcoin in any of its many guises is not for the risk-averse. Bitcoins are a rival to government currency and may be used for black market transactions, money laundering, illegal activities, or tax evasion. As a result, governments may seek to regulate, restrict, or ban the use and sale of bitcoins (and some already have). Others are coming up with various rules.

For example, in 2015, the New York State Department of Financial Services finalized regulations that would require companies dealing with the buy, sell, transfer, or storage of bitcoins to record the identity of customers, have a compliance officer, and maintain capital reserves. The transactions worth $10,000 or more will have to be recorded and reported.

The lack of uniform regulations about bitcoins (and other virtual currency) raises questions over their longevity, liquidity, and universality.

Security Risk

Most individuals who own and use bitcoin have not acquired their tokens through mining operations. Rather, they buy and sell bitcoin and other digital currencies on any of a number of popular online markets, known as bitcoin exchanges.

Bitcoin exchanges are entirely digital and, as with any virtual system, are at risk from hackers, malware, and operational glitches. If a thief gains access to a bitcoin owner's computer hard drive and steals their private encryption key, they could transfer the stolen bitcoin to another account. (Users can prevent this only if bitcoins are stored on a computer that is not connected to the internet, or else by choosing to use a paper wallet printing out the bitcoin private keys and addresses, and not keeping them on a computer at all.)

Hackers can also target bitcoin exchanges, gaining access to thousands of accounts and digital wallets where bitcoins are stored. One especially notorious hacking incident took place in 2014, when Mt. Gox, a bitcoin exchange in Japan, was forced to close down after millions of dollars' worth of bitcoins were stolen.

This is particularly problematic given that all Bitcoin transactions are permanent and irreversible. It's like dealing with cash: Any transaction carried out with bitcoins can only be reversed if the person who has received them refunds them. There is no third party or a payment processor, as in the case of a debit or credit card—hence, no source of protection or appeal if there is a problem.

Insurance Risk

Some investments are insured through the Securities Investor Protection Corporation. Normal bank accounts are insured through the Federal Deposit Insurance Corporation (FDIC) up to a certain amount depending on the jurisdiction.

Generally speaking, bitcoin exchanges and bitcoin accounts are not insured by any type of federal or government program. In 2019, prime dealer and trading platform SFOX announced it would be able to provide bitcoin investors with FDIC insurance, but only for the portion of transactions involving cash.13

Fraud Risk

While bitcoin uses private key encryption to verify owners and register transactions, fraudsters and scammers may attempt to sell false bitcoins. For instance, in July 2013, the SEC brought legal action against an operator of a bitcoin-related Ponzi scheme. There have also been documented cases of bitcoin price manipulation, another common form of fraud.

Market Risk

Like with any investment, bitcoin values can fluctuate. Indeed, the value of the currency has seen wild swings in price over its short existence. Subject to high volume buying and selling on exchanges, it has a high sensitivity to any newsworthy events. According to the CFPB, the price of bitcoins fell by 61% in a single day in 2013, while the one-day price drop record in 2014 was as big as 80%.

If fewer people begin to accept bitcoin as a currency, these digital units may lose value and could become worthless. Indeed, there was speculation that the "bitcoin bubble" had burst when the price declined from its all-time high during the cryptocurrency rush in late 2017 and early 2018.

There is already plenty of competition, and although bitcoin has a huge lead over the hundreds of other digital currencies that have sprung up because of its brand recognition and venture capital money, a technological break-through in the form of a better virtual coin is always a threat.

Imposter Websites

You may be following a solid tip from someone with a lot of expertise but still become a victim by accidentally visiting a fake website. There's a surprising number of websites that have been set up to resemble original, valid startup companies. If there isn't a small lock icon indicating security near the URL bar and no "https" in the site address think twice.

Even if the site looks identical to the one you think you're visiting, you may find yourself directed to another platform for payment. For example, you click on a link that looks like a legitimate site, but attackers have created a fake URL with a zero in it instead of a letter 'o'. That platform, of course, isn't taking you to the cryptocurrency investment that you've already researched. To avoid this, carefully type the exact URL into your browser. Double check it, too.

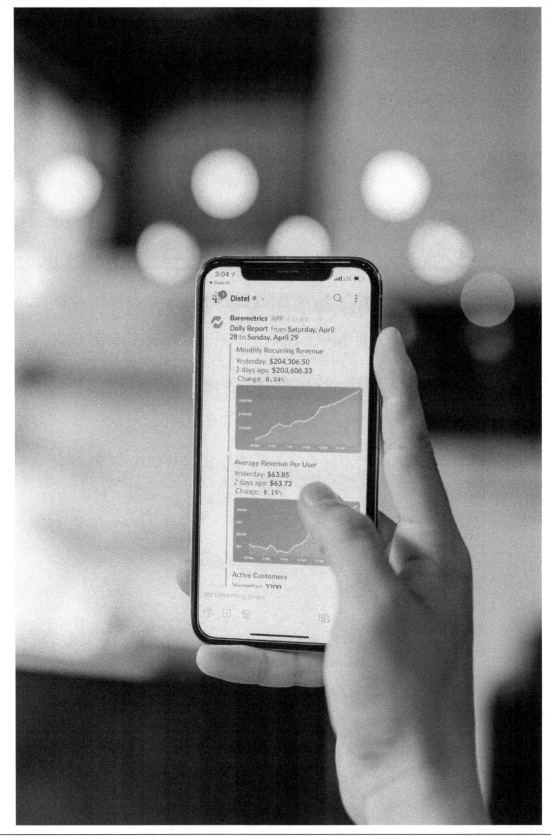

Fake Mobile Apps

Another common way scammers trick cryptocurrency investors is through <u>fake apps</u> available for download through Google Play and the Apple App Store. Although stakeholders can often quickly find these fake apps and get them removed, that doesn't mean the apps aren't impacting many bottom lines. Thousands of people have already downloaded fake cryptocurrency apps, <u>reports Bitcoin News</u>.

While this is a greater risk for Android users, every investor should be aware of the possibility. Are there obvious misspellings in the copy or even the name of the app? Does the branding look inauthentic with strange coloring or an incorrect logo? Take note and reconsider downloading.

Bad Tweets and Other Social Media Updates

If you're following celebrities and executives on social media, you can't be sure that you're not following impostor accounts. The same applies to cryptocurrencies, where malicious, impersonating bots are rampant. Don't trust offers that come from Twitter or Facebook, especially if there seems to be an impossible result. Fake accounts are everywhere.

If someone on these platforms asks for even a small amount of your cryptocurrency, it's likely you can never get it back. Just because others are replying to the offer, don't assume they aren't bots, either. You have to be extra careful.

Scamming Emails

Even if it looks exactly like an email you received from a legitimate cryptocurrency company, take care before investing your digital currency. Is the email the exact same, and are the logo and branding identical? Can you verify that the email address is legitimately connected to the company? The ability to check on this is one reason why it's important to choose a company that has real people working for it. If you have doubts about an email, ask someone who works there. And never click on a link in a message to get to a site.

Scammers often announce fake ICOs, or initial coin offerings, as a way to steal substantial funds. Don't fall for these fake email and website offers. Take your time to look over all the details.

Unfortunately, there are many ways that some Internet users exploit unsecure computing systems to mine or steal cryptocurrency.

How to Buy Bitcoin using PayPal

It is likewise feasible to shop for Bitcoin through charge processor PayPal. There are two ways to buy Bitcoin the usage of PayPal. The first, and maximum handy technique, is to purchase cryptocurrencies through the use of your PayPal account. The second choice is to apply the stability of your PayPal account to buy cryptocurrencies from a third-celebration issuer. This choice isn't always as handy as the first one due to the fact very few third party sites allow users to purchase Bitcoin with the use of the PayPal button.

Four cryptocurrencies – Bitcoin, Ethereum, Litecoin, and Bitcoin Cash – can be purchased without delay thru PayPal. With the exception of Hawaii, citizens of all states can both use their existing PayPal accounts or set up new ones.

To set up a crypto account with PayPal, the subsequent pieces of information are required: Name, Physical cope with, Date of Birth, and Tax Identification Number. There are some of the methods by which you may purchase Bitcoin via PayPal.

Some of them are:

- Existing balance in PayPal account.

-
  - Debit card linked to PayPal account

-
  - Bank account linked to PayPal account

-

It is not feasible to apply for a credit card to buy Bitcoin using PayPal. During the purchase system, PayPal will show a price. However, the inherent volatility of cryptocurrency charges method that those prices can exchange fast. You have to make sure which you have enough finances in your account to make the purchase.

When you buy Bitcoin without delay from PayPal, it makes cash off the crypto spread or the distinction between Bitcoin's marketplace charge and change fee among USD and the cryptocurrency. The enterprise additionally expenses a transaction fee for each purchase. These charges rely upon the dollar quantity of buy. For instance, a flat rate of $zero.50 is charged for purchases between $a hundred to $2 hundred. Thereafter, the fee is a percentage of the general dollar amount. For instance, a fee of two% of the whole quantity is charged for crypto purchases among $100 to $two hundred.

One downside of buying cryptocurrencies via PayPal is that you can't switch crypto outside the price processor's platform. Therefore, it isn't always feasible to switch cryptocurrencies from PayPal's pockets to an outside crypto wallet or your private wallet.

The other downside of using PayPal is that very few exchanges and online investors allow the charge processor to purchase payment. EToro is many of the few online investors who use PayPal to buy Bitcoin on its platform.

How to Buy Bitcoin with Credit Card

The technique to purchase Bitcoin with credit playing cards is just like getting the cryptocurrency with debit cards or thru computerized clearing house (ACH) transfers. You will want to go into your credit card details with the trade or online buying and selling firm and authorize the transaction. In trendy, however, it isn't always a terrific concept to purchase Bitcoin with credit cards. There are multiple motives for this.

First, not all exchanges permit Bitcoin purchases using credit cards because of associated processing expenses and the chance of fraud. Their selection to accomplish that may fit out inside the quality hobbies of customers. This is because credit card processing can tack extra fees onto such transactions. Thus, similarly to paying transaction charges, you will emerge as processing expenses that the alternate may also bypass onto you.

The 2nd motive is that credit card purchases can be high priced. Credit card issuers treat Bitcoin purchases as coins advances and charge hefty charges and interest quotes on such advances. For example, American Express and Chase both count purchases of cryptocurrencies as coins boost transactions. Thus, if you purchase $100 well worth of Bitcoin using an American Express card, you will pay $10 (current cash boost fee for such transactions) plus an annual percentage charge of 25%.

An oblique technique of buying Bitcoin using a credit card is to get a Bitcoin Rewards creditcard. Such playing cards characteristic like your normal rewards creditcard; besides, they offer rewards in the shape of Bitcoin. So, they make investments cash again earned from purchases into Bitcoin. An instance of a Bitcoin Rewards card is the BlockFi Bitcoin Rewards Credit Card.

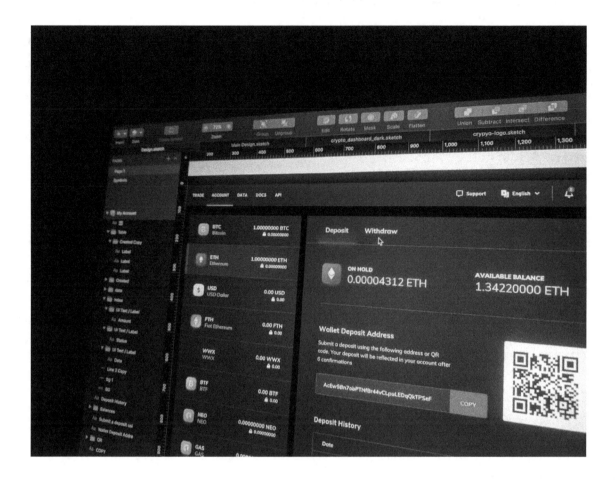

Beware, however, that the annual price on these playing cards may be steep, and there can be extra expenses associated with the conversion of fiat currencies into crypto.

Alternate Ways of Buying Bitcoin

While exchanges like Coinbase or Binance remain some of the most popular ways of purchasing Bitcoin, it is not the only method. Below are some additional processes Bitcoin owners utilize.

Bitcoin ATMs

Bitcoin ATMs act like in-person Bitcoin exchanges. Individuals can insert cash into the machine and use it to purchase Bitcoin that is then transferred to a secure digital wallet. Bitcoin ATMs have become increasingly popular in recent years; Coin ATM Radar can help to track down the closest machines.

P2P Exchanges

Unlike decentralized exchanges, which match up buyers and sellers anonymously and facilitate all aspects of the transaction, there are some peer-to-peer (P2P) exchange services that provide a more direct connection between users. Local Bitcoins is an example of such an exchange. After creating an account, users can post requests to buy or sell Bitcoin, including information about payment methods and price. Users then browse through listings of buy and sell offers, choosing those trade partners with whom they wish to transact.

Local Bitcoins facilitates some of the aspects of the trade. While P2P exchanges do not offer the same anonymity as decentralized exchanges, they allow users the opportunity to shop around for the best deal. Many of these exchanges also provide rating systems so that users have a way to evaluate potential trade partners before transacting.

How to Sell Bitcoin

You can sell Bitcoin at the same venues that you purchased the cryptocurrency, such as cryptocurrency exchanges and peer-to-peer platforms. Typically, the process to sell Bitcoin on these platforms is similar to the process used to purchase the cryptocurrency.

For example, you may only be required to click a button and specify an order type (i.e., whether the cryptocurrency should be sold instantly at available prices or whether it should be sold to limit losses) to conduct the sale. Depending on the market composition and demand at the venue, the offering price for Bitcoin may vary. For example, exchanges in South Korea traded Bitcoin at a Kimchi premium during the run up in its prices back in 2018.

Cryptocurrency exchanges charge a percentage of the crypto sale amount as fees. For example, Coinbase charges 1.49% of the overall transaction amount as fees.

Exchanges generally have daily and monthly withdrawal limits. Therefore, cash from a large sale may not be immediately available to the trader. There are no limits on the amount of cryptocurrency you can sell, however.

Chapter 3. Before You Begin

There are numerous matters that every aspiring Bitcoin investor desires. A cryptocurrency change account, private identity documents in case you are using a Know Your Customer (KYC) platform, a comfy connection to the Internet, and a method of charge. Likewise, it is recommended that you have your own private wallet outside of the trading account. Valid strategies of payment using this path consist of financial institution accounts, debit playing cards, and credit playing cards. It is likewise viable to get Bitcoin at specialized ATMs and via P2P exchanges. However, be aware that Bitcoin ATMs have been increasingly requiring authorities-issued IDs as of early 2020.

Privacy and protection are vital issues for Bitcoin traders. Even though there are no physical Bitcoins, it is also a bad idea to gloat approximately huge holdings. Anyone who profits the personal key to a public address at the Bitcoin blockchain can authorize transactions. Private keys must be kept in mystery; criminals might also attempt to steal them if they analyze large holdings. Be conscious that anybody can see the balance of a public deal you use. That makes it a good idea to maintain vast investments at public addresses that aren't immediately linked to ones that are used for transactions.

Anyone can view a history of transactions made at the blockchain, even you. While transactions are publicly recorded at the blockchain, figuring out user information isn't always. Most effective, a person's public key appears next to a transaction— making transactions exclusive however not nameless on the Bitcoin blockchain. In an experience, Bitcoin transactions are greater transparent and traceable than coins, but the cryptocurrency can also be used anonymously.

Following are some steps you need to follow if you want to invest in cryptocurrency:

Step One: Choose an Exchange

Signing up for a cryptocurrency trade will permit you to shop for, sell, and maintain cryptocurrency. It is generally an exceptional exercise to apply a change that lets its customers additionally withdrawal their crypto to their very own non-public online wallet for more secure preservation. This feature might not depend on the ones trying to change Bitcoin or other cryptocurrencies.

There are many styles of cryptocurrency exchanges. Because the Bitcoin ethos is about decentralization and man or woman sovereignty, some exchanges permit customers to remain anonymous and do not require users to go into private information. Such exchanges perform autonomously and, generally, decentralized, which means that they no longer have a primary factor of manipulation.

While such structures may be used for nefarious sports, they're extensively utilized to offer offerings for the arena's unbanked population. For certain classes of human beings – refugees or those dwelling in international locations with little to no infrastructure for authorities' credit or banking – anonymous exchanges can help convey them into the mainstream economy.

Right now, but, the maximum popular exchanges now not decentralized and do require KYC. In the United States, these exchanges include Coinbase, Kraken, Gemini, and Binance U.S., to name some. Each of those exchanges has grown appreciably inside the variety of capabilities they offer.

Coinbase, Kraken, and Gemini offer Bitcoin and a growing wide variety of altcoins. These 3 are probably the perfect on-ramp to crypto in the entire enterprise. Binance caters to a more superior dealer, imparting greater critical trading functionality and a better style of altcoins to choose from.

A vital thing to note whilst creating a cryptocurrency change account is to apply secure net practices. This consists of the usage of -aspect authentication and using a precise and lengthy password, together with a variety of lowercase letters, capitalized letters, special characters, and numbers.

Step Two: Connect Your Exchange to a Payment Option

Once you have chosen an exchange, you now want to collect your non-public documents. Depending on the exchange, these may consist of snapshots of a driving force's license, social security variety, in addition to statistics approximately your business enterprise and supply of funds. The records you could need can depend upon your location and the laws inside it. The system is largely the same as putting in place a standard brokerage account.

After the trade has ensured your identity and legitimacy, you can now join a payment choice. At most exchanges, you may connect your financial institution account without delay, or you could join a debit or credit card. While you may use a credit card to buy cryptocurrency, it's miles usually something that should be avoided because of the volatility that cryptocurrencies can revel in.

While Bitcoin is legal inside the United States, some banks no longer take too kindly to the idea and might query or even forestall deposits to crypto-associated web sites or exchanges. It is a great idea to test to make sure that your financial institution deposits at your chosen alternate.

There are various costs for deposits thru a financial institution account, debit, or credit card. Coinbase is a stable exchange for beginners and has a 1.49% charge for financial institution money owed, with a 3.99% rate for debit and credit playing cards. It is essential to analyze the charges associated with every fee choice to assist in pick out and trade or pick out which price choice works great for you.

Exchanges additionally rate fees in step with the transaction. This rate can both be a flat fee (if the trading quantity is low) or a per cent of buying and selling quantity. Credit cards incur a processing rate similarly to the transaction costs.

Step Three: Place an Order

Once you have selected trade and connected a charged alternative, you may now buy Bitcoin and other cryptocurrencies. In latest years, cryptocurrency exchanges have slowly turn out to be more mainstream. They have grown notably in terms of liquidity and their breadth of capabilities. The operational modifications at cryptocurrency exchanges parallel the exchange notion for cryptocurrencies. An industry that became as soon as the notion of as a rip-off or one with questionable practices is slowly morphing right into a valid one that has drawn interest from all huge players in the economic offerings industry.

Now, cryptocurrency exchanges have gotten to some extent where they have almost identical functions as their stock brokerage counterparts. Once you have located an exchange and linked a charging method, you are geared up to move.

Crypto exchanges these days provide some order types and methods to invest. Almost all crypto exchanges offer each marketplace and limit orders, and some also provide stop-loss orders. Of the exchanges stated above, Kraken gives the most order kinds. Kraken lets in for market, restriction, prevent-loss, prevent-restrict, take-earnings, and take-profit limit orders1

.

Aside from diffusion of order types, exchanges also provide approaches to set up habitual investments allowing clients to dollar fee average into their investments of desire. Coinbase, for instance, we could users set habitual purchases for every day, week, or month.

Step Four: Safe Storage

Bitcoin and cryptocurrency wallets are a place to shop virtual property extra securely. Having your crypto out of the trade doors and your personal wallet guarantees that only you have manipulated the personal key to your funds. It additionally gives you the ability to shop funds far away from an exchange and avoid the threat of your change getting hacked and losing your funds.

Some wallets have extra capabilities than others. Some are Bitcoin best, and some provide the potential to shop numerous types of altcoins. Some wallets also offer the capability to change one token for any other.

When it involves deciding on a Bitcoin wallet, you have some options. The first element you will need to understand about crypto wallets is hot wallets (online wallets) and cold wallets (paper or hardware wallets).

Hot Wallets

Online wallets also are called "hot" wallets. Hot wallets are wallets that run on internet-related devices like computer systems, phones, or capsules. This can create vulnerability due to the fact these wallets generate the private keys on your coins on those net-related devices. While a hot pockets may be very convenient in the way you're capable of access and make transactions along with your belongings quickly, storing your non-public key on a web-linked tool makes it greater vulnerable to a hack.

This can also sound far-fetched, but individuals who are not the usage of sufficient protection whilst using those hot wallets may have their price range stolen. This isn't always an rare prevalence and it can take place in some of approaches. As an instance, boasting on a public discussion board like Reddit about how a good deal Bitcoin you keep while you are the usage of little to no safety and storing it in a hot pockets would not be smart. That said, these wallets may be made to be relaxed so long as precautions are taken. Strong passwords, two-component authentication, and safe internet surfing have to be considered minimum requirements.

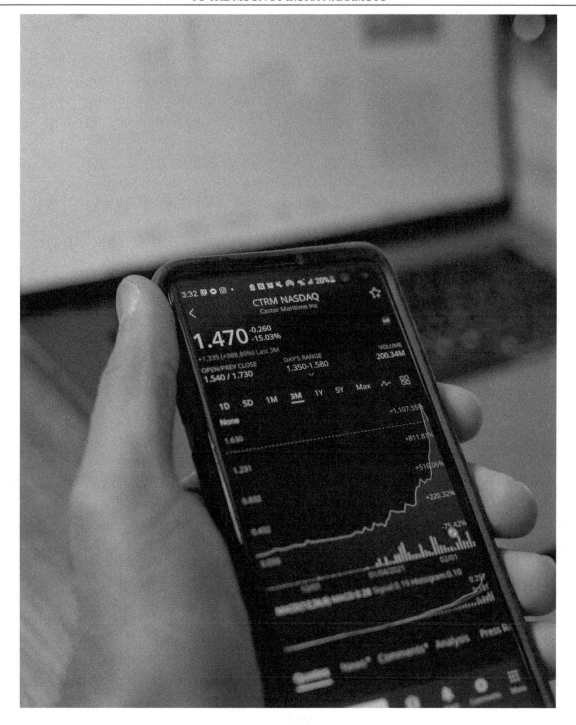

These wallets are nice used for small quantities of cryptocurrency or cryptocurrency that you are actively buying and selling on an exchange. You should liken a hot pockets to a bank account. Conventional financial wisdom might say to preserve handiest spending money in a bank account at the same time as the majority of your cash is in savings debts or different funding bills. The identical could be said for hot wallets. Hot wallets embody cell, computer, net, and exchange account custody wallets.

As stated previously, change wallets are custodial accounts provided by way of the alternate. The consumer of this pockets kind isn't always the holder of the personal key to the cryptocurrency that is held in this wallet. If an event were to arise where the change is hacked or your account becomes compromised, your budget could be lost. The phrase "now not your key, no longer your coin" is closely-repeated within cryptocurrency boards and groups.

Cold Wallets

The most effective description of a cold wallet is a pockets that is not related to the internet and consequently stands at a much lesser risk of being compromised. These wallets can also be referred to as offline wallets or hardware wallets.

These wallets keep a person's private key on some thing that is not linked to the internet and may come with software program that works in parallel in order that the user can view their portfolio with out putting their personal key at chance.

Perhaps the most secure manner to keep cryptocurrency offline is through a paper pockets. A paper wallet is a wallet that you can generate off of certain websites. It then produces each public and personal keys that you print out on a bit of paper. The capacity to get admission to cryptocurrency in these addresses is simplest viable if you have that piece of paper with the private key. Many people laminate those paper wallets and shop them in protection deposit packing containers at their financial institution or even in a safe of their home. These wallets are meant for excessive safety and long-time period investments because you can not quick sell or alternate Bitcoin saved this manner.

A more usually used type of cold wallet is a hardware pockets. A hardware pockets is commonly a USB power device that stores a person's non-public keys securely offline. Such wallets have serious benefits over hot wallets as they're unaffected by viruses that might be on one's pc. With hardware wallets, personal keys in no way are available contact together with your network-related computer or doubtlessly prone software. These gadgets are also commonly open supply, allowing the network to decide its protection thru code audits rather than a organisation declaring that it is safe to apply.

Cold wallets are the most cozy way to shop your Bitcoin or other cryptocurrencies. For the maximum component, but, they require a piece greater understanding to installation.

A proper way to installation your wallets is to have three matters: an alternate account to shop for and sell, a hot wallet to keep small to medium quantities of crypto you desire to change or promote, and a cold hardware pockets to keep large holdings for long-term periods.

Best cryptocurrencies on the market to invest in

Cryptocurrencies are almost always designed to be free from government manipulation and control, although as they have grown more popular this foundational aspect of the industry has come under fire. The currencies modeled after Bitcoin are collectively called altcoins, and in some cases "shitcoins," and have often tried to present themselves as modified or improved versions of Bitcoin. While some of these currencies may have some impressive features that Bitcoin does not, matching the level of security that Bitcoin's networks achieves has largely yet to be seen by an altcoin.

Below, we'll examine some of the most important digital currencies other than Bitcoin. First, though, a caveat: it is impossible for a list like this to be entirely comprehensive. One reason for this is the fact that there are more than 4,000 cryptocurrencies in existence as of January 2021. While many of these cryptos have little to no following or trading volume, some enjoy immense popularity among dedicated communities of backers and investors.

Beyond that, the field of cryptocurrencies is always expanding, and the next great digital token may be released tomorrow. While Bitcoin is widely seen as a pioneer in the world of cryptocurrencies, analysts adopt many approaches for evaluating tokens other than BTC. It's common, for instance, for analysts to attribute a great deal of importance to the ranking of coins relative to one another in terms of market cap. We've factored this into our consideration, but there are other reasons why a digital token may be included in the list, as well.

1. Bitcoin (BTC)
2.

The closest thing you'll get to a blue-chip cryptocurrency, <u>Bitcoin</u> has dominated the market since the first bitcoins were mined in January 2009 – but that doesn't mean it has always been smooth sailing. Bitcoin prices hit a high of around $20,000 in December 2017 before collapsing in 2018, reaching a bottom at $3,234 by the end of that year. Since then, however, Bitcoin has enjoyed a comeback as prices surged to more than $40,000 in January 2021 for a market cap of more than $1 trillion – meaning bitcoins accounted for more than 69% of the cryptocurrency market. Bitcoin has its fair share of volatility, as prices have pulled back since hitting this high, but being the biggest name in crypto gives it a worldwide acceptance that lesser-known rivals don't have, arguably making it the best cryptocurrency to buy for investors new to the asset class.

1. Bitcoin Cash (BCH)
2.

<u>Bitcoin Cash</u> (BCH) holds an important place in the history of altcoins because it is one of the earliest and most successful <u>hard forks</u> of the original Bitcoin. In the cryptocurrency world, a fork takes place as the result of debates and arguments between developers and miners. Due to the decentralized nature of digital currencies, wholesale changes to the code underlying the token or coin at hand must be made due to general consensus; the mechanism for this process varies according to the particular cryptocurrency.

When different factions can't come to an agreement, sometimes the digital currency is split, with the original chain remaining true to its original code and the new chain beginning life as a new version of the prior coin, complete with changes to its code.

BCH began its life in August of 2017 as a result of one of these splits. The debate that led to the creation of BCH had to do with the issue of scalability; the Bitcoin network has a limit on the size of blocks: one megabyte (MB). BCH increases the block size from one MB to eight MB, with the idea being that larger blocks can hold more transactions within them, and therefore the transaction speed would be increased. It also makes other changes, including the removal of the Segregated Witness protocol which impacts block space. As of January 2021, BCH had a market cap of $8.9 billion and a value per token of $513.45.

1. Litecoin (LTC)

2.

Litecoin, launched in 2011, was among the first cryptocurrencies to follow in the footsteps of Bitcoin and has often been referred to as "silver to Bitcoin's gold." It was created by Charlie Lee, an MIT graduate and former Google engineer. Litecoin is based on an open-source global payment network that is not controlled by any central authority and uses "scrypt" as a proof of work, which can be decoded with the help of CPUs of consumer-grade. Although Litecoin is like Bitcoin in many ways, it has a faster block generation rate and hence offers a faster transaction confirmation time. Other than developers, there are a growing number of merchants who accept Litecoin. As of January 2021, Litecoin had a market cap of $10.1 billion and a per token value of $153.88, making it the sixth-largest cryptocurrency in the world.

1. Ethereum (ETH)
2.

The first Bitcoin alternative on our list, <u>Ethereum</u>, is a decentralized software platform that enables <u>Smart Contracts</u> and Decentralized Applications (DApps) to be built and run without any downtime, fraud, control, or interference from a third party. The goal behind Ethereum is to create a decentralized suite of financial products that anyone in the world can have free access to, regardless of nationality, ethnicity, or faith. This aspect makes the implications for those in some countries more compelling, as those without state infrastructure and state identifications can get access to bank accounts, loans, insurance, or a variety of other financial products.

The applications on Ethereum are run on its platform-specific cryptographic token, ether. Ether is like a vehicle for moving around on the Ethereum platform and is sought by mostly developers looking to develop and run applications inside Ethereum, or now, by investors looking to make purchases of other digital currencies using ether. Ether, launched in 2015, is currently the second-largest digital currency by market cap after Bitcoin, although it lags behind the dominant cryptocurrency by a significant margin. As of January 2021, ether's market cap is roughly 19% of Bitcoin's size.

In 2014, Ethereum launched a pre-sale for ether which received an overwhelming response; this helped to usher in the age of the initial coin offering (ICO). According to Ethereum, it can be used to "codify, decentralize, secure and trade just about anything." Following the attack on the DAO in 2016, Ethereum was split into Ethereum (ETH) and Ethereum Classic (ETC). As of January 2021, Ethereum (ETH) had a market cap of $138.3 billion and a per token value of $1,218.59.

In 2021 Ethereum plans to change its consensus algorithm from proof-of-work to proof-of-stake. This move will allow Ethereum's network to run itself with far less energy as well as improved transaction speed. Proof-of-stake allows network participants to "stake" their ether to the network. This process helps to secure the network and process the transactions that occur. Those who do this are rewarded ether similar to an interest account. This is an alternative to Bitcoin's proof-of-work mechanism where miners are rewarded more Bitcoin for processing transactions.

1. Binance Coin (BNB)
2.

Like Ethereum, Binance Coin is much more than a cryptocurrency – as a matter of fact, Binance Coin was originally hosted on Ethereum until the Binance decentralized exchange, or DEX, went online in 2017. The Binance DEX is a platform much like Ethereum, albeit with a different mission. The Binance DEX is a decentralized platform where users can not only buy and sell binance coins but also use BNB to convert other cryptocurrencies from one to another. This has made the Binance DEX the biggest cryptocurrency exchange on the planet by volume and has helped fuel the popularity of the digital asset. Most importantly, the Binance DEX offers a discount to users who pay transaction fees on the exchange with BNB – a smart strategy that keeps users on the platform and helps sustain Binance Coin's growth.

1. Tron (TRX)
2.

The past year brought extreme upheaval within the entertainment industry, leaving it ripe for disruption. This is exactly the sort of opportunity the founders of Tron must have been hoping for when they built a decentralized, blockchain-based platform for sharing content. Whereas many of the biggest entertainment companies in the world profit from gathering and selling data about their users, using Tron leaves no such footprints behind. While it protects users, Tron also allows creators to monetize their content directly via Tronix, Tron's form of cryptocurrency. The platform has gained fame and notoriety in equal measure over the last few years due to the antics of Tron Foundation founder Justin Sun, but no matter how you feel about him, it's undeniable that Tron is an ambitious idea – and while it isn't going to overthrow <u>Netflix</u> (ticker: <u>NFLX</u>) tomorrow, it is an excellent speculative investment.

1. Chainlink (LINK)
2.

Chainlink is a decentralized oracle network that bridges the gap between smart contracts, like the ones on Ethereum, and data outside of it. Blockchains themselves do not have the ability to connect to outside applications in a trusted manner. Chainlink's decentralized oracles allow smart contracts to communicate with outside data so that the contracts can be executed based on data that Ethereum itself cannot connect to.

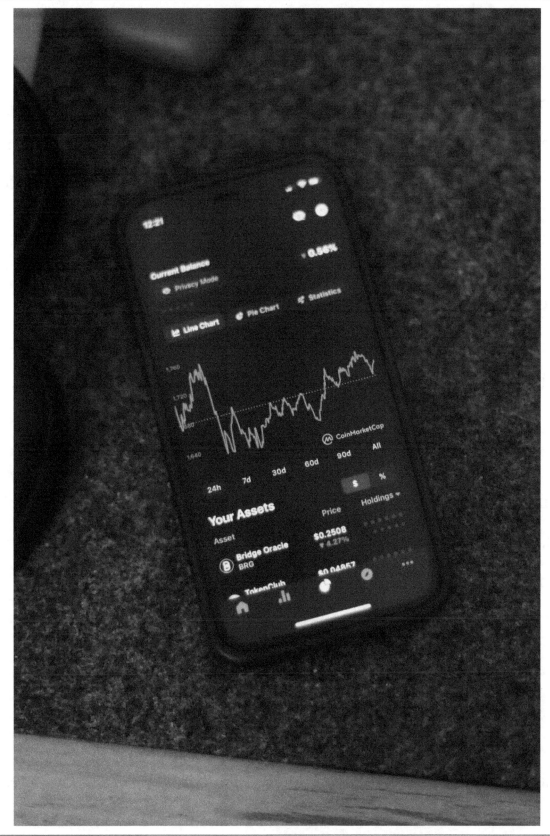

Chainlink's blog details a number of use cases for its system. One of the many use cases that are explained would be to monitor water supplies for pollution or illegal syphoning going on in certain cities. Sensors could be set up to monitor corporate consumption, water tables, and the levels of local bodies of water. A Chainlink oracle could track this data and feed it directly into a smart contract. The smart contract could be set up to execute fines, release flood warnings to cities, or invoice companies using too much of a city's water with the incoming data from the oracle.

Chainlink was developed by Sergey Nazarov along with Steve Ellis. As of January 2021, Chainlink's market capitalization is $8.6 billion, and one LINK is valued at $21.53.

1. USD Coin
2.

The stablecoin, which hit the markets in September 2018, is managed by a consortium called CENTRE, launched by peer-to-peer company Circle and crypto exchange Coinbase. Their aim, according to their website, is to "bring stability to crypto". It was trading at $1 with a market cap of $9.12bn as of 9:38am GMT on 9 March.

1. Cardano
2.

Cardano is an "Ouroboros proof-of-stake" cryptocurrency that was created with a research-based approach by engineers, mathematicians, and cryptography experts. The project was co-founded by Charles Hoskinson, one of the five initial founding members of Ethereum. After having some disagreements with the direction Ethereum was taking, he left and later helped to create Cardano.

The team behind Cardano created its blockchain through extensive experimentation and peer-reviewed research. The researchers behind the project have written over 90 papers on blockchain technology across a range of topics. This research is the backbone of Cardano.

Due to this rigorous process, Cardano seems to stand out among its proof-of-stake peers as well as other large cryptocurrencies. Cardano has also been dubbed the "Ethereum killer" as its blockchain is said to be capable of more. That said, Cardano is still in its early stages. While it has beaten Ethereum to the proof-of-stake consensus model it still has a long way to go in terms of decentralized financial applications.

Cardano aims to be the financial operating system of the world by establishing decentralized financial products similarly to Ethereum as well as providing solutions for chain interoperability, voter fraud, and legal contract tracing, among other things. As of January 2021, Cardano has a market capitalization of $9.8 billion and one ADA trades for $0.31.

1. Tether (USDT)
2.

Tether was one of the first and most popular of a group of so-called <u>stablecoins</u>, cryptocurrencies that aim to peg their market value to a currency or other external reference point in order to reduce volatility. Because most digital currencies, even major ones like Bitcoin, have experienced frequent periods of dramatic volatility, Tether and other stablecoins attempt to smooth out price fluctuations in order to attract users who may otherwise be cautious. Tether's price is tied directly to the price of the US dollar. The system allows users to more easily make transfers from other cryptocurrencies back to US dollars in a more timely manner than actually converting to normal currency.

Launched in 2014, Tether describes itself as "a blockchain-enabled platform designed to facilitate the use of fiat currencies in a digital manner." Effectively, this cryptocurrency allows individuals to utilize a blockchain network and related technologies to transact in traditional currencies while minimizing the volatility and complexity often associated with digital currencies. In January of 2021, Tether was the third-largest cryptocurrency by market cap, with a total market cap of $24.4 billion and a per-token value of $1.00.

1. Monero (XMR)

2.

<u>Monero</u> is a secure, private, and untraceable currency. This open-source cryptocurrency was launched in April 2014 and soon garnered great interest among the cryptography community and enthusiasts. The development of this cryptocurrency is completely donation based and community driven. Monero has been launched with a strong focus on decentralization and scalability, and it enables complete privacy by using a special technique called "ring signatures."

With this technique, there appears a group of cryptographic signatures including at least one real participant, but since they all appear valid; the real one cannot be isolated. Because of exceptional security mechanisms like this, Monero has developed something of an unsavory reputation—it has been linked to criminal operations around the world. While this is a prime candidate for making criminal transactions anonymously, the privacy inherent in Monero is also helpful to dissidents of oppressive regimes around the world. As of January 2021, Monero had a market cap of $2.8 billion and a per-token value of $158.37.

1. Stellar

2.

Stellar is an open blockchain network designed to provide enterprise solutions by connecting financial institutions for the purpose of large transactions. Huge transactions between banks and investment firms that typically would take several days, a number of intermediaries, and cost a good deal of money, can now be done nearly instantaneously with no intermediaries and cost little to nothing for those making the transaction.

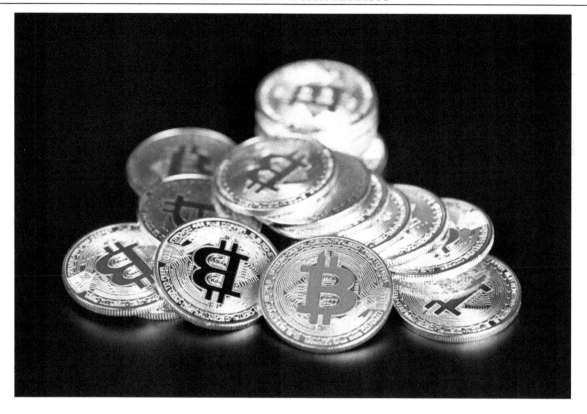

While Stellar has positioned itself as an enterprise blockchain for institutional transactions, it is still an open blockchain that can be used by anyone. The system allows for cross-border transactions between any currencies. Stellar's native currency is Lumens (XLM). The network requires users to hold Lumens to be able to transact on the network.

Stellar was founded by Jed McCaleb, a founding member of Ripple Labs and developer of the Ripple protocol. He eventually left his role with Ripple and went on to co-found the Stellar Development Foundation. Stellar Lumens have a market capitalization of $6.1 billion and are valued at $0.27 as of January 2021.

1. Ripple (XRP)
2.

XRP is a digital asset built for payments. It is the native digital asset on the XRP Ledger—an open-source, permissionless and decentralized blockchain technology that can settle transactions in 3-5 seconds.XRP can be sent directly without needing a central intermediary, making it a convenient instrument in bridging two different currencies quickly and efficiently.

Ripple diverges from much of its cryptocurrency competitors in a number of ways. Ripple is an invention of Ripple Labs, and the Ripple token is being used in high-speed and low-cost money transfers worldwide.

Ripple Labs has announced a number of partnerships with leading money transfer services, with more financial market partnerships expected in the future.

Unlike many cryptocurrencies that trade on hopes and dreams, Ripple is being used in the real world today, showing signs of future adoption within the financial market community. Ripple rise in value over 36,000% in 2017, but similar gains may not be likely going forward

1. EOS (EOS)
2.

<u>EOS</u> is the native cryptocurrency for the EOS.IO blockchain platform with smart contract capabilities. The company <u>Block.one</u> created EOS.IO in September 2017 and it now has over 100 dapps with thousands of daily active users. It enables decentralized apps, or dapps, to be created by software developers. The platform is more scalable than many other blockchain networks, with the ability to process one million transactions per second without any fees. Its dapp development capability makes

EOS similar to <u>Ethereum</u> with the notable distinction that transaction confirmations are done through a different type of consensus system. Block producers are chosen by the EOS ecosystem through a voting mechanism known as delegated-proof-of-stake (DPoS). In order to vote, users must stake tokens for three days without selling them, putting them at risk of losing money should the price of the token drop during that time. There is no maximum supply limit of EOS tokens. The delegated proof-of-stake model uses inflation, capped at 5% annually, to fund transactions and pay block users. Many competitors, including Ethereum, have a transaction fee for transferring coins or tokens from one wallet address to another. EOS concluded its year-long ICO in May of this year, raising a total of $4 billion. The longer-duration ICO was done in an attempt to create an orderly market for EOS without the dramatic run-up and sudden crash common to cryptocurrencies when launched.

YTD performance for EOS is flat, with less volatility than has been seen with some competitors. Enthusiasm for the project remains high, and EOS is one of the most actively traded cryptocurrencies on exchanges.

1. Polkadot (DOT)
2.

Polkadot is a unique proof-of-stake cryptocurrency that is aimed at delivering interoperability between other blockchains. Its protocol is designed to connect permissioned and permissionless blockchains as well as oracles to allow systems to work together under one roof.

Polkadot's core component is its relay chain that allows the interoperability of varying networks. It also allows for "parachains," or parallel blockchains with their own native tokens for specific use cases.

Where this system differs from Ethereum is that rather than creating just decentralized applications on Polkadot, developers can create their own blockchain while also using the security that Polkadot's chain already has. With Ethereum, developers can create new blockchains but they need to create their own security measures which can leave new and smaller projects open to attack, as the larger a blockchain the more security it has. This concept in Polkadot is known as shared security.

Polkadot was created by Gavin Wood, another member of the core founders of the Ethereum project who had differing opinions on the project's future. As of January 2021, Polkadot has a market capitalization of $11.2 billion and one DOT trades for $12.54.

Chapter 4. Are cryptocurrencies a good investment?

Cryptocurrencies may go up in value, but many investors see them as mere speculations, not real investments. The reason? Just like real currencies, cryptocurrencies generate no cash flow, so for you to profit, someone has to pay more for the currency than you did.

That's what's called "the greater fool" theory of investment. Contrast that to a well-managed business, which increases its value over time by growing the profitability and cash flow of the operation.

As NerdWallet writers have noted, cryptocurrencies such as Bitcoin may not be that safe, and some notable voices in the investment community have advised would-be investors to steer clear of them. Of particular note, legendary investor Warren Buffett compared Bitcoin to paper checks: "It's a very effective way of transmitting money and you can do it anonymously and all that.

A check is a way of transmitting money too. Are checks worth a whole lot of money? Just because they can transmit money?"

For those who see cryptocurrencies such as Bitcoin as the currency of the future, it should be noted that a currency needs stability so that merchants and consumers can determine what a fair price is for goods. Bitcoin and other cryptocurrencies have been anything but stable through much of their history. For example, while Bitcoin traded at close to $20,000 in December 2017, its value then dropped to as low as about $3,200 a year later. By December 2020, it was trading at record levels again.

This price volatility creates a conundrum. If bitcoins might be worth a lot more in the future, people are less likely to spend and circulate them today, making them less viable as a currency. Why spend a bitcoin when it could be worth three times the value next year?

Legal Risks for Cryptocurrency Investors

Along with the explosion of interest in digital currency and all of its implications for both new and traditional businesses, there is a growing need for clarity regarding the legal implications of these new technologies and currencies. As governments around the world, regulatory agencies, central banks, and other financial institutions are working to understand the nature and meaning of digital currencies, individual investors can make a great deal of money investing in this new space. On the other hand, <u>investors assume certain legal risks when they buy and sell cryptocurrencies</u>.

While digital currency might be easy to confuse for conventional electronic money, it is not the same; similarly, it is unlike conventional cash currencies because it cannot be physically owned and transferred between parties. Much of the murkiness of the legal standing of digital currency is due to the fact that the space has only recently become popular as compared with more traditional currency and payment systems. Below, we'll explore some of the emerging legal implications associated with investing in cryptocurrencies.

Cryptocurrencies as Property

One of the most critical legal considerations for any cryptocurrency investor has to do with the way that central authorities view cryptocurrency holdings. In the U.S., the IRS has defined cryptocurrencies as property, rather than as currencies proper. This means that individual investors are beholden to <u>capital gains tax</u> laws when it comes to reporting their cryptocurrency expenses and profits on their annual tax returns, regardless of where they purchased digital coins.

This aspect of the cryptocurrency space adds layers of confusion and complexity for U.S. taxpayers, but the difficulty does not end there. Indeed, it remains unclear whether digital currency investors who have purchased their holdings on foreign exchanges must face additional reporting measures come tax time. <u>According to a report by CNBC,</u> "anyone with more than $10,000 abroad usually needs to fill out the Report of Foreign Bank and Financial Accounts (FBAR)...with the Treasury Department each year. Another law--the <u>Foreign Account Tax Compliance Act</u>, or FATCA--requires certain U.S. taxpayers to describe their overseas accounts on Form 8938, when they file their taxes with the IRS."

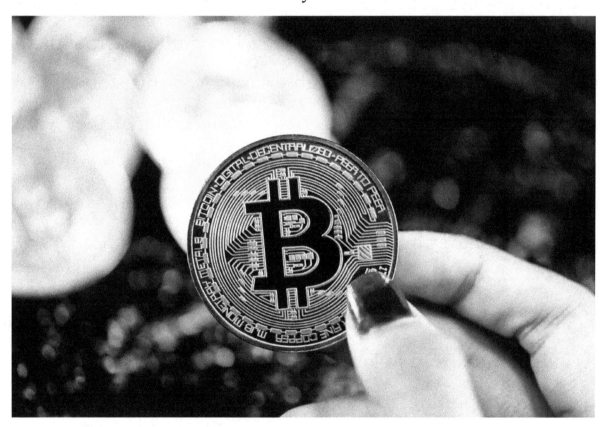

Former federal tax prosecutor Kevin F. Sweeney offered a hint as to how foreign cryptocurrency exchanges could complicate tax matters for U.S. digital currency investors: "there probably is an FBAR requirement, but I wouldn't go as far as to say there always is one," he explained, adding that the lack of guidance from the IRS has created a "black hole" of uncertainty for investors and tax professionals alike. "It would seem awfully unfair if they would expect taxpayers to know that--and to then issue penalties for taxpayers who didn't do that--when practitioners can't even 100% figure out if there's an FBAR requirement," Sweeney added.

All of this suggests that digital currency investors should take special precautions to follow the advice of tax professionals when it comes to reporting cryptocurrency profits and losses. Because the rules are constantly changing, what may have been legally permissible last year or even months ago may now be cause for legal concern.

Decentralized Status

One of the great draws of many digital currencies is also a potential risk factor for the individual investor. Bitcoin (BTC) has paved the way for other cryptocurrencies in that it is <u>decentralized</u>, meaning that it has no physical presence and is not backed by a central authority. While governments around the world have stepped in to assert their regulatory power in various ways, BTC and other digital currencies like it remain unattached to any jurisdiction or institution. On one hand, this frees investors from being beholden to those institutions. On the other hand, however, this status could result in legal complications. The value of digital currencies is dependent entirely upon the value that other owners and investors ascribe to them; this is true across all currencies, digital or fiat. Without a central authority backing the value of a digital currency, investors may be left in the lurch should complications with transactions or ownership arise.

Another potential risk associated with cryptocurrencies as a result of their decentralized status has to do with the particulars of transactions. In most other transactions, currency with a physical presence changes hands. In the case of <u>electronic money,</u> a trusted financial institution is involved in creating and settling deposits and debt claims. Neither of these concepts applies to cryptocurrency transactions. Because of this fundamental difference, legal confusion between parties in various types of digital currency transactions is a real possibility. Once again, because of the decentralized state of these currencies, the path of legal recourse in these situations can be difficult to assess.

Business Registrations and Licensing

A growing number of businesses are taking advantage of digital currencies as a form of payment. As in other financial areas, businesses may be required to register and obtain licensure for particular jurisdictions and activities. Owing to the complex and evolving legal status of digital currencies, this area is significantly less clear for businesses operating in the crypto market. Companies which only accept cryptocurrencies, for example, may not need to register or obtain licenses at all. On the other hand, they may be required to submit to special considerations depending upon their jurisdiction. The onus of responsibility falls on business owners and managers to insure that they are following proper legal procedure for their operations at both the local and state levels. At the federal level, for example, financial institutions must maintain certain activities related to protections against <u>money laundering</u> and fraud, transmission of funds, and more. Considerations like these also apply to businesses dealing with digital currencies.

Fraud and Money Laundering

There is a widespread belief that cryptocurrencies provide criminal organizations with a new means of committing fraud, money laundering, and a host of other financial crimes. This may not directly impact most cryptocurrency investors who do not intend to use this new technology to commit such crimes. However, investors who find themselves in the unfortunate position of being a victim of financial crime do not likely have the same legal options as traditional victims of fraud.

This issue also relates to the decentralized status of digital currencies. When a cryptocurrency exchange is hacked and customers' holdings are stolen, for instance, there is frequently no standard practice for recovering the missing funds. <u>Digital currency investors thus take on a certain amount of risk by purchasing and holding cryptocurrency assets</u>. It is for this reason that developers and startups related to digital currency have focused such a great deal of attention on creating secure means of holding digital coins and tokens. Still, while new types of wallets are being released all the time, and while cryptocurrency exchanges are always improving their security measures, investors have so far not been able to fully eliminate the legal risks associated with owning cryptocurrencies, and it's likely that they never will.

Private Label Crash Course

Build Your First 6-Figure Business Supported by a Collection of 9+1 Profitable Strategies. Find the Best Products, Build an Enlighten Team and Start Your Personal Brand

By

Iruka Nakamoto

Table of Contents

Introduction 251

Chapter 1: Getting Started-Private Label 258

1.1 What is Private Label? 259

1.2 Private Label Categories 259

1.3 Different types of Private Label as profitable strategies 260

1.4 White Label vs. Private Label Dropshipping? 262

1.5 Dropshipping Private Label 267

1.6 Deciding What to Private Label 269

Chapter 2: Profitable Strategies in Building Six-Figure Business .278

2.1 Private Label for Profitability 278

2.2 9+1 Pricing Strategies 284

2.3 Best Practices in Private Label Branding 291

2.4 Positives and Negatives of Private Label 294

2.5 Keys to Private Label Greatness 297

Chapter 3: Finding the Products & Starting Your Personal Brand
....304

3.1 How to Start Your Private Label Brand from Scratch? 306

3.2 Understand the costs of private labeling 308

3.3 Choosing the Right Products 322

3.4 Building a Team and Starting your Personal Brand 327

Conclusion 334

Introduction

A private label is where a person or corporation paying another business to make a commodity without its name, emblem, etc. The person or business then applies to the packaging their name and design. So, what sorts of items should be labeled privately? From skincare and dietary treatments and infant essentials, pet products, and kitchen utensils, pretty much all under the sun. The benefit of private labeling is that nothing innovative needs to be produced or developed by you. You can add your mark on it as long as it's not a proprietary commodity and label it yours. For the last ten years, private labels have risen by at least double the number of popular household products. In reality, there is a lot of conversation about the rise of private labels or retail brands around the world these days. Or we need to claim private brands, maybe since they are indeed labels by the end of each day. Opportunities to have ever-better-value offerings for both of us as consumers. Possibilities for everyone to push the main factors transforming the world of today and tomorrow. Yes, it's not the Private Label curse. It could well, in truth, be a present. A blessing that pushes us all to question the status quo again. A gift that pushes one to step positively with some of the main big forces that form the world of today to collaborate together more successfully and collaboratively. A blessing that is increasingly important to all of us, whether in the United Kingdom, the United States, China, or Scandinavia. If we like it or not, Private Label will soon have a single category of quick products in the country. In the last ten years, private labels have risen at least double the amount of popular consumer packaged goods brands. How did the Private Label expand at the above remarkable pace, and what lessons does it give players in the more narrowly established markets of fast-moving consumer goods? We like to think of it as a food event, but it's increasingly a complete experience of consumption. Flavors' globalization, marketers, and individuals have made Private Label a global fact. More and more, Private Label is the face of today's retailer. Comprehend it. This isn't going to go away. Act about it. Perhaps we should name them PRIVATE Companies from now on. Perhaps we might create very different tactics to survive if we began naming them brands instead of labels. Brands are concerned about combating their closest competing brand. Will they behave as though their closest advertised rival is the Private Label? Maybe they could, because maybe if they did, they might behave very differently in reality. The commodity has gone on. In turn, as Private Label has become a brand power in its own right, it has become privatized. It cannot be ignored as a single mark anymore. It's something a ton more. While taken out of context, Private Label is turning controversial for this cause, maybe more than any other, placing owners on the backhand side and retail section on the offensive. Neither group appears especially keen to publicly address it or cooperate on something outside development. Products have brought copycatting stores to court, and dealers have de-listed popular brands from their racks. There's a tiny concession space. It increasingly distorts agreed shopping habits and usage trends in order to exacerbate problems more. It is a brand that can often account for two out of three physical transactions made by your consumer. A brand that is gradually seen as an alternate product and value of parity. A company that will out-weigh and out-image any typical brand by exploiting the retailer's corporate strength and spending. A brand that can drive producers into a vicious cycle of loss in the market. A trillion-dollar market that, as you realize its sheer scale and future effects, must be the least evaluated and poorly understood industry around. An industry that in the years to come is going to get a lot larger. There would theoretically be billions of dollars of sales redirected by brand owners to this power. Are you confident your plans are ready? The remedies? But, as the solution, what do people recommend? Lower costs, increase efficiency, and be more imaginative. This is not just a remedy that you can pursue as a standard component of your business growth. It is simply not sufficient. This is an opportunity that requires the unusual and the unconventional. Or else rise to the challenge. The Private Label is a wake-up call from a brand creator. Wake up to the truth in the company. Wake up in search of a shopper. Wake up to what you might theoretically do for your company. Wake up to proactivity for real. Wake up to a chance to get the rest of the planet back into communication with your company. Private label has arisen from the conventionally held assumption that firms will benefit and conquer the competition by providing either higher value at a higher cost for their consumers (or shoppers) or fair value at a cheaper cost (retailer brands). In other terms, it's a preference between distinction (or innovation) and low cost, and it's safe to assume that only then have retailers fallen into the former to offer the latter to the shopper reliably in spades. As Coke (and Tesco) can also inform you, it pays dividends to see the brand on any street corner. However, as some of our research highlights would demonstrate, there is still a significant perception difference between Private Label and existing manufacturer labels in terms of quality/value. As long as the shopper is concerned, at least, without the other, one will not thrive, and broadly speaking, maker labels are better positioned to offer sound 'innovation' and 'value' to retailers. Just 16% of shoppers in all regions sincerely agree that a supermarket of retailer-owned goods can only be expected in the future. So, we think there is a potential for brands to constantly reinvent themselves through shopper intuition, deeper brand commitment, and creativity. The potential for retailers to continuously add value is there. The potential exists for producers to maximize their manufacturing ability and for interactions to be reinvented by agencies. But most critically, the potential is there to constantly impress and entertain the shopper, far beyond all their hopes. The other alternative frequently provided is to get yourself into making a private label. However, you may be compelled by Private Label to analyze the very simple essence of the company in which you are and to doubt whether it is strong enough to move you further. Ask for your goods. Ask how and to whom you are offering. Ask if you still are tuning into the agents of transition. Your corporate purpose issues. Ask if you have the best staff and processes to meet this crucial problem. Finally, Private Label is a concern for manufacturers alike. Knowing how to profitably manage it without undermining the very essence of the organization you are with. And the manufacturers that you work with. Yes, you may assume that you can survive without them. Yet we're advising, be very, very patient. If you want to be a genuinely successful marketing tool in terms of bringing to the shopper, you need one another. In comparison, we exist in an age in which the newspapers are building up major global supermarket chains as the latest businesses to despise. Why are you stopping this? As the messenger, you use Private Label, a messenger that not only reveals that you deliver excellent value and costs but also indicates that you think for your consumer and their long-term social needs. And you are really doing what you can to support them. Now, even more on this. The private label is, to a great degree, a hidden force. The conservative nature of the subject-matter literature tends to downplay its actual place in the world, a function far from conservative in fact, and a role in which Private Label is undeniably the single greatest influence on our businesses and goods today. Brands, engagement professionals, and scholars have consistently ignored or underestimated this. That's got to change.

Chapter 1: Getting Started-Private Label

A private label is where a person or corporation paying another business to make a commodity without its name, emblem, etc. The person or business then applies to the packaging their name and design. So, what sorts of items should be labeled privately? From skincare and dietary treatments and infant essentials, pet products, and kitchen utensils, pretty much all under the sun. The benefit of private labeling is that nothing innovative needs to be produced or developed by you. You can add your mark on it as long as it's not a proprietary commodity and label it yours. A private label product is made and marketed under a retailer's brand name through a contract or third-party maker. You specify all about the commodity as the distributor-what goes into it, how everything is packaged, what the logo looks like-you pay to get it manufactured and shipped to your shop. This is in relation to purchasing goods with their corporate logos on them from other businesses. A successful brand identity can be the crucial base for building loyal customers, customer growth, and a competitive edge. Care of your corporate name as your company's face is how you are viewed by the audience. Without a detailed, excellently defined brand identity, the consumer might not realize who you are. In the end, you need to create a personal link. The potential exists for producers to maximize their manufacturing ability and for interactions to be reinvented by agencies. But most critically, the potential is there to constantly impress and entertain the shopper, far beyond all their hopes. The other alternative frequently provided is to get yourself into making a private label. However, you may be compelled by Private Label to analyze the very simple essence of the company in which you are and to doubt whether it is strong enough to move you further.

1.1 What is Private Label?

A private label product is made and marketed under a retailer's brand name through a contract or third-party maker. You specify all about the commodity as the distributor-what goes into it, how everything is packaged, what the logo looks like-you pay to get it manufactured and shipped to your shop. This is in relation to purchasing goods with their corporate logos on them from other businesses.

1.2 Private Label Categories

Almost every consumer product category has both branded and private label offerings, including:

- Condiments and salad dressings

- Cosmetics

- Personal care

- Frozen foods

- Dairy items

- Beverages

- Household cleaners

- Paper products

1.3 Different types of Private Label as profitable strategies

Generic Private Label

Generic private-label goods are one of the conventional private label tactics used to provide the price-conscious consumer with a low-price alternative. The brand doesn't matter to these consumers. With limited advertising and no marketing, the goods are inexpensive, undifferentiated, poor inconsistency. In commoditized and low-involvement goods, these private labels are primarily present. For both discount stores in Western nations, this technique is widespread.

Copycat Brands

In order to draw buyers, manufacturers play on the price point, retaining the packaging identical to a national brand that offers a sense of the product's similar consistency. These goods are reverse engineered, utilizing factories of identical technologies from national brand products. In wide categories that have a clear market champion, certain private labels are mostly present. In the detergent group, Massive Corporation blindly embraces the copycat brand approach. Detergents against rival products with identical packaging have been launched, albeit at a cheaper price.

Premium store brands

Retailers now have started utilizing private labels, rather than just as a pricing strategy, as a store point of difference. Premium store brands are valued higher and are also high in performance than the national brands. Here, the customer proposal is to be the greatest brand that money will purchase. In the retailer's shop, these products get influential eye-catching locations. In the advertising, the manufacturer insists on the excellent consistency of the goods.

Value innovators

Retailers manufacture goods that have all the value-adding characteristics and eliminate the non-value-adding characteristics in order to reduce costs, one point ahead of the copycat approach, and thus provide the customer with the best value deal. The danger of being imitated also rests in these labels. As it produces furniture under a modern market paradigm that involves self-service, assembling, and transporting yourself, Ikea is renowned for its better goods.

1.4 White Label vs. Private Label Dropshipping?

You can select between white label and private label dropshipping if you want to launch an online store. Both words define goods that have been branded by a reseller, but the two definitions very distinctly. Particularly to beginners, they may seem quite complicated, so let's go through each one and explain their relative benefits.

Private Labeling

Private marking is where a company selectively makes a commodity for a store that offers it under its own name. Costco utilizes private marking, for instance, by marketing its own "Kirkland" brand that no other store can offer. As a consequence, goods with private labels are typically less pricey than national brands. Plus, they can be very lucrative if they're promoted properly. Dropshipping is a convenient method for private-label goods to be distributed. You will find a dropshipping provider if you are an online shop owner who can offer items directly to you and incorporate your branding. Dropshipping is an e-commerce market concept in which no inventory is held by the manufacturer. The retailer, instead, manages the packaging, packing, and delivery of goods to the end customer. In other terms, for dropshipping, the goods are delivered directly to consumers, and they are never used by stores.

White Labeling

A white-label product is a manufactured product that a company makes but is rebranded by marketers to make it look as though it had been produced. Each dealer is authorized to resell the item under its own title and labeling. Unlike private labels, several retailers may market a white-label commodity. For e.g., you can have your own branding and labels on the goods that are delivered if you wish to market a product under your brand name utilizing the dropshipping business strategy. It is often safer to search at something that already has a market when it comes to items with a white mark. It's dangerous to produce goods with white marks that consumers are not comfortable with. It's safer to go for existing brands that people regularly use. As with private labels, dropshipping makes it simple to market online white-label goods. Again, the items are delivered directly from the producers to customers, and the commodities are seldom seen by dealers.

Advantages & Disadvantages of White Labeling

You won't have to go through the complicated logistics of making a commodity in one of these two e-commerce market models. You can save a lot of time and money without significant expenditure of time and energy in product design and production. In essence, you will concentrate on selling the commodity to the target group and branding it. In order to expand your company, you won't spread yourself thin and can concentrate on other areas of expertise. So, let's go through the common advantages and disadvantages of each business model:

Advantages of White Labeling

There are some real benefits of the white labeling market model, including:

- **It saves time and money.**

It's just cheaper to white mark an established commodity instead of wasting resources on developing a product from scratch.

- **Gain a large profit**

In general, white label goods are exclusively marketed by suppliers and may be bought at cheap market rates.

Disadvantages of White Labeling

There are, on the other side, some risks of white marking, including:

- **Limited options for branding**

Because it will be the producer or retailer who makes the white label product's bottle, label, and packaging, depending on the concept, you can just decide what it will deliver for you.

- **Limited choices of products**

Just the goods that the maker produces will be preferred, and you will not be allowed to produce anything special to the market.

- **Competition is tough**

It is challenging to stand out from the other online vendors that, white-label or not, sell the same items.

1.5 Dropshipping Private Label

We have addressed that different dropshipping products are among the simplest methods for private or white label items to be distributed. So, let's go about how private or white label items can be dropshipped.

Finding a supplier

In order to achieve the sustainability of online shops, having a successful dropshipping supplier is utterly crucial. In quest of finding a directory of dropshipping vendors who sell private label facilities, you should look at business websites or just do a search on Google. Seeking a niche will allow you and your business to stand out from other retail vendors. Make sure that you conduct consumer analysis to figure out what sort of thing you would prefer to rebrand or distribute.

Establishing the identity with the brand

A successful brand identity can be the crucial base for building loyal customers, customer growth, and a competitive edge. Care of your corporate name as your company's face is how you are viewed by the audience. Without a detailed, excellently defined brand identity, the consumer might not realize who you are. In the end, you need to create a personal link. Brand awareness must be expressed in the products, slogan, website, and packaging. It can offer a' derived from human attributes' to your brand. Brands with a very well-established personality make the brand intimately relatable, connecting consumers at a relational level and having to have the commodity in their lives. This is relevant for dropshipping products, including the private and white labels.

Increase awareness about your label and brand

Growing your brand recognition is another important move towards building a profitable brand. If the product is fresh, then identifying your target customers and discovering ways to draw consumers to your shop is the very first thing you'll want to achieve. This is so if it's the private label dropshipping goods. Here are some forms that brand recognition can be improved without any expense:

- Build content on your website with the addition of a blog

- Developing your social network online identity

- To engage and network with more clients and get product feedback.

- To maximize your keyword scores, perform SEO.

1.6 Deciding What to Private Label

You might be wondering about what's a competitive commodity to private label. The secret to this phase and probably the most crucial step in beginning a private label company is researching and putting efforts into finding a good product. You ought to figure out which products/services are in the market to ensure if your product would sell. To see what people, look for on the internet and get ideas about what you can offer from there, you can use programs available online. If you intend to launch your private label company on online marketplaces, you'll want to use a testing method that actually monitors what individuals are searching for on that platform. For this, popular programs include

Helium 10 and Jungle Scout. They both provide several resources to help you continue your market path with your private label.

What Makes A Good Private Label Product?

The biggest point to hold in mind when applying for a private label for a commodity is to find one that:

It is in strong market demand and has limited competition from sellers.

This can help you stop being trapped with things that you will not offer.

Has a strong margin for benefit

Taking into consideration how much the item would cost you vs. how much you will market it for. If the item is held in a warehouse, plus the expenses involved with sale online, don't neglect to take into account the delivery costs from your source to you and from you to your client, packing and storage fees.

If you can manage the expenses

If you have a $1,000 or $10,000 startup investment budget, you need to take into consideration how many units you will need/want to buy and how much of the budget you will spend.

How to Find Suppliers

It's time to search for a producer or trade firm that provides private label service once you have a commodity in mind that you would like to private label. You can select anywhere in the world to make your goods. And several times, the type of service/product you select would rely on where you choose to get your product made. For e.g., China might be worth considering if you are trying to sell toys or gadgets because they seem to produce a ton of these types of items at very low prices. Consider looking for Alibaba or AliExpress if you want to go on this path. Both of these platforms are bulk markets where the goods are identified by suppliers and trade houses, where you can find almost everything. Because with all our federal rules, it's a great choice to source in the U.S. whether you want to offer food, dietary foods, cosmetic goods, or something else you bring in or on your body. Check on Google for items sourced domestically. Say you're searching for vegan deodorant source, just type in Google "vegan perfume private label

U.K." to get a list of companies that can use vegan deodorants for private label.

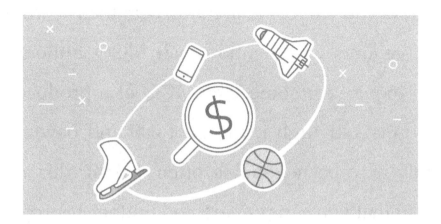

What to Ask Private Label Suppliers

Once you've drawn up a list of possible vendors, calling each one and posing some questions is a smart idea.

Pricing Per Unit

The price would usually already be accessible for you to see on the website for each item. However, depending on how many units you order, most manufacturers give a discount. Knowing this data would also assist you in estimating the gross margin.

MOQ

In the private label/wholesale environment, this is a generic word used because it stands for "minimum order" or the minimum number of units you will order at a time. On their website/product listing, most vendors will mention their MOQ, although you will only have to inquire for some. The MOQ of a producer can be as few as five units, although it can be 1,000 and beyond for some. Although this may be negotiable often, asking this upfront is a smart move so that you can prepare and budget appropriately.

Customization

It is nice to know what the factory is and will not do in advance so that you can stop trying to swap vendors later unless you are seeking to apply your branding to the package, customize packages, or make modifications to the product.

Production Time

It is helpful to know how long it would take your provider to meet orders when your private label company continues to expand, and you continue to prepare for potential orders. Typically, the norm is around 15 days (depending on the commodity and order size), so it can go up from there.

Response Time

Take notice of how long it takes for the supplier to get back to you, bearing in mind that you are initiating a long-term future trading partnership. You would want to make sure that your communication individual is trustworthy, prompt, and specifically addresses your questions. If your provider is based in another country, take into consideration that they are in a separate time zone and that you will not automatically obtain a reply. During their business hours, being present will allow the operation easier.

Samples

Ask for prototypes such that the consistency and particular requirements can be measured. Many vendors can submit a sample free of charge, while others may start charging a small fee. Anyway, it's certainly not something you'd skimp on, especially if you're trying to give the highest service to your customers.

Customizing Your Product

In how your product can market, customizing your product will play a huge role. Question yourself, "What's going to set my version apart from the competition?" The response to this is key in having a prospective customer select your product over the product of a more known, well-reviewed business. Perhaps it's as quick as providing color combinations or getting fancy packaging, or it might be easier to enhance a function that you want more in-depth. Such customizations, such as packaging upgrades, are likely to be achieved by your supplier, and some can be accomplished through yourself or by your suppliers, such as custom marking with product specifics and a logo. Customizing the goods in any form is the main message here. Stand out by having it different (and better) than the rivals '. By basically slapping the mark on it, you don't want to sell the same exact thing as another brand.

You are selling your Private Label product.

You may pick anywhere to market your private-label line of items. Here's an extensive list of online sales places or suggestions on how to get into shops.

A Personal Online Store

Such customizations, such as packaging upgrades, are likely to be achieved by your supplier, and some can be accomplished through yourself or by your suppliers, such as custom marking with product specifics and a logo. Customizing the goods in any form is the main message here. Stand out by having it different (and better) than the rivals '. By simply yanking your tag on it, you wouldn't want to give the same product as yet another brand.

Brick-And-Mortar

Sitting the goods on the shelf of a physical shop offers consumers the ability to see your product that they would never have dreamed of it otherwise. In other words, customers have to practically "search" for services or products they want to buy online. But if they don't think about it, they're not going to search and probably won't find it unless you pay serious bucks promoting it. If shoppers are still in a shop and happen to see it, it builds brand/product recognition at least. Fees and requirements for getting shelf-space vary by store, but it can be a decent place to start from local, family-owned stores. Read more regarding boutique collaborations or having your own storefront.

Markets

Markers and art fairs for producers are on the increase. Consumers love to shop locally and want to help their community's artisans. They're a perfect way to get instant input from customers, too. Find out how to start trading and find craft markets at farmer's markets.

Don't limit yourself.

Start with a variety of channels, in-person shops, and websites. You would be able to see over a span of time how many sales you create from each one, how much money each produces, etc. You should just stick doing what's profitable, then. It is certainly a road to launch your private label company, and it will be months until you can bring the goods on the market. But the trip can be well worth it if you do your product testing, pick the best source, separate the product from the market, and price it right.

Chapter 2: Profitable Strategies in Building Six-Figure Business

For private-label products, manufacturers may raise gross margins by managing the whole supply chain from manufacture to distribution. Clothing traders have been pushing different private-label options for years. Costco has the Kirkland private-label name. Nordstrom's got Caslon. And Kohl's has Sonoma as its in-house, billion-dollar brand. Although online stores have supplied other industries with private label labels, basic products for tangible products focused on low-cost hardware and office equipment, the move to clothes implies a brazen policy expansion. Any volume seller is looking at the advantages of growing private-label brand's goods in order to drive sustainability and connect with a more aware and conscious millennial generation who are known for not being very brand loyal.

2.1 Private Label for Profitability

Profits are powered by private labels. A private-labeled commodity or product with parity in operation and consistency with major labels will cost manufacturers 40 to 50 percent less to develop and sell to consumers. In order to negotiate with online marketplace empires and other online suppliers who offer low-cost products without caring about reducing margins, merchants will then switch around to provide greater discounts. Online, where customers have 100 percent pricing transparency, this is especially essential. This functions on both luxury and commodity items. Building and maintaining a private label often enables manufacturers to develop exclusive goods for higher prices or to manufacture commodity products below brands at a sustainable price. To boost their inventory rotation, manufacturers are now using private-label tactics. Retail stores with services from private labels could also have more than four seasons a year. An innovative team in private label, such as the JCPenney team of 250 designers working in-house or the internal production and procurement departments of Nordstrom, will contend on an equal footing with fast-trending fashion stores like H&M.

Factors to be Considered

It may be dangerous to hop into this business without carefully thinking it over. Before investing and dedicating time to a privately-label approach, here are some factors to be considered:

- ## Identifying low cost and high-quality manufacturer

A colossal advantage is strong production suppliers, while poor manufacturers or suppliers are a horrific liability. Spend the effort to do it correctly. There are hundreds or thousands of suppliers capable of producing stuff that you would need. Find the producer that fits all the requirements for price and consistency; often, identifying the markets that are relevant. You may also want to learn from Portugal or Vietnam for clothing. Vietnam, South Korea, and China have manufacturing expertise in electronics. Take note that costs for suppliers differ greatly depending on the order's size.

- ## Strengthen the Skills in Design and Procurement

The private label includes relationships with producers of agricultural and consumer goods, component retailers, multinational warehouses, and distribution suppliers. Will you broaden the current partnerships between suppliers? If not, determine whether to consult the staff or purchase the expertise that will render the retail company a key competency of the strategy regarding the private label. Consider a completely dedicated bet on vertical trading, too.

- **Using brand pricing and external signs as guiding principles for pricing policy**

Research your rival brands closely while designing your own products under the banner of a private label. Retailers ought to make up their mind whether to generate the product as a luxury product and expend marketing expenses or to position it as an alternate brand by selling below national labels. If product attributes can be readily contrasted and placed as a substitute brand, it is important to consider the price point of comparable goods to position them correctly against competitors' national brand/products label brands. In other situations, were comparing features is not something very straightforward. Retailers can use a number of internal market pointers for pricing, such as site traffic, ratings, consumer feedback, and retailers can recognize the popularity of the product. Today, if a commodity is popular/interest-generating, but the converging performance is low, this can cause a price reduction/promotion intervention.

- **Acknowledge the differences in categories and manage them smartly**

Consumers can browse for functionality within a particular perceived cost sub-set for white and hard goods. Buyers searching for features are opting for a dryer or washing machine. Potential customers are looking for other qualities, such as cloth, shape, trendiness, for soft items like clothing. Those features deter similarities.

- **Decide Efficient Customized Label Blend**

The best combination of private label and branded items has to be determined by retailers. Are buyers looking for a feature in a certain product category or range on the website? Collecting web search data can help marketers make a choice. They have to remember the client base as well. If the consumer pool is predominantly 28- to 51-year-old buyers, private label goods can be more value aware and prefer small-scale proliferation.

- **Implement Algorithmic, Data-Driving Pricing Methods**

With constantly evolving customer preferences, at every given level in time, you should be able to recognize demand levels and continually seek the optimum price value. Factor in leveraging algorithms based on technology systems to easily evaluate price levels and strategies; when priced carefully with supporting data, private-label brands also deliver unexpected revenues. For e.g., the commodity was priced well below the national brand by a generic manufacturer of merchandise with a very well private label refrigerator brand, just to experience a drop in revenue. The store began checking multiple price ranges, steadily pushing up the segment. Sales started to fall with the first $200 onwards. And, magically, revenue and traffic boomed until the price reached a hidden barrier. This sounds counterintuitive, but the private-label company has already been put in a competitive area with national labels in the view of the consumer. Instead of seeing it as a lower quality commodity, clients began to see it as domestic brands.

They were prepared to move since the price levels were always cheaper than domestic brands. In a considerably more profitable buyer zone, it was repositioned by moving the idea up the continuum. If consumers interpret things the same way with analytic pricing, the same SKU will gain double the profits. These are some of the most important elements in successfully initiating your private label initiative at any major retailer. Going over these basics will strip the efforts of the bulk of danger.

2.2 9+1 Pricing Strategies

Want to maximize profit on your product sales?

Aside from other publicity and business tactics, a strong pricing policy is indeed something you need to concentrate on. When setting the price for your goods or services, what considerations do you consider? When determining the prices for your goods or services, there are a number of considerations, including:

- Production cost

- positioning strategies

- competitor's products

- Distribution cost

- Target consumer base

When buying a commodity, price is a very important consideration for a buyer. A productive pricing system can also have a profound influence on the company's performance. And often, it decides whether or not the organization can succeed. So, what are those tactics you should suggest in order to improve the revenue and be more profitable?

Premium Pricing

Marketers put rates higher than their competitors or rivals for this promotional policy. However, it is used where there is a major competitive edge, and a relatively cheaper price is safe for the marketer or the organization to charge. For small businesses that offer exclusive services or products, high pricing is perfect. A corporation, however, can check that the packaging of the goods, its promotional campaigns, and the décor or luxury facilities of the store all fit to maintain the fixed price.

- **Example of Premium Pricing**

Let's take the example of luxury specialty retail stores that charge you a little extra but sell you exclusive styles and tailored clothing.

Penetration Pricing

To try to draw buyers? Ok, this technique is going to help you with the purpose. Lower rates are given on utilities or goods under this strategy. Although this technique is used by many emerging firms, it does appear to lead to an initial reduction of profits for the business. Over time, though, the growth of product or service recognition will drive revenues and allow small businesses to stand out. In the long run, as a business succeeds in entering the sector, its costs always end up growing to represent the condition of its role in the sector.

Economy Pricing

The advertisement expense of a service or commodity is held at a low in this strategy. The technique is used during a certain period where the organization does not invest much in promoting the service or product.

Example of Economy Pricing

The first few budget airlines, for instance, are offered at low rates in discount airlines to fill in the jet. A broad variety of businesses, from discount stores and generic grocery manufacturers, use Economy Pricing. The technique, though, maybe dangerous for small firms when they lack the market scale of larger corporations. Small companies can fail to make a sufficient profit with low rates, but strategically tailoring price-cuts to your most loyal customers or consumers may be a successful way to guarantee their loyalty for years to come.

Price Skimming

This technique is meant to assist enterprises in focusing on the sale of innovative services or goods. During the preliminary process, this strategy means setting high prices. The rates are then reduced steadily when the competitor's goods or services arrive on the market. When the product is first released in the marketplace, this price approach produces an image of exclusivity and good quality.

Psychology Pricing

This method of pricing deals with a client's psychology. For e.g., setting the price of a ring at $99 is likely to draw more clients than setting prices at $100. But the concern is, in terms of a very limited gap, why are consumers more drawn to a product's former price? Psychology suggests that on a price tag, customers prefer to give greater attention to the first digits. When stores apply $0.99 on product tags of $1.99 or $2.99, you can find identical promotional strategies. The purpose of this approach, therefore, is to build an image of greater value for the consumer.

Bundle Pricing

How often have you been persuaded to purchase a multipack of 6 packets for $2.99 instead of purchasing one packet for $0.65? Or an SMS kit instead of texting on the individual rates? Without sacrificing efficiency, we all enjoy commodities that cost us less. This is why package selling is a success for both the vendor and the consumer and is profitable. The vendor gets to sell more of their inventory, and for less cost, the consumer gets to purchase the product in bulk. For instance, if bundle package of chips is for $1.30 and 3 multipacks for2.50$. The probability of purchasing three packs is more than purchasing only one. Bundle pricing enhances the worth sense when you are actually offering your consumers anything for free.

Value Pricing

This technique is used when external forces such as increased rivalry or unemployment cause corporations to offer valuable promotional offerings or goods, e.g., combo offers or value meals at KFC and other restaurants, to sustain sales. Quality pricing lets a buyer know like for the same price, they are receiving a ton of product. In several respects, profit pricing is analogous to economic pricing. So, let's make this very clear that there is added benefit with regard to service or product in value pricing. Generally speaking, price cuts should not rise in value.

Promotional Pricing

Promotional pricing is a really common method for sales and can be used in different department stores and restaurants, etc. Part of this promotional policy are methods such as money off coupons, Buy One Get One Free, and promotions.

Cost-based Pricing

This method entails determining cost-based rates for the commodity to be made, shipped, and sold. In addition, a fair rate of profit is usually added by the corporation or sector to compensate for the risks as well as initiatives. Businesses such as Walmart and Ryanair are seeking to become low-cost suppliers. These businesses may set lower rates by constantly lowering costs whenever feasible. This undoubtedly contributes to lower profits but better profits and revenues. Companies with higher costs can, therefore, often rely on this approach to pricing. Yet, in general, in order to demand greater profits and rates, these businesses purposely generate higher costs. The aforementioned techniques are the most widely adopted strategies used by corporations to increase profit from sales of their product or service. In its own unique way, any pricing strategy is effective. Therefore, consider your marketplace and other conditions before selecting a pricing plan for your good or service to bring the most out of the strategy used. Therefore, becoming mindful of the competitive place when setting a price is important. What the clients or buyers anticipate in terms of the price should be considered in the marketing mix.

2.3 Best Practices in Private Label Branding

Can you recall when generic or non-national branded items with large black lettering and bad product consistency indicated simple white or yellow packing materials? After the unmemorable early days of supermarket labels, stores have clearly come a long way. In fact, many private label labels today are practically indistinguishable from their producer-branded equivalents on the shelves.

Align with and support the master (retail) brand

It is certainly no accident that some of the best private label company portfolios are those that tend to be in tune with the supermarket master brand's positioning and strategic purpose. Preferably, their positioning is strongly complementary to the supermarket master brand, enhancing the latter's equity and beneficial relationships.

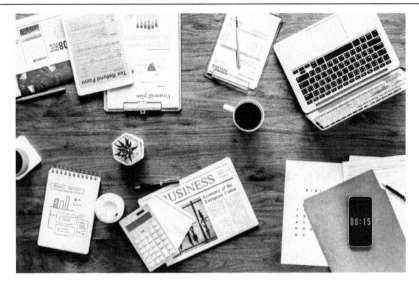

Bring differentiation to the category; fulfill unmet customer needs.

When their products are additive to the supermarket, or better still, the overall competition, private label labels are maybe at their strongest. One way to achieve this is to bring the category to something completely differentiated. Another similar approach is to resolve consumer expectations that are not fulfilled by the big national labels. Importantly, this difference can be more than just a cheaper price than the brands of the manufacturer. In the good or service offering itself, private label labels can often be exclusive. Safeway is a perfect illustration of introducing distinction to the market and thereby addressing an increasingly unmet desire of the customer. Finally, creativity is another form in which private label labels may offer category and consumer distinction.

Establish clear boundaries for private label brands

There is also a temptation to expand it everywhere and anywhere in the shop once retailers effectively establish a good private label brand. This extends horizontally across types of goods and vertically across ranges of price/value. However, the tendency to over-extend or dilute the private label brand properties is resisted by better practice retailers.

Define brands based on emotional attributes

Since they feel an intrinsic bond to them, customers prefer to gravitate towards (and stay faithful to) products. There is no more for products with private labels than for brands with national suppliers. For private label labels, it is important that they stand for something more than just price/value and much more than a commodity attribute. They need to have an emotional advantage to which customers may connect. This essential nuance is understood by marketers that have become popular with exclusive labels and find ways to distill emotional equity through their private label brands.

Distinguish brands with a distinct identity and appropriate brand linkages

Finally, a distinctive and highly identifiable visual identity is established by leading label labels and embraces a clear messaging approach. They still maintain clear rules specifying the degree to which the private label mark may and should be identifiably affiliated with the supermarket master brand. An attractive visual presence and strategically advantageous brand design are undeniably part of what makes private label companies popular or leads to their downfall if overlooked.

2.4 Positives and Negatives of Private Label

Advantages

There is a legitimate explanation for retailers that are involved in flooding their stores with items with their brand name. Many of the main benefits of goods with private labeling include:

- **Handling Production**

Third-party suppliers operate at the behest of the supplier, providing full influence over the ingredients and consistency of the goods.

- **Control overpricing**

Retailers may also assess sales cost and efficient selling due to leverage over the product.

- **Adaptability**

In reaction to growing consumer demand for a new feature, smaller stores have the opportunity to move rapidly to bring a private label product into development, whereas larger firms might not be involved in a product or niche category.

- **Managing branding Decisions**

The company name and package concept produced by the manufacturer carry private label items.

- **Managing profitability**

Retailers monitor the amount of profitability their goods offer due to control over manufacturing expenses and pricing.

- **Increased margins**

Private labels enable manufacturers to sell and raise the profit margin more competitively on their goods. Compared to producing brands, several manufacturers gain 25-30 percent higher profit profits on private labels.

- **Customer loyalty**

Nowadays, consumers want goods manufactured locally, and they would like more if they enjoy the private label products. You would be the only outlet who would be willing to supply them with such goods. It is challenging to win the trust of individuals in the retail sector.

Disadvantages

As much as you have the financial capital to spend in creating such a commodity, the risks of introducing a private label brand are few. Primary drawbacks include:

- **Manufacturer dependency**

Since the manufacturing of your product range is in possession of a third-party vendor, working with accomplished businesses is critical. Otherwise, if the manufacturer gets into challenges, you might lose out on opportunities.

- **Difficulty building loyalty**

In a number of retail stores, existing household brands have the upper hand and can always be found. Only in your shops can your goods be sold, restricting consumer access to it. Restricted supply, of note, may also be an asset, providing clients an incentive to come back and purchase from you. Although private label goods are usually offered at a lower price point than their brothers of the corporate name, certain private label brands are also branded as luxury products, with a higher price tag to show it.

2.5 Keys to Private Label Greatness

As of late, we are doing a lot of innovative work in the Private Label sector, and here is a good refresher of The Core Values that we believe in for developing our own labels that are strategically convincing. We also see that there are particular fundamental stories in their creation throughout all great store brand cases, but there are seven values that they must abide by to be genuinely strategically convincing.

Principles of Equity and Environment

From a branding and design point of view, there has never been more interest in the grocery store and how we connect, affect purchasing decisions, and even construct theatre inside it. This is real in every part of the world. Of course, there is a reverence we all have to have for the cultural uniqueness of the grocery store, from country to country, since some customers are in the store just once a week, to other food and market experience where customers connect every day. Even with these diverse regional variations in frequency, familiarity, and satisfaction inside the retail shop, there is a common emphasis on making the store brand function more credibly and more convincingly with consumers in general.

The equity connection

Immersing oneself in the retailer's overarching goal, its perception and equity distinction as it is now, and what is achievable in the future is important. To achieve this, the right branding collaborators coordinate with the senior brass of the distributors with which they operate, as well as the organization's top merchants and store name specialists. They take into account all the main targets for which a merchant is fishing and then see how to enhance store brands as being one of the key tools to accomplish their task. Store products strengthen the retailer's total equity and vice-versa, and they struggle because they do not.

Environmental support

A kit can only do too many. Your store brand will get overloaded if it does not have the off-shelf environmental help in the vast stream of 40,000+ items that many of the largest supermarkets carry today. Beyond the box, give it existence and speech. To help your brand, use the theatre in the shop.

Be preferential

For supermarket brands, own products, exclusive brands, and the like, there are loads of common nomenclatures. "But whatever the language, don't treat your store brands to the larger national brands as weaker "stepchildren. Don't be afraid to handle your supermarket labels preferentially in the store, beyond the incisive box template for your company. In their importance, in their distribution of space, in their positioning of shelves, and in their show and cross-merchandising all throughout the shop. No need to apologize to the CPGs or succumb to the study of planograms.

Don't blindly follow.

For years, there has been a "follow the herd" attitude of store labels, and today it still persists. Because of what Walmart has achieved with Such Prices, many retailers we talk to now are terrified of "white" packaging. So often, individuals are hyper-attentive to the competition and norms and what's going around the market of store labels. The bottom line is that you can build your own vision in a very creative and special way. Do not blindly obey the naming conventions, color conventions, or typically mundane price-centered store brands set by broad categories and how they have traditionally behaved in order to reconsider anything intelligently.

Three layers have to work together.

Make sure you are not concerned with visual language alone with the positioning of the store labels and how they are to be fully distinguished for the future. This is the responsibility of a number of production agencies, who feel they are only employed to rewrite the store brand's aesthetic vocabulary. If we want to encourage these products to be produced differently, we need to understand how the graphic language is created, indeed, but also how it is structurally packaged and the language we use to orally convey the item. Graphic, systemic, and verbal languages all cohesively operate together.

Steve Jobs never asked the consumer.

Apple is one of the world's most creative and well-thought-out, profitable enterprises. When questioned what Steve Jobs felt about research in a New York Times report and how Apple uses it to direct new product creation, he replied, "None... it's not the job of consumers to know what they want." There are so many retailers that use research to store products in their innovative development phase, and this is a mistake. Customers will still turn to the protection and what is comfortable with them, but if they are the only sounding board, you will not have the most creative performance.

On the brand's positioning

In using the name of the shop on the individual store brand packaging, there are no universal guidelines, just as there are no generalizations to create about how large the store brand should stretch. Both of these brands had a very definitive strategic positioning when producing Greenway, Hartford Reserve, and Via Roma for A&P, and this relationship that established the role of the company was a very significant part of the process. Clearly describe it, know that you want to distinguish the brand rather than sheer costs, own it thoroughly in the consumer's head, and correctly reiterate it. In the development of an ambitious store brand platform, these ideals would suit you well because they are standards that the best supermarket brands live by with true conviction. The name brand industry continues to be guided by continuing innovative creativity, a true steel hand in spreading out from the single "price" veil, and to be persuasive in their own right. And store brands need to be promoted with vigor, motivation, and media support.

Chapter 3: Finding the Products & Starting Your Personal Brand

You should concentrate on creating a reputation before you start your company, one that is recognizable and valued, and a private label benefits both you and the retailer or supplier you select. The first move with your organization is importing the goods you choose to market, products that do not crack easily, which have satisfaction for the customer. The second and most significant move is to make your brand known to current and future clients. The more customers remember your brand, the higher it is possible that your revenue rate will be. Through selecting producers or suppliers who will submit your goods via Private Label, you will help this along. This operates by encouraging the consumer to position their orders with you, then deliver them to the retailer and directly dispatching the product. The return home address would be that of the company in most situations, but for Private Label, this will be yours. This ensures that whether they have any concerns or queries, the consumer would assume that the service/product has come from you, and they will only contact you. This helps you build up a brand reputation, but using trustworthy vendors, depends on you, and you deliver top-quality customer support. In general, manufacturers are willing to use private labels since it suggests that they do not have to be interested in any consumer problems. To sum up, while you are looking to get your brand out and develop a company without leeching on mainstream online market place/websites' popularity, a private label makes perfect sense. It will require a bit extra time to select a supplier since you must do the job yourself and guarantee that you work for the right supplier. Still, you will also gain a better profit when you take responsibility for the client support and are willing to negotiate the supplier's rates. A private label is where a person or corporation paying another business to make a commodity without its name, emblem, etc. The person or business then applies to the packaging their name and design. So, what sorts of items should be labeled privately? From skincare and dietary treatments and infant essentials, pet products, and kitchen utensils, pretty much all under the sun. The benefit of private labeling is that nothing innovative needs to be produced or developed by you. You can add your mark on it as long as it's not a proprietary commodity and label it yours.

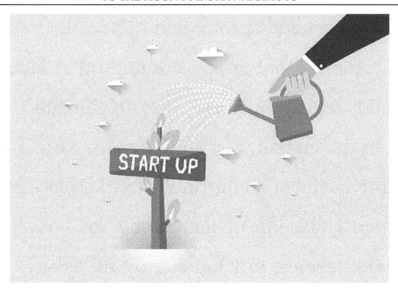

3.1 How to Start Your Private Label Brand from Scratch?

Because of its profitability and consumer benefits, private labeling has boomed in prominence in recent years. To distinguish between larger vendors, more and more sellers create their products on and off e-commerce marketplaces. With 50 percent of one of the online markets, private labeling vendors, the rivalry is fierce. You need to realize what you're doing if you want to excel. To start a strong private label, you need the know-how, expertise, and money. When you place your logo and name on a standardized commodity, private labeling is. This separates the brand from related rivals and retailers. You have full power over your brand, with a private label. You establish a distinctive identity that is essential for successful promotion and the acquisition of consumers. Customers, not goods, are faithful to labels. Customer satisfaction and repeat business may be created through the private label. In the market, you still have the power of your price and place. A private label on the online marketplace enables you to build a different collection of items only for your product. This gives real estate devoted to your brand and assures that you are not vying against other retailers for the Buy Box. Since they get higher value, clients love private labels. Private-label goods are usually cheaper, but major stores' efficiency is the same, if not higher. In reality, at least one form of private label product is purchased by approximately 98 percent of customers. Depending on their lifestyle, customers may even buy goods. One study showed that clients prefer private labels for the price and choose them based on expertise. They buy from private labels that they most associate with. Ultimately, in a sea of rivals, a private label separates the name, allows you greater leverage over your revenues, and appeals to a niche client target. So, you have agreed to launch a private label of your own. The measures to take to help you start a profitable private label from design to launch are below.

3.2 Understand the costs of private labeling

Before digging deeper into a private label, it's important to consider the initial start-up costs. In comparison to reselling, private tagging is more costly. However, this capital input usually results in a better return on your expenditure in the long term.

Manufacturing

Typical development expenses, such as supplies, processing, manpower, and transportation, would have to be accounted for. You may need to consider the customization charge, too. For customizing a product with your mark, packaging, or specs, most manufacturers will charge a fee.

Brand

Even to design the brand itself, you would require money. To create the logo and package template, you'll definitely want to employ a graphic artist. To stress the voice of your company, you will also want to develop a content strategy.

Marketing

Marketing is a significant part of private labeling. Customers don't know about your company, so to become more noticeable, you need to spread knowledge. A large cost may be generated through ads such as promoted and boosted blogs. A website creator and domain name would presumably both need to be charged for. For any other unforeseen fees or modifications that pop about at the beginning of the start of a new company, you can also add a sizable buffer.

- **Choose the products you want to sell**

The majority of corporations and labels start with a commodity. The brand is how you create your cash and profits. The item is the guiding force of your business. Starting a commodity with your name helps determine your margins, demand, and availability. The brand is the consumer service, but you will need to offer your consumers a valuable product in the end. You would typically choose a branded commodity that you place your own logo on while you market a private label. This suggests that a single generic product begins with your "brand." How do you further build and broaden your branding using that product? You want high-rank and high-margin units when buying a commodity. To lower warehousing and shipping costs, you will want thin, lightweight goods. If the first product you offer doesn't work out or you choose to shift paths, you can still move goods. The aim is to stick less to one commodity than to use product testing as a prism in your overall business and niche instead. You should also accept complimentary commodities with this in mind. If you market key items, you want to think of a range of similar goods that would still blend with your brand when choosing key products. For starters, you can grow inside the travel domain or beverage industry if you sell travel mugs. You will market some eco-friendly home products as well if you sell environmentally efficient cleaning products.

- **Define your target market**

Who is the perfect consumer for you? Who would be more willing to buy your unique product? This can assist you in deciding the sorts of goods you are trying to produce and how you are going to promote such products. The consumer is your market and your brand's secret. Getting a well-defined target demographic is more relevant than ever, considering the current condition of the economy. No one is willing to afford to target everyone. By approaching a niche segment, small enterprises may successfully compete with big firms. Many firms say they are targeting "anyone interested in my services." Others say they are targeting buyers, renters, or stay-at-home moms in small businesses. These priorities are all too common. Targeting a certain market does not mean that you exclude entities that may not follow the standards. Instead, focus marketing helps you to concentrate your advertising money and brand message on a single demographic that is more inclined than other markets to purchase from you. This is a means of meeting prospective consumers and creating a business that is far more accessible, accessible, and effective. For instance, an interior design business might opt to sell to households between the ages of 34 and 63 with incomes of $160,000-plus. The business could opt to approach only those involved in kitchen design remodeling and conventional designs in order to define the segment any better. This business may be broken into two niche markets: parents on the move and baby boomers leaving. It is much simpler to decide where and how to advertise your brand with a well-specified target audience. To help you identify your target market, here are some ideas.

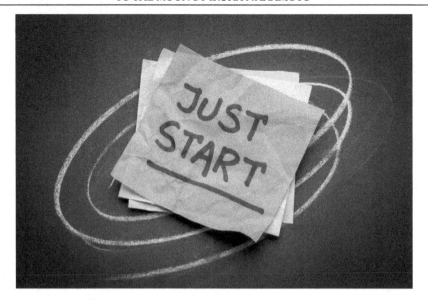

Look at your current customer base.

Who are your new clients, and why are they buying from you? Look for features and desires that are popular. What ones do other businesses carry in? It is also possible that your product/service will also help other individuals like them.

Check out your competition.

What are your adversaries targeting? Who are the clients at present? Don't try the same business. You might discover a niche market they are missing.

Analyze your product/service

Write up a description of each of the product or service specifications. List the advantages it offers next to each function. A graphic artist, for instance, provides high-quality design services. The advantage is the picture of a professional organization. More clients would be drawn to a professional image when they perceive the business as professional and trustworthy. So, basically, attracting more clients and earning more profits is the advantage of high-quality design. When you have your advantages identified, make a list of persons that have a need that suits your benefit. A graphic designer may, for instance, opt to approach organizations involved in increasing their consumer base. Although this is already too common, you now have a foundation on which to proceed.

Choose specific demographics to target.

Find out not only who wants the products or service and also who is most willing to order it. Consider the reasons that follow:

- Location

- Education level

- Occupation

- Gender

- Ethnic background

- Marital or family status

- Age

- Income level

- Ethnic background

Consider the psychographics of your target.

Psychographics is a person's more intimate traits, including:

- Personality

- Values

- Interests/hobbies

- Attitudes

- Lifestyles

- Behavior

Assess how your service or product would blend with the lifestyle of your destination. How and where is the item going to be used by your goal? What characteristics are most enticing to your goal? What media for details does your goal switch to? Can the newspaper read the destination, check online, or attend unique events?

Evaluate your decision

Make sure to consider these issues after you have settled on a target market:

- Are there enough individuals that meet my criteria?

- Is my goal actually going to benefit from my product/service?

- Are they going to have the use for it?

- Do I know what guides my aim to make choices?

- Can they afford my service/product?

- With my post, may I meet them? Are they readily accessible?

Don't smash the goal so far down there. Know, there is more than one niche opportunity you may have. Consider how, for each niche, the marketing message can be different. If you can successfully hit all niches with the same post, then maybe you have broken down the market so much. Also, if you notice that there are only 50 individuals that match all of your requirements, you may need to reevaluate your objective. Finding the right combination is the trick. You might be wondering, "How do I gather all this data?" Attempt to look online for analysis that others have done on your aim. Look for posts and blogs in publications that speak to or around the target group. Check for blogs and sites where thoughts are shared by people in the target market. Check for sample findings, or try doing your own survey. Ask for input from the new clients. The hard part is identifying your target demographic. It is much simpler to find out which platforms you should use to attract them, and what advertisement campaigns can connect with them if you know who you are approaching. You should give it only to people that suit your requirements instead of delivering direct mail to anyone in your ZIP code. In identifying the target demographic, save money and have a greater return on investment.

• **Consider your differentiating factor.**

You've settled on demand and a commodity. Now, what is going to make you distinctive in your business from your competitors? Look at the rivalry. What is their emphasis? And where are they missing? A perfect spot for you to put the brand is the field that they struggle the most. You could find, for example, that all of your rivals have a formal language; with your brand, you might take a goofy and enjoyable tone. In order for it to become a good differentiator, it doesn't have to be a big improvement. The core of your identity becomes your differentiator. Keep in mind that price may also be a defining factor. You would get a different demographic and competition than a cheap or discounted commodity, whether you are quality or luxury product.

- **Create your brand look**

Your "brand" consists of the goods, the demand, and the distinguishers. Yet, it is your material and aesthetic as well. You need a clear emblem that represents the name while private labeling is used. How you are and where the stuff comes from, the logo tells. This emblem can be included in all communications, packaging, and marking. Be sure it's accessible as a corporation and website prior to picking the brand name. This would mean that you do not infringe on any patents or fight with companies with identical names. To build the logo and package template, you'll definitely want to employ a graphic artist. This is the perfect approach to make things look respectable and trustworthy to the private label.

- **Create an experience**

A brand is, ultimately, more than a slogan, though. Your "brand" is how your business is experienced by the client. It's a consistent way for your audience to communicate. You need to work out how consumers can uniquely perceive your brand based on brand differentiation. What is your content going to look like? What could you provide that is unique to the experience of your brand? You may produce visually enticing social media photographs, for instance, that contribute to the lifestyle around your dog collars. Or you should make sure that you react to and respond to any social network statement or post. To keep your label on the edge, you can use special and exclusive packaging. Build an atmosphere, and you can turn your one-time consumers into long-term customers.

- **Find a supplier**

Acting with a good provider is an important aspect of private marking. The manufacturer must have private labeling expertise so they can help you make a return from your products. For a variety of consumers, several overseas factories will produce a standardized commodity and modify such items with private packaging for marking. You collaborate with a retailer, for instance, that produces bottles of water and T-shirts. They have ten buyers, each with their own special emblem written on the bottles, that offer water bottles. A customization and packing fee will normally be paid by the factory.

- **Build the brand**

You have put yourself in a role, built a differentiator, and found a supplier. It's time to start developing your organization now. You have to:

- Name and image copyright.

- Website configuration

- Creating a voice on social media

- Shape an LLC

Just like you would like any other legal corporation, recognize your e-commerce firm. You need yourself, your goods, and your income to be covered. You would also like to start naming the lists with online items. A private label means you don't have to fight for a Buy Package. "With a different page for your branded goods, you hold your own "real estate." In line with the brand background, this is a good chance to customize the listing.

3.3 Choosing the Right Products

Choosing the best market and the right goods to spend your efforts on is the greatest challenge you would have to conquer. This decision is vital to the success or failure of your company. The only biggest mistake you're going to make is selecting a product based on your own interests or personal preferences, particularly if you want to create a genuinely profitable company. You have to provide what other customers want, not what you want. Especially if you are not the type of individual to embrace patterns or the type of individual that is always perceived to be "outside of the box." We can't tell you what products to offer, but we can definitely give you some ideas about how to pick the right ones.

How to choose the right product

Your organization would have an uphill struggle to become profitable without a strong product portfolio. It may seem impossible to try to find out what you are trying to market, with potentially millions of items out there. The item you chose will also pose other concerns that you may need to work on. For starters, shipping may become an issue if you are planning to sell freezers.

Depending on where the clients work, whether you are selling alcohol, there could be regulatory limits. Market analysis can sound daunting, but knowing the product can cater to the people you are going to attract through your site is important. You should monitor the industry dynamics if you already have an understanding of what you intend to do to see how the commodity is actually performing on the market. If you are really not sure what you'd like to offer, trends can still be helpful to you. Business dynamics will offer you an indication about what items consumers are purchasing or are interested in buying at the moment. Look for items that address a dilemma the target group is experiencing. If your consumer is fed up with the current product range, open a unique and better product to deliver them. Choosing a commodity that is not reasonably available nearby or a national brand that is coveted by a region outside of where it is actually accessible may also be a brilliant choice. Another recommendation is to find a service/ product based on your target audience's interests. This may be in the shape of a new TV show that is beginning or a fashion trend. It often applies to aiming for a difference in chances. If you choose a product that many different competitors are already selling, find something that you can do differently or better than everybody else. This can be an enhanced product characteristic, a market that your competitors totally miss, and maybe something in your marketing plan. If you are trying to market a commodity-based on something that is trending at the moment, ensure that you capitalize early on the pattern. There tend to be more individuals who buy the product at the beginning of a trend. Everybody else is now also moving along to the next thing if you get on the hype train at the end of the trend. Do not wait too long to profit on a trend in the market unless you think that you're going to revive a dead trend. When you make your choices, it is important to take into account product turnover. It would take a lot of time and resources on a product range that varies year after year to guarantee that the product selection is held up-to-date and does not include last year's choices, which could no longer be eligible. A reduced churn product would enable you to engage in a more informative website that will be applicable for a longer time span. Don't be frightened of looking at smaller segments and niches of products. Although there may be fewer prospective customers, there will also be less competition, making it easier to get it to the top of the search engines and much more cost-effective in terms of marketing. The right product is an essential part of your success. Take your time and also don't rush into the first good-looking product.

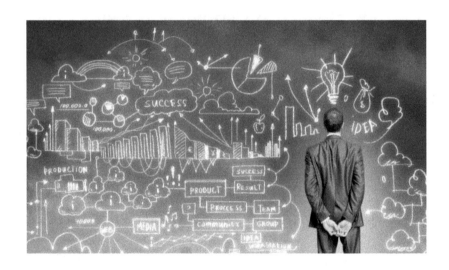

Looking for Product Ideas

There is no need to start a shop without a commodity to sell. Begin with something you already have, or how you can fix your own issues or the challenges of people you meet before you start looking for fresh ideas on what you can sell. There are some ways to consider:

- Which items or niches are you involved in?

- What items are your mates excited about?

- Which challenges do you have with your own life?

- Whose goods can address this?

- What kind of firms are based in your community?

- Can they be translated into a definition online?

- What will organizations in your culture cater to individuals outside of your community?

- In other areas of the planet, what items are trending?

- Is there a need inside your society for them?

- Will you build in your society a market for them?

- Is there a certain sector you like to be interested in if you are confused regarding products? In that industry, what products are popular?

- What items can you find useful from that industry?

- In other online retailers, what items are popular?

- Will this commodity have a niche that you should specialize in in sales?

- What's the social curation website trend?

- Is there an undiscovered thing out there that individuals would want to see open to them?

3.4 Building a Team and Starting your Personal Brand

Choosing the Right Supplier

It can be tricky to pick a supplier for your private label company, but it can help you to realize that there are a variety of suppliers who have been doing this for several years. Some lead the industry in broad industries, and this may be the perfect place to get started in your new company since the goods you offer are already established and have gained appreciation from the market. You can have to trade-off or work in restricted strategies with your profitability, and you need to be careful in reviewing the terms and conditions of each corporation, but each of these can create a backdoor into which you can start a profitable long-term business. Not all private labels are made equally, and to guarantee that your organization is effective, you want to make sure you chose the best provider. There are certain items that your provider wants to provide and some things that are less essential but can have greater convenience. Any of the items you'll be searching for in a provider include:

- Will the retailer have members who are knowledgeable?

- Will the supplier devote them to a particular entity committed to your account?

- Are they invested in being advanced technologically?

- How can you send orders?

- Where are they situated?

- Are they a coordinated business?

- How fast are their orders shipped?

- How are they keeping you throughout the loop on product returns and items out of stock?

- How fast can they send you the tracking details and purchase order?

- What payment types do they approve?

- What kind of fees are they charging?

It may seem impossible to locate the legal firms and distinguish them from the fraudulent as you are searching for a provider. There are some tricks to choosing a decent provider for private labels. One crucial point to bear in mind when you start approaching suppliers is that they could very well be the secret to selecting the best supplier, even though they are not the right match for you. Make sure you always ask every supplier you meet if they can guide you in the appropriate path to reach a supplier that suits your company. As they're in the business, they are sure to have connections that will help you and are typically prepared to share the details. Looking at social media is another way one can improve the chances of having a reliable supplier to deal with. Often, through a family member, neighbor, or acquaintance who might be in the industry or meet someone in the industry, you may find a lead. Any lead is a successful lead, even though it leads to a dead end. In order to strengthen the partnership, you have with your supplier, there are a few items you should do:

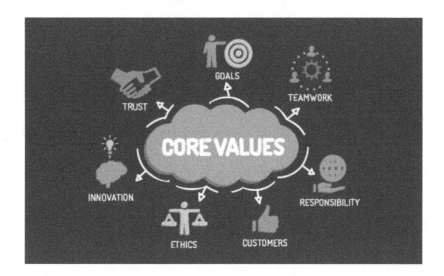

- Pay on time to develop trust and then become a reliable client.

- Set simple and realistic targets if an estimation of the goods you plan to sell in a specified period is requested

- Remember that they have other clients and do not belong to you alone.

- Learn what you need when you put orders to speed up the operation.

- If there is a malfunction, do not accuse the representative, but collaborate with them to find a remedy.

- Knowing somebody on a personal level seems to make them more likely to help you out. Build relationships with your delegate

- Train them to identify what you need, such as fresh product photos and product update updates, items out of stock, and products were withdrawn.

Finding the Right Suppliers and Working with Them

The one crucial part you have to do before you continue the quest for the right suppliers is learned how to say the difference between a true wholesale supplier and a department store that works like one. The manufacturer orders their stock from a genuine wholesaler and delivers far higher deals than a supermarket would. To create a good organization, you need to be able to do all of the following:

Have Access to Exclusive Distribution or Pricing

Being able to negotiate unique product agreements or exclusive prices would offer you the advantage without the need to import or produce your own product to sell online. These are not quick items to arrange, and you can notice that you are still out-priced, and at wholesale rates, some private label brands would still offer the same or equivalent. You need to find a way to persuade the buyers that the commodity you sell is of greater quality than the competitor, whether you can have exclusive distribution, particularly if the competition sells a knock-off product at a cheaper price. This is where the website's "about us" page becomes much more useful as it is a good way to share the fact that you are unique to the product.

Sell at the Lowest Possible Price

You will rob clients from such a chunk of your niche market if you are willing to sell your goods at the lowest costs. The main thing is that since you actually won't be able to appreciate the gain, you are destined to struggle. The low price is not often the primary motivating factor behind the choice of a consumer to shop. Customers seem to choose to invest their cash on the best benefit and lowest cost of a commodity. This suggests that you ought to persuade them that the best decision is to invest a little extra cash in your goods, so there is less downside and more appeal to them.

Add Your Value Outside of the Price

Think in terms of having data that complement the items selected. A real capitalist can fix challenges, and at the same time offering goods at high rates. In your unique niche, make sure you give suggestions and insightful recommendations. Your customer support is one extremely efficient way to bring value to the goods outside of the costs. If you are willing to address all the queries of your consumer without needing to call you and are willing to respond to any emails easily, your store website will stick out from the rest.

Conclusion

A private label is where a person or corporation paying another business to make a commodity without its name, emblem, etc. The person or business then applies to the packaging their name and design. So, what sorts of items should be labeled privately? From skincare and dietary treatments and infant essentials, pet products, and kitchen utensils, pretty much all under the sun. The benefit of private labeling is that nothing innovative needs to be produced or developed by you. You can add your mark on it as long as it's not a proprietary commodity and label it yours. Dropshipping is a convenient method for private-label goods to be distributed. You will find a dropshipping provider if you are an online shop owner who can offer items directly to you and incorporate your branding. Dropshipping is an e-commerce market concept in which no inventory is held by the manufacturer. The retailer, instead, manages the packaging, packing, and delivery of goods to the end customer. In other terms, for dropshipping, the goods are delivered directly to consumers, and they are never used by stores. There is a legitimate explanation for retailers that are involved in flooding their stores with items with their brand name. Third-party suppliers operate at the behest of the supplier, providing full influence over the ingredients and consistency of the goods. In reaction to growing consumer demand for a new feature, smaller stores have the opportunity to move rapidly to bring a private label product into development, whereas larger firms might not be involved in a product or niche category. You should concentrate on creating a reputation before you start your company, one that is recognizable and valued, and a private label benefits both you and the retailer or supplier you select. The first move with your organization is importing the goods you choose to market, products that do not crack easily, which have satisfaction for the customer. The second and most significant move is to make your brand known to current and future clients. The more customers remember your brand, the higher it is possible that your revenue rate will be. Through selecting producers or suppliers who will submit your goods via Private Label, you will help this along. This operates by encouraging the consumer to position their orders with you, then deliver them to the retailer and directly dispatching the product. To sum up, while you are looking to get your brand out and develop a company without leeching on mainstream online marketplace/websites' popularity, a private label makes perfect sense. It will require a bit extra time to select a supplier since you must do the job yourself and guarantee that you work for the right supplier. Still, you will also gain a better profit when you take responsibility for the customer support and are willing to negotiate.

Short Stays Real Estate with No (or Low) Money Down

The 7+1 Creative Strategies to Create Passive Income from Home Using the AirBnb Business Model in 2021

By

Iruka Nakamoto

Table of Contents

Introduction...341

CHAPTER 1: Understand Income and Importance of Passive Income 345

1.1 Active Income...345

1.2 Portfolio Income..348

1.3 Passive Income 350

1.4 Taxing of passive income 354

1.5 Why Passive Income Beats Earned Income...................355

1.6 Reasons Why Passive Income Is So Important 357

CHAPTER 2: Passive income ideas to help you make money in 2021 364

2.1 How many streams of income should you have? 365

2.2 Passive income ideas for building wealth 366

2.3 Selling information products 366

2.4 Rental income 367

2.5 Affiliate marketing 369

2.6 Flip retail products 371

2.7 Peer-to-peer lending..372

2.8 Dividend stocks..374

2.9 Create an app...375

2.10 REITs...376

2.11 A bond ladder...378

2.12 Invest in a high-yield CD or savings account 380

2.13 Buy Property...381

2.14 Rent out your home short-term through Airbnb..................382

2.15 Air BnB Business as a Passive income Strategy 383

2.16 Advertise on your car...388

2.17 Invest in Stocks...389

2.18 Make Your Car Work for You...................................390

2.19 Sell your Videos 391

2.20 Create YouTube Videos 392

2.21 Write an eBook 392

2.22 Sell Digital Products 393

2.23 CPC Ads (Cost Per Click) 394

2.24 Minimize your taxes on passive income 395

CHAPTER 3: Airbnb Offers The Best Passive Income Generation Strategy...397

3.1 Understand the Vacation Rental Industry 398

3.2 Create a Maintenance Management System 399

3.3 Put Together a Vacation Rental Marketing Strategy..............400

3.4 Invest in Property Management Tools 401

3.5 Outline Your Guest Management Strategy 403

3.6 Set a Reasonable (But Competitive) Price..........................404

3.7 How an Airbnb Business Works 405

3.8 The Bottom Line...417

Conclusion 419

Introduction

If you are a forward-focused person, you can dream of leaving the profession to enjoy a retirement life that is simpler, or you might even consider early retirement. But a dream is only a wish without a plan. You need to contemplate passive income to put a few wheels on the dream. There are also plenty of different options for passive income and rationales of how to build it. Passive income is the money you collect that doesn't cause you to do a lot of "active" work in order to continue to earn it. In essence, you may do much of the work in advance and do some extra effort to earn an income. For instance, to keep the money flowing, if you develop an online course, you only need to update the content. Likewise, passive income strategies like renting out property and/or building a blog can take some effort to get up and running, but while you sleep, they would eventually earn you cash. You've already heard the word, "make money when you're sleeping." This is the main attraction that allows individuals to generate passive income. Even when you're not working, you can develop something (a course, a blog, e-book, videos, and/or an online store) which generates income. Or you can own something that helps you to earn passive income (property or stocks).

So why do you need to build passive income?

In the presence of a full-time job, your salary is your biggest income tool, a tool that usually requires your active involvement. Even if you enjoy your career, you wouldn't mind making some additional money without the tears, blood, sweat, and time commitment of another job. If you lose your job or want to generate an extra source of income when you are no longer productive or if you outlive your retirement fund, developing a passive income will improve your wealth-building strategy, create the opportunity to retire early, and save you from a total loss of income.

And how much money can passive income generate?

Generally, passive income won't make you wealthy overnight, so ignore those get-rich-quick schemes you've read about. But, over the long term, consistent, profitable passive income strategies will produce some serious money. Depending on the income stream, we're talking about anything from two to three thousand dollars to thousands of dollars.

Some people like to think of investing when we mention "passive income" because, with the least amount of effort, it can yield the greatest returns. But you should think about your retirement plan & passive income as two distinct subjects. The entire premise behind the long-term investment is to produce retirement income. If your fund options are good and they offer a match, you want to make sure you invest in your company retirement plan, like that of a 401(k). These are great choices for establishing a powerful pension plan, but before a certain age, you will face taxes as well as penalties for every withdrawal. You need to let your money grow only for the long term with retirement planning and not touch it. However, a form of low-effort income which can be accessed at any time should be passive income. After you are debt-free and have some cash left, one way to build passive income is by buying real estate and leasing it out to tenants. Rental property may be a fantastic source of additional income, but it is not the most passive option because, unless you employ a property management company, you will have to put a lot of effort and time into maintaining the property. You need to be in charge of your property if you go on the rental property route. Pay off your own home first before you buy a rental property, and buy your investment property with cash. You must not go into debt in order to purchase property for rent. You could develop something like an informative blog and/or a YouTube tutorial series to be able to generate online traffic if you have a bright idea that appeals to a particular audience. You might sell commercial space on your blog or ad spots on your channel if your content is engaging and it sees ample regular traffic. You can sit back, relax, and reap sources of passive income after you put in the heavy lifting. The list of ideas for passive income could go on indefinitely. Never go for any passive income strategies that promise a fast return or require large sums of money upfront. Your other financial targets would be sabotaged by them. In this book, we will present ideas that are steady, profitable, and trustworthy.

CHAPTER 1: Understand Income and Importance of Passive Income

There are three main categories of income:

Active income

Portfolio income

Passive income

1.1 Active Income

Active income alludes to money made as a result of the provision of service. Examples of active income are wages, tips, salaries, fees, and income from companies in which there is material involvement. The owner must meet the criteria for "material participation," which is based on hours worked or other factors, in order for income from a company to be considered active rather than passive. The most popular example of active income is income earned in the form of a paycheck from an employer. "Money from business activities is deemed "active" for the self-employed or someone else with an ownership interest in a corporation if it meets the criteria of material participation by the Internal Revenue Service (IRS). That implies one of the following is valid, at least:

- The taxpayer works during the year in the corporation for 500 or more hours.
- The taxpayer performs the majority of the company's work.
- Over the year, the taxpayer works for more than 100 hours in the company and no other employee works more hours than the taxpayer.

However, income earned is treated as passive income if someone earns income from a company in which they do not actively participate. Meanwhile, portfolio income is income from investments, like dividends and capital gains. Depending on the legislation at the time, these various forms of income can be taxed differently. At present, for instance, portfolio income is taxed at lower rates than active income.

Example of active income from a business

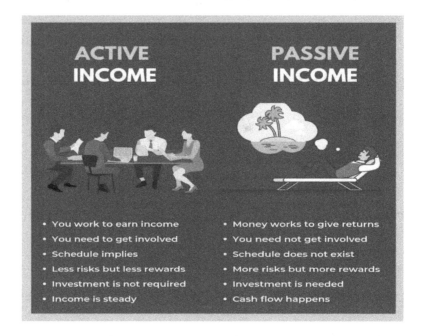

John and Laura are not married to each other. They have a 50% interest in an online business. John performs the majority of the day-to-day work in the business. Therefore, his income is considered active by the IRS. On the other, Laura helps with the marketing activities. She, however, works less than 100 hours a year in the business. It is for this very reason that her income from the business is considered passive income by the IRS. The material participation rule was established to prevent individuals that do not actively participate in a business from using it to generate tax losses which they, otherwise, could have written off against their active income.

1.2 Portfolio Income

Income from the portfolio is money received from investments, interest, dividends, and capital gains. Portfolio income streams are often known to be dividends received from investment properties. It is one of three main income groups. Active income and passive income are the others. Most income from the portfolio enjoys favorable tax treatment. Dividends and capital gains are charged at a much lower rate as compared to active income. Furthermore, portfolio income is not subject to Medicare or Social Security taxes. Income from the portfolio contains dividends, interest, and capital gains. Compared to active or passive income, portfolio income typically enjoys favorable tax treatment. Money from the portfolio is not subject to withholding from Social Security or Medicaid. One way to maximize portfolio income is to invest in an ETF that purchases dividend-paying stocks. Income from the portfolio does not come from passive investments. Moreover, portfolio income is not received from daily business activity. It is earned because of dividends, taxes, and capital gains or interest paid on loans. For tax purposes, the categories of income are important. Passive income losses can not necessarily be offset against portfolio or active income.

Ways to Increase Portfolio Income

Following ways can be employed for increasing portfolio income:

Purchase High-Paying Dividend Stocks

Investors can enhance their portfolio income by purchasing stocks that pay above-average dividends. Dividends can be paid directly to the shareholder. Moreover, dividends can also be used to buy additional shares in the company.

Purchase Dividend Exchange-Traded Funds

A cost-effective way to maximize portfolio income is to buy ETFs that explicitly track high-paying dividend stocks. For example, the FTSE High Dividend Yield Index is tracked by the Vanguard High Dividend Yield ETF. There are 396 stocks that have high dividend yields and are included in the index. For other dividend ETF options, the selection criteria concentrate on how many consecutive years the company has paid a dividend and/or on companies that have a history of raising their annual dividend payments.

Write Options

An investor can write call options against their stock holdings to enhance his portfolio income.

1.3 Passive Income

Passive income are earnings that come from a limited partnership, rental property, or another enterprise in which an entity is not actively engaged, such as a silent investor. Proponents of passive income tend to be boosters of the working lifestyle of a work-from-home and/or be-your-own-boss. Colloquially, it has been used on the part of the person receiving it to describe money being earned periodically with little or no effort. When used as a technical term, passive income is defined by the IRS as either "net rental income" or "income from an enterprise in which the taxpayer does not participate materially" and may include self-charged interest in some cases. Passive income is a source of income that may require some initial effort or investment but continues to generate payments in the future. Examples are music and book royalties and house rent payments. Passive income is the return on savings accounts. Passive income is created by a limited partnership in which a person owns a share of a company but does not engage in its functioning. Passive income consists of earnings generated from rental property, a limited partnership, or some other enterprise in which a person does not engage actively. Usually, taxes are charged on passive income. Portfolio income is perceived by a few analysts as passive income, and interest and dividends will also be considered as passive income. In order to earn and maintain, passive income needs little to no effort. When an earner puts in one of those little efforts to produce income, it is called progressive passive income. In many ways, a passive income investment can make an investor's life easier. This is true when a hands-off strategy is followed. Examples of passive income investment strategies include - Peer-to-Peer Lending, Real Estate, Dividend Stocks, and Index Funds. These four choices suggest different risk and diversification levels. As with any kind of financial investment, calculating the anticipated returns in relation to a passive income opportunity versus the loss potential is important. The main types of passive activities are explained below:

Cash flows from property income, including cash flows from a property or from any piece of real estate, capital gains, rent through resource ownership such as rental income, and in the form of interest from financial asset ownership.

Trade or business-related activities in which an individual does not engage in a company's operations other than investing during the year.

Royalties, that is, payments initiated by one corporation (the licensee) to another firm/person (the licensor) for the right to use the intellectual property of the latter (music, video, book).

Standards for Material Participation

The standards for material participation include:

- Five hundred plus more hours toward an activity or a business from which you are earning
- If the participation for that tax year has been "substantially all."
- Up to 100 hours of commitment and at least as much as every other person involved in the operation
- Material involvement in at least five of the past 10 tax years
- For personal services initiatives, material engagement at any point in three previous tax years

According to the IRS, there are two passive activity categories. Rentals, including equipment and real estate, are the first type; and businesses are the second type, where the individual does not engage materially on a daily, continuous and significant basis.

Examples of passive activities

The following are considered passive activities:

- Equipment leasing
- Limited partnerships

- Partnerships, S-Corporations, and LLCs where the individuals do not materially participate

- Rental real estate (some exceptions apply)

- Sole proprietorship or farm where the individual does not materially participate

1.4 Taxing of passive income

There are various forms of passive income, ranging from capital gains and dividends. Then the question arises whether the passive income is taxable or not. The brief response is, yes. Tax rates can differ depending on how long the assets are kept, the amount of benefit gained, and/or net income on each form of passive income.

Short-Term Passive Income Tax Rates

For assets retained for a year or less, short-term gains apply and are taxed as ordinary income. In other words, at the same rate as your income tax, short-term capital gains are taxed. The prevailing tax rates for short-term gains are as follows: 10 percent, 12 percent, 22 percent, 24 percent, 32 percent, 35, and 37 percent.

Long-Term Passive Income Tax Rates

Long-term capital gains (assets that are held for more than one year) are taxed at three rates: zero percent, fifteen percent, and twenty percent, based on your income bracket.

Taxing of real estate income

With lower tax rates, investing in real estate and high yield rental assets is now even more advantageous for individuals. The authorized business income deduction is now a twenty percent deduction on the taxable income while buying and holding real estate. This deduction of 20 percent now requires investors to subtract a portion of the real estate investment holdings, which may lead to a higher ROI.

1.5 Why Passive Income Beats Earned Income

income Earned is the income that you earn when you work the job full-time or run a business. Notice that, in most instances, "running business" doesn't require rent real estate corporate. Money gained from royalties, rents, & stakes in the limited partnerships is passive income. Income from the portfolio is the income from interest, dividends, and stock sales capital gains. Earned income would be subject to heavy taxation at all levels. Earned money should be utilized to rapidly create wealth, but your wealth must be transferred into the portfolio and passive income pools in order to reduce your tax position. Earned incomes are subject to FICA taxation and the full marginal income tax rate. There are undoubtedly ways of minimizing tax liability, such as operating an S-earned Corporation's revenue, investing in the firm and currently earning deductible expenditures, etc., but high marginal tax rates would also be subject to net income. The issue with earned money is that you still have to spend more cash in order to minimize tax liability. Passive incomes from the rental property aren't subject to the high operational tax rates. Rental property income is privileged by amortization and depreciation and contributes to a much lesser effective rate of tax.

Let's assume, for instance, you now own a rental property, which nets 10,000 dollars before the depreciation & amortization. Let's just say that $8,000 is the total amount of depreciation and amortization. It leaves with a taxable revenue of $2,000. You can pay a tax equivalent to 740 dollars if you fall in the 37 percent tax bracket. Yet you see an effective rate tax of just 7.4 percent as we equate the $740 with the amount raised ($10,000). If you made the same 10,000 dollars in the earned income, in order to minimize the amount available to tax, you would need to expend more. Otherwise, with $10,000 into taxable income, you'd pay $3,700, meaning you're in 37 percent tax brackets. With the rental real-estate, every year, you don't have to be paying for depreciation. It's a ghostly cost which you have to claim. That's why, from a tax standpoint, passive income knocks out earned income.

1.6 Reasons Why Passive Income Is So Important

It's no wonder passive income's, and for a good cause, one of the most thought about, sought after aspects of personal finance. Passive income will have an incredibly positive effect on only about any financial situation, from creating vast wealth to avoiding a paycheck-to-paycheck lifestyle. But that poses the question: why does passive income matter so much? In short, passive income's essential because in financial life, it provides flexibility, prosperity, and independence. In addition, because your time & resources do not limit passive income, it may have a beneficial and important impact on the ability to build wealth. Passive income, in different words, is 1 of the easiest ways to upgrade the financial condition. But if that's not compelling enough, we've listed the top reasons why passive income's important.

Improved financial stability

One of the most significant milestones you will hit on the road to prosperity is monitory stability. In different words, even if you really can see your financial position and realize, with certainty, that you're capable of coping with a powerful financial storm, so then you're on a very stable path. If you may count on the money rolling inside without having to fight for every cent of it, even more than that, so financial security is just a nearby corner. More money which comes in more you can be secure and comfortable in the finances. It helps you in relaxing, look at the bigger picture, & make smarter financial decisions because you don't have to grind for every dollar you earn, which, in turn, increases your financial health. This is a magnificent little cycle & one of key reasons why passive income is playing such a major role in personal finance.

Less reliance on a paycheck

The discomfort that comes with living paycheck to paycheck is not comparable by any means. And if it is your case, then one of the best moves you can take is to add a bit of the passive income in your life. There is no secret in that sometimes it may get a bit stressful as you trade time for dollars. And the more you will distance yourself from a focus on the next paycheck, the lighter it can be in your life. One of the greatest advantages of passive income is avoiding the paycheck-to-paycheck lifestyle.

It's easier to achieve your goals

Did you ever say to yourself, " only If I made extra money, then I could accomplish my monetary goals much more quickly...”? Well, that's just another explanation why the passive income's so awesome. It doesn't what financial targets you're trying to attain; you can accomplish your goals much quicker if you build certain passive income sources that enable you to make money all the time of day.

More freedom to pursue your passions

You will unexpectedly find yourself with the opportunity to pursue your passions or, for that matter, your ideal job, along the same line as avoiding the paycheck to the paycheck lifestyle, while you get some of the passive income flowing through the bank account. Remember that it's easy to end up trapped in a position you can't bear when you focus on the active income to make ends meet. It is tough enough to leave a career. But it is particularly tough to leave a job if you don't have sufficient money to pay the rent that is due in two weeks. On the other hand, you have the opportunity to do the things you really want to do when you have a stable stream of passive income running into the finances of yours. Passive income, to put plainly, offers you choices. & with those choices, independence comes.

Location independence

Likewise, in many ways, passive income encourages you to live and working from anywhere you like. Since you don't have to work constantly to earn a passive income, so you don't have to be working from a particular position either. You could tour the world if you like, as far as you earn passive income sufficient to support your lifestyle. And plenty of people do.

Early retirement

Retirement is, to some degree, for many people, that may only be done later in life. Although, if you're building any passive income sources, retirement may not be far away as you thought. Really, if you love the thought of retirement at a young age, so then your primary financial priority should be passive income. If it means creating a company that operates even without you needing to be present there, participating in real estate, or a mix of few different sources of income, if you desire to stop working at a young age, passive income is necessary.

More financial margin

more financial margins you will build in life, better off you will be in personal finance. In different words, the more distance you've between the expenditures & your income, the better it will get for financial life. And when you produce a constant stream of the passive income per month, it becomes much simpler to build the financial margin. Let's say, for instance, that your monthly gross expenditures increase up to 3,000 dollars. Now, if you're earning $4,000 inactive household revenue, then the monthly margin is $1,000. Yeah, that's not bad. However, if you add an additional $2,000 in passive monthly income in to the mix, life just got a lot better.

Reduced stress

There's one unity between all, after everything we've spoken about so far. It's plain; passive revenue has a distinctive way to reduce the financial burden. A passive income life is considerably less difficult than a life deprived of it. Because your financial security, margin, independence, and too much more are improved by passive income, it's only logical that it will help alleviate your financial burden. So, if financial condition makes you feel a little tightened around the collar, you may just want to give passive income a little more priority.

It's exciting

Passive income is not constrained by the effort and time that you can put into it. In different words, at all the hours of night and day, passive income can be earned, including while you are sleeping.

Yet, at the same time, making money is incredibly thrilling. There's nothing like waking up in the morning thinking that you've won a few hundred bucks while you're sleeping. And the more you are enthusiastic about the financial condition, the more probable you are to continue to improve it.

CHAPTER 2: Passive income ideas to help you make money in 2021

Passive income may be a wonderful way of helping you produce more cash flow, & global upheaval created primarily by the pandemic is evidence of the importance of having many income sources. Passive income lets you cross the gap whether you unexpectedly become jobless or even whether you willingly take the time from work away with the pandemic tossing the working condition of most people into disarray. You might get the cash rolling in from passive income even while you follow your primary career, or if maybe you can build up a good passive income pool, you may need a little to kickback. Anyway, you are granted additional protection from passive income. And if you are concerned about being capable of saving enough money to reach your retirement objectives, accumulating capital through passive income also is a tactic that could be appealing to you. Regular earnings from a party other than the employer or the contractor are counted as passive income. IRS (Internal Revenues Service) notes that passive revenue will come from 2 sources: a company or a rental property in which one is not directly participating, such as paying book royalty or dividends on securities. Most individuals agree that passive income's about getting more for nothing. It's got get-wealthy-quick charm, but it also includes work in the end. What you offer is work upfront. You may do any or all the job upfront in practice, but the passive income also requires some extra labor along the way too. To keep the passive dollars flowing, you might have to save your merchandise updated or well-maintained rental property. But if you're dedicated to the approach, it could be a perfect way to make income, and by the way, you'll build some more financial stability for yourself.

2.1 How many streams of income should you have?

"When it comes to generating revenue sources, there is no "one size fits all" advice. How many revenue streams you have can depend on where you are financially and what your potential financial targets are? But it is a decent beginning to get at least a handful. "With multiple lines in the sea, you'll attract more fish. Rental assets, revenue-producing shares, and company ventures are a perfect way to diversify your income stream, in addition to the earned income produced by your human capital. You'll want to make sure, of course, that bringing work into a new passive income stream would not cause you to lose sight of the other sources. So, you want your efforts to be aligned and make sure you pick the right options for your time.

2.2 Passive income ideas for building wealth

So, if you're considering building a passive income source, look at these techniques and absorb what this takes to succeed with them, whereas still recognizing the dangers involved with each strategy.

2.3 Selling information products

One common passive income approach is to produce information products, such as e-books, or video or audio lessons, and then kick back while cash rolls inside from product sale. Via platforms such as Skillshare, Udemy, and Coursera, courses could be distributed & sold. Otherwise, you may think of a "freemium model"-making a free content follow-up and only charging for the more comprehensive details or for the ones who wish to learn more. Language teachers or / & stock-picking guidance, for instance, can use the model. Free material serves as a demonstration of talents and can draw those who want to be going to the next stage. You may use advertising (or sponsor) to make your revenue as the third alternative for this concept while offering information or material on a free forum like YouTube to a growing audience. Take the love of music or video games, for instance, and transform it into the content.

Opportunity

The Information products will have an outstanding revenue stream, so after the initial time outlay, you quickly make money.

Risk

development of this product typically requires a huge amount of effort. And it needs to be good in order to make great money off it. There isn't space out there for trash. If you wish to be competitive, you must create a strong base, advertise your products & prepare for other products. Unless you get very lucky, one product isn't business. Generating more outstanding products is the easiest way to market an established good. You could create a strong income stream once you understand the business model.

2.4 Rental income

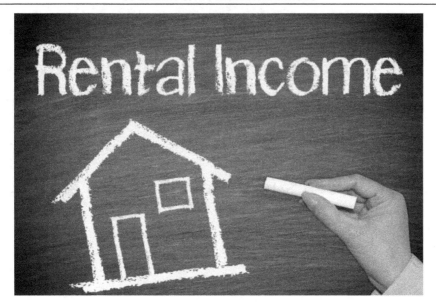

A successful way of earning passive income is to invest in rental properties. But more work is always needed than people expect. You could risk your money if you do not take the time to know how to create a profitable venture.

Opportunity

If you want to earn the passive incomes from the rental properties, then you must determine three things:

- Financial risk of owning property.
- Property's total expenses and costs.
- How much profit you need on investment.

For example, suppose your objective is to make $10,000 in a year in the rental income. At the same time, your property has monthly mortgages of 2,000 dollars and charges another 300 dollars in one month for the taxes & other expenses. In this scenario, you will have to cost 3,133 dollars in the monthly rent for accomplishing your objective.

Risk

 few questions should be considered: Is there a marketplace for a property? How if you have a homeowner who pays off the property late or harms it? Suppose you cannot rent the property out? The passive income could be significantly impacted by any of the variables. And pandemic also has raised new threats. You could suddenly have occupants who could no longer afford their rent because of the economic crisis, although you may already have a mortgage of your own to be paying. Or, if earnings fall, you couldn't be capable of renting out homes for as far as you did before. So, to secure yourself, you'll want to consider these threats and have a contingency plan in place.

2.5 Affiliate marketing

However, with affiliate advertising, website owners, "influencers" on social media or blogs support the goods of third parties by including a link to the product on the forum or the social media network. The best-known associate partner maybe Amazon, but Awin, ShareASale and eBay, are all among the bigger brands. And for those watching to develop a following and sell goods, TikTok and Instagram have become major websites. To attract attention to the blog or else steer people to goods and services which they may like, you might also start growing an email list.

Opportunity

The site owner receives a fee if visitors click on the link and make a transaction from a third-party associate. The commission may vary from 3-7 %, so it would obviously need substantial traffic to the site to produce serious revenue. But you could be able to make some serious coin if you may expand the following or even have a more profitable niche (like tech, fitness, or financial services). Affiliate advertising is deemed passive, and, in principle, only by adding a link to your social media platform or website, you will gain money. In fact, if you cannot draw readers to the site to tap on the link and purchase anything, you won't earn anything.

Risk

You'll have to be taking time to develop content and generate traffic if you're just starting out. Building a following will take important time, and you'll need to discover the best formula to reach the crowd, a task that could take a while on its own. Worse, the audience might be likely to fly to the next famous influencer, topic, or social media site after you've expended all that energy.

2.6 Flip retail products

Make use of online sales sites like Amazon or eBay, and offer goods you find nowhere at prices of cut-rate. You will arbitrage the difference between the prices between your purchase & selling, and you will be able to create a following of the people who monitor your transactions.

Opportunity

The price disparities between what you'll find & what average customer will be capable of finding would encourage you to take advantage of them. If you've contact that may help you obtain affordable goods that some other individuals can locate, this might work extremely well. Or you might be capable of uncovering useful products which others have completely missed.

Risk

Although deals can happen online at any moment, you'll probably have to rush to find a reputable source of goods to help keep this strategy passive. And you're just going to have to know the competition so that you don't buy at a price that's too much. Otherwise, in order to market, you can finish up with goods that nobody needs. Moreover, you may be forced to slash the price drastically in order to make the product worthwhile for the buyers.

2.7 Peer-to-peer lending

Peer-to- peer (or P2P) loan's personal loan supports by the intermediary of third-party like LendingClub or Prosper between you & borrower. Funding Circle that targets firms & has greater borrowing caps, and Payout, which targets better collateral losses, are other players.

Opportunity

You generate income as a lender from interest payments made on loans. Yet, you face the possibility of default because the loan is insecure, implying you might end up with nothing. You must do two things to cut the risk:

By paying smaller sums on different loans, diversify the lending portfolio. Minimum investment for each credit is $25 at Prosper.com and LendingClub.

To make educated choices, evaluate old data on the prospective borrowers.

Risk

It takes time to learn the lending metrics of P2P because it's not completely passive, and you'll want to vet your prospective borrowers closely because you ought to pay particular attention to payments earned when you're engaging in several loans. If you intend to create profits, whatever you make for interest can be reinvested. Economic recessions may also make the high-yielding personal loans more likely to default candidates because if the COVID-19 manages to harm the economy at higher than historical rates, these loans will go bad.

2.8 Dividend stocks

The Shareholders in companies with dividend-yielding securities receive a payout from the company at regular intervals. The Companies pay the cash dividend out of the earnings on a quarterly basis, and what you need to be doing is to own stock. Per-share of stock, dividends are funded, meaning the more shares that you hold, the larger your compensation.

Opportunity

Since stock income is not linked to any operation other than the actual financial investment, it may be one of the most passive ways of money-making to own dividend-yielding securities. In your bank account, the money will simply be deposited.

Risk

Choosing the correct stocks is a tricky aspect. Without carefully researching company issuing stock, too many novices leap into the market. You have to study the website of each organization and be acquainted with their financial statements. 2 to 3 weeks you can spend researching each venture. That said, without wasting a massive amount of time analyzing firms, there are some ways to participate in the stocks dividend-yielding. ETFs, or Exchange-traded fund, are strongly recommended for income generation. ETFs are hedge vehicles containing collateral such as equity, commodities & bonds but trading like stocks. The ETFs are an excellent alternative for novices because, due to much lower prices than mutual funds, they are easier to understand, affordable, highly liquid, and offer much higher potential returns. Another key risk's that the stocks or the ETFs will decrease dramatically over short periods of time, particularly in times of volatility, such as when the financial markets were shocked by the Coronavirus crisis in 2020. Economic uncertainty may also cause certain firms to fully cut the dividends, while the diversified funds can experience less of a pinch.

2.9 Create an app

Creating an app may be a method to invest time in advance and then enjoy rewards over time. Your software may be a game or one that allows smartphone users to execute any feature that is difficult to do. Users download it once the application is public, & you can generate revenue.

Opportunity

There's a big upside to an app if you can create something that captures your audience's fancy. You'll think about how it's best to generate revenue. You could run in-application advertisements, for example, or else make users pay a small fee to use the app. You'll definitely add incremental improvements to keep the product current and popular as the app gains attention or you get feedback.

Risk

Perhaps the greatest risk here's that you spend your time unprofitably. You have no financial drawback here if you contribute little to no money to the project (and/or money which you'd have spent otherwise, for instance, on hardware). It's a competitive market, though, and genuinely popular applications must give consumers a persuasive benefit of experience. If your app gathers some data, you would also want to ensure that it is in accordance with privacy rules, which vary across the globe.

2.10 REITs

For a corporation that owns and manages real assets, REIT is a real estate investment trust, which is a fancy word. REITs have a special legal arrangement such that although they pass over any of their income to owners, they pay no or little corporate income tax.

Opportunity

In the stock exchange, you can purchase REITs much as every other business or dividend stock. You're going to earn whatever the REITs payout as a payout, and the strongest REITs have an annual record of growing their dividend, meaning over time, you might have an increasing supply of dividends. Specific REITs could be more expensive, like dividend stocks, than buying an ETF composed of hundreds of REIT stocks. Fund offers instant diversification, which is inherently much better than owning specific stocks & you can always earn a good return.

Risk

You'll have to be capable of selecting good REITs, much like dividend stocks, that means you'll have to evaluate any of the firms you might purchase, which indeed is a time-taking process. Also, while it is a passive activity, if you do not know what you're doing, you might lose a lot of money. And neither are REIT dividends safe from difficult economic times. If REIT does not produce enough income, this would possibly have to slash or totally remove its dividend. So just when you want it, most of the passive income could get hit.

2.11 A bond ladder

 bond ladder's sequence of bonds maturing over a number of years at various periods. The phased maturities help you to reduce the risk of reinvestment, which is a risk of locking up your cash as bonds offer interest rates that are too low.

Opportunity

bond ladder's a traditional passive investment that for decades has attracted near-retirees and retirees. You will sit back to collect the interest payments, and you "extend the ladder," transferring the principle into different package of bonds as the bond matures. For starters, you could start off with one year, three years, five years, and seven years of bonds. In the year that 1st bond matures, you have two years, four years, and six years of bonds left. You may use proceeds from the newly aged bond to purchase another one year or roll out an eight-year bond with a longer-term, for example.

Risk

Bond ladder reduces one of the big dangers of purchasing bonds, the possibility that you may have to purchase a new bond as the bond develops when the interest rates will not be attractive. Bonds, too, come with the other risks. Although the federal government backs Treasury bonds, corporate bonds aren't, meaning you could risk your principal. And to diversify the exposure & eliminate the risk of someone bond harming your total portfolio, you'll want to buy multiple bonds. Many investors move to bond the ETFs because of these issues, which include a diversified fund of bonds that you may put up on a ladder, removing the possibility that a single bond will harm your returns.

2.12 Invest in a high-yield CD or savings account

Investing in an online bank's high-yield deposit certificate (CD) or savings account will help you to produce passive income and get one of the country best interest rates as well. In order to make money, you won't even have to leave home.

Opportunity

You'll want to do a fast check of the nation's great CD rates or the top savings accounts to make the most of your CD. Going to the online bank instead of the local bank is typically far more advantageous since you will be able to pick the highest rate available in the region. And if the financial firm is backed by the FDIC, you will also receive a fixed return of principal of up to 250,000 dollars.

Risk

Your principal is secure as far as the bank is backed by FDIC and under limits. So, it is just as secure a return as you'll find to invest in a CD or savings account. Nevertheless, though the accounts are secure, these days, they return even less than before. And with Federal Reserve aiming at 2% inflation, the least in the short run, you're going to miss out on inflation. A savings account or CD can, though, yield less than keeping your cash in cash or in a non-interest paying checking account where you will earn about zero.

2.13 Buy Property

Real estate can be a decent way to make a passive income, depending on where you invest and when. There has been a rapid growth in the value of property in common cities such as Toronto-44 percent in Canada alone in the last five years. You will find some lower-cost properties by purchasing pre-construction condos, which will rise in value by the time it is eventually completed, enabling you to sell the property once it is complete for a profit. Like for all investments, it can be dangerous, so if you're new to the market, it's better to talk to a real estate agent to help you purchase the correct investment property.

2.14 Rent out your home short-term through Airbnb

This simple approach takes advantage of space that you don't need anyway, and converts it into an opportunity to make some money. Whether you're leaving for summer and/or have to be outside of the town for some time, or maybe even you want to fly, try renting your present space out while you're gone.

Opportunity

On a variety of websites, including Airbnb, you may list space and set rental conditions yourself. With limited additional work, you'll receive a check for efforts, particularly if you rent to a tenant who might be in place for a couple of months.

Risk

You do not have a lot of financial downsides here, but it's a gamble that's atypical of the most passive investors to let strangers stay in your house. Tenants can, for instance, even deface or ruin your property or steal valuables even.

2.15 Air BnB Business as a Passive income Strategy

Airbnb is an online website for selling and renting urban homes. It ties hosts and travellers and promotes the rental process without owning any rooms on its own. Moreover, it cultivates a cooperative economy by allowing private flats to be leased by property owners. Airbnb is an internet platform which links individuals that wish to rent the homes to an individual in that area who are searching for a room. It currently surrounds more than 100 thousand cities in the world and 220 countries. The name of the business derives from the "air mattress B and B." Engaging in Airbnb is a way for hosts to gain some money from their home, but with the possibility that it may be damaged by the visitor. The benefit could be comparatively cheap lodging for visitors, but with the possibility that property wouldn't be as advisable as the listing has made it look. For less than the cost of a hotel bed, travellers may also book an Airbnb. The traveler's biggest concern is that the property could not live up to its listing. The primary concern for hosts is that their property may be badly damaged by guests.

Airbnb

Business Model **Toolbox**

The Advantages of Airbnb

It offers the following advantages:

Wide Selection

Airbnb hosts list several different categories of properties on the Airbnb website, like single rooms, a suite of rooms, moored yachts, , whole homes, studios, houseboats, even castles.

Free Listings

In order to list the assets, hosts don't have to be paying. Listings may contain written descriptions, captioned photographs, and user profiles so prospective visitors can have the knowledge about hosts a little better.

Hosts Can Set Their Own Price

It is the host's prerogative to decide how much to charge per night, per week, or /and per month.

Customizable Searches

The Guests can filter the Airbnb database and not only through date & location, however also by price, property type, amenities, and the host's language. To further limit their search, they may also add keywords (such asclose to the Louvre').

Additional Services

Airbnb has increased its services to include events and restaurants in recent years. In addition to a list of available hotels for the dates they expect to visit, individuals searching by the venue can see a list of opportunities provided by nearby Airbnb hosts, like classes and sightseeing. Restaurant listings also contain Airbnb hosts' reviews.

Protections for Guests and Hosts

As a protection for customers, before transferring the funds to the host, Airbnb keeps the guest's payment for 24 hours following check-in. For guests, Airbnb's Host Guarantee program "provides security for up to $1,000,000 in damage to covered property in eligible countries in the rare incident of guest damage."

The disadvantages of Airbnb

It has the following demerits:

What You See May Not Be What You Get

Booking Airbnb accommodation is not like booking a space with a big hotel chain, where you have a fair promise that the property will be as described. Individual hosts, though some may be more truthful than others, create their own listings. Previous visitors, however, often post updates about their experiences, which may offer a more critical perspective. To make sure the listing is correct, review the reports of other guests who have stayed at the Airbnb house.

Potential Damage

The greater concern for hosts is potential that their property will be damaged. Although most stays go without incident, when the Airbnb hosts assumed they were renting to a peaceful household, there are reports of entire houses being trashed by thousands of partygoers. Some insurance is offered by Airbnb's Host Guarantee program, mentioned above, but it does not cover anything, like cash, rare artwork, jewellery, and pets. Also, hosts whose homes are destroyed can experience significant inconvenience.

Added Fees

A number of extra charges are imposed by Airbnb (just like, of course, hotels and other lodging providers). To cover Airbnb's customer care and other programs, travelers pay a guest management fee of 0 percent to 20 percent on top of the reservation fee. Prices are shown in the currency that the customer chooses, provided it is sponsored by Airbnb. Banks or issuers of credit cards can, where applicable, add fees. And though listings are free, to cover the cost of handling the transaction, Airbnb charges a service fee of at least 3 percent for each reservation.

It Isn't Legal Everywhere

Would-be hosts need to review their municipal zoning codes before listing their properties on Airbnb to make sure it is legal to rent their properties. To receive special permits or licenses, hosts may also be required.

2.16 Advertise on your car

By merely driving your car across town, you can be able to raise some additional income. Contact a specialized advertisement firm to determine your commuting patterns, like when and how many miles you drive. The firm will "wrap" your car with the ads at no cost to you if you're a match with one of their advertisers. Newer vehicles are being searched by agencies, and drivers should have a clear driving record.

Opportunity

If you're still putting in the miles anyway, though you may have to get out and drive, then this is a perfect way to earn hundreds every month at little to no added expense. It is reasonable to pay drivers by the mile.

Risk

Be extra cautious about locating a reputable operation to work with if this idea seems good. In this space, many fraudsters set up schemes to try to bilk you out of thousands.

2.17 Invest in Stocks

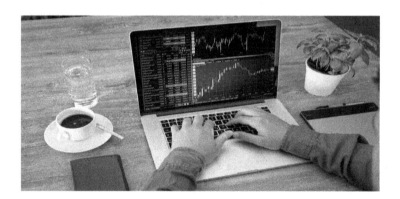

When you look at the wealthiest people in the world, it's pretty fair to conclude that their deep, endless savings accounts are a result of their major investment in stocks. Warren Buffett reads 500 pages a day, but he doesn't read your usual mystery novel. He reviews the annual corporate reports. He better knows whether or not a company is doing well by reviewing annual reports each day, which helps him improve his decision to invest in stocks. While the act of investing in stocks is very passive, the analysis that goes into it is active. Nevertheless, investing in shares will help you gain passive income that goes well beyond what your value is worth at your 9 to 5 work. So, if you enjoy reading about the success of different firms, consider this passive income approach.

2.18 Make Your Car Work for You

Driving is another everyday practice that you can translate into passive income. When you're just walking around, why not pick up a commuter or two to run errands? Uber can help you make money by taking people to their designated destination by driving your vehicle. You may also put ads on your vehicle to collect cash as you drive around. When your car is not used while you're on holiday, driving, or just during a normal workday, it will still make money. You will make thousands of dollars with an app like Getaround by renting out your car if you're not using it. Plus, drivers of Getaround vehicles get the best parking spaces in town, a $50 monthly rental credit on any vehicle they want, and one million U.S. dollars in primary insurance coverage.

2.19 Sell your Videos

We live in a day and age where video content fascinates hundreds and thousands of humans. You would want to take out your phone and hit the record if you still find yourself in the middle of drama and excitement. To allow you to make some passive income, you can sell stored content. Why? It is because the video can be sold to a news site. And you can make some recurring income for weeks, months, and maybe even years if the video takes off. Of course, being at cultural gatherings such as marches, rallies, and festivals is the best way to get in on the action. You'll find ways for your material to be sold anywhere there's controversy. And corporations will pay you to make viral videos along with providing a share of total earnings if you are successful at creating engaging content.

2.20 Create YouTube Videos

The passive income source that just keeps on giving is YouTube. You'll find that you can make a regular income from your YouTube channel, from funded videos to ad sales. Creating videos on a regular basis for a long time is the key to creating a profitable YouTube channel. If you stick with it in the long run, you will finally start reaping the benefits of passive income.

2.21 Write an eBook

In 2009 and 2010, e-books came onto the scene and are now a hugely successful content medium. While they first became popular a few years ago, to this day, there is still a very decent chunk of individuals who make passive income from writing e-books. It's an insanely dynamic business, of course. Yet, you might find yourself with a nice slice of the profits if your writing chops are stellar. You could build a fanbase of loyal readers by designing how-to e-books on famous niches and marketing them.

2.22 Sell Digital Products

You can make digital goods if you're trying to create your own products rather than selling someone else's. You can sell your digital goods online using Shopify. From e-books, educational classes, PDFs, custom graphic templates, stock images, or some other digital goods, digital products will contain anything. Selling these items is the epitome of passive income, and with immediate updates, the whole operation can be streamlined on Shopify.

Car Wash

Car wash is a perfect way to earn a semi-passive income. Although a car wash will need daily cleaning, it is something you can either contract out or do once a week. We are talking about the very simple car wash that is cinderblocks, a pressure washer, and the powered coin, as a side note. It's certainly a corporation vs. a passive income stream if you're trying to run a drive-through car wash.

2.23 CPC Ads (Cost Per Click)

You get really paid whenever anyone clicks on your link and signs up for something or orders something through affiliate ads. On the other hand, show advertisements charges depend on the volume of traffic and eyeballs that you receive on their ads. On the other hand, for CPC advertisements, also known as "cost per click" ads, anytime someone clicks on an ad, you get paid no matter what they do after that. You don't have to hope or pray that they're buying anything or signed up for something. Any single click takes money into your account with the bank. Does that mean that all day long you can go to your own website and click on ads? It is not realistic since the corporation will inevitably find out what you are doing and cut you off. With all that in mind, it should not be a part of your plan here to click on your own ads. Instead, aim to build up traffic so that more and more viewers every day see the ads.

2.24 Minimize your taxes on passive income

A passive income may be a wonderful side-income generation strategy, but you can still create a tax burden for your effort. But by setting yourself up as a business and building a savings portfolio, you can reduce the tax bite and plan for your future, too. However, this solution will not work with all these passive strategies because to qualify. You will have to be a legal organization.

Register with the IRS to make your company receive a tax identification number.

Then call a broker, such as Charles Schwab or Fidelity, who will open a self-employed retirement account.

Determine the type of savings account that will fit well for your needs.

CHAPTER 3: Airbnb Offers The Best Passive Income Generation Strategy

rental vacation industry is rising quickly. It is real quick indeed as a matter of fact. The sector is currently generating 57,669 million dollars in sales, according to recent analysis reports from Statista.com. The revenue is awaited to grow to a market value of 74,005 million dollars by 2023 and is projected to see an average growth rate of 6.4 percent. This data illustrates just how broad & robust the holiday rental management industry is. And you should expect demand for Airbnb property management to pursue to grow over the coming years with the growth of Airbnb rental properties in recent years. Therefore, if one day you are aiming to become a manager of Airbnb property, now is a great time to be entering the business. But how are you able to get started? We will supply you with what you have to know regarding how to be an Airbnb vacation rental property manager. We're going to teach you what this takes to handle rental Airbnb properties, particular instruments you're going to be needing before you start, and stop points for the beginners for achieving successful property management. So, without further ado, over here are all six steps to beginning an Airbnb property management career in real estate.

3.1 Understand the Vacation Rental Industry

Just like some other business, without learning at least the fundamentals of this area, you can't succeed. However, no formal qualification is necessary to become an Airbnb property manager, and many find success with the only diploma of high school in this profession. Thorough knowledge of how the holiday rental industry & Airbnb run is what you need to have. So, if you don't already have it, having this information now is the 1st step to being the manager of the Airbnb properties. Ideally, as Airbnb hosts yourself, you should have some experience. If you've already hosted your rental property on Airbnb, run it yourself, you can show to potential buyers which you know exactly what you are doing. Furthermore, this will allow you to be prepared better to predict challenges, recognize potentially troublesome travelers, and cope with common issues. But if you don't have the experience, through online guides and classes, you can empower yourself about the rental vacation industry & how Airbnb works.

There are plenty of those out there that can help you create a good base on which you have to learn. For instance, you may take marketing coursework to know how to extend your scope and get bookings more and business courses to know how to manage a company, keep records, & file tax. As an Airbnb property manager, it'll help you improve your creditability. Before you start, another significant point to learn is where the Airbnb hosts invest in rentals for the short-term. You'll know the place to find customers looking for management support with this detail.

3.2 Create a Maintenance Management System

Managing rental of short-term rentals ensures that you'll get visitors checking in & out repeatedly. One of many duties of the property managers, of course, is to review property before visitors visit & after they depart. Every now & then, operators of holiday rentals must also conduct repairs to ensure that the properties are in perfect shape. This is vital to ensure the happiness of both your customer and guests. For instance, imagine having visitors who had parties and had rental property trashed before leaving. Nobody with such a situation is going to be happy to step into a rental. As a consequence, before addressing the issue, the manager of Airbnb property can never leave the maintenance as an afterthought or even wait for the property owner to receive several inquiries. In addition, to offer high-quality care on their behalf, great short-term property rental operators often work alongside a dependable maintenance team. Your staff should include, among others, plumbers, house cleaners, and electricians. For any check-in, these entities will ensure that Airbnb assets you handle are tip to top.

3.3 Put Together a Vacation Rental Marketing Strategy

The most significant tasks of property managers are promoting and selling holiday rentals to attract prospective visitors. Today, there are millions of listings on Airbnb & more rental sites for the short-term, which is creating rivalry among the Airbnb hosts. It is why one of the first things potential users would like to know is how you're going to get reservations and increase their occupancy rates for Airbnb. As a consequence, you must have a basic comprehension of tactics and methods for property marketing. Therefore, having a marketing campaign that will draw Airbnb visitors to the holiday rentals you run is the next step towards being Airbnb properties manager. Start by writing an enticing listing that will maximize the probability of retaining a high rate of occupancy & a positive flow of cash. To make rental properties under your management stand out, think about investing in advanced photography & videography facilities, also branding services. Moreover, selling holiday rentals suggests that you have to go outside the listing platform. It is why active rental managers of Airbnb use social media and also SEO to meet the target tenant audience. If you don't know how it works, before you begin handling rentals in the short term, we strongly suggest that you begin to read about real estate marketing.

3.4 Invest in Property Management Tools

You can handle them with hard work and a few spreadsheets as you become manager of Airbnb property for the first time when you have only some rental properties underneath your belt. This becomes difficult, though, as you continue to add more assets to manage. How are thirty check-ins & cleanings going to be done in 1 day? At an early point, it is best to begin thinking about it so that you're planning yourself & your company for success and expansion. Using real estate management of property software that allows to automate & remain structured is the best approach for this.

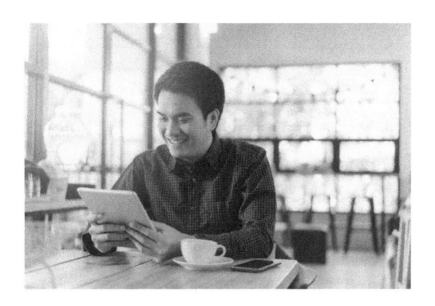

In order to operate their businesses more effectively, modern holiday rental property supervisors rely a lot on technology. There are several high-tech solutions that make it easy to handle Airbnb rental, from the smart lock to invoicing, pricing, and the guest screening software systems. You will even find holiday rental apps which will synchronize schedules and handle multiple Airbnb profiles for free from different platforms. Not only does the use of such instruments make your life more effective as a manager of real estate properties, but they can also give you the strategic edge to keep rising. Mashboard, for instance, is a software that lets managers of Airbnb property connect with their customers and find the right properties for those to expand their business.

3.5 Outline Your Guest Management Strategy

Amazing client care is one of the abilities that any manager of real estate property wants to provide when handling both conventional and holiday rentals. It is how effective operators of Airbnb assets set themselves away from the audience. A good selling point, particularly for Airbnb travelers, is customer service that goes beyond and beyond. Getting a guest engagement plan ensures that during their visit, the services can be open to visitors and their demands at whatever time. Expect the short-term visitors to have to inquire or inquire over something. You must be capable of responding in a timely way to such unannounced requests. How can you treat a case, for instance, where the visitor has misplaced keys to a holiday rental and can't get in? There will be a contingency in it and other cases for a successful Airbnb property manager. In addition, to manage communication with visitors, managers of top-performing properties also have automation tech systems in place. Airbnb guests really enjoy great customer service & show this by posting favorable feedback. This, in essence, helps to get more bookings & boost cash flow, that will surely make the customers happier. As you could see, one of the most critical skills for good management of Airbnb property is definitely customer service, so don't consider it as an afterthought.

3.6 Set a Reasonable (But Competitive) Price

To become a manager of Airbnb property, the only thing you need is a pricing plan. Usually, the holiday rental manager takes a percentage cut from the real host's secured rental fee. A selection of online outlets recommends anywhere from ten to twenty-five percent. At the same time, others believe that more consumers would be drawn by charging the lowest price; that isn't the case. Customers base their options on the quality o facilities rendered by property managers-not dependent on costs. Thus, providing the lowest price means that you don't have top-tier facilities for owners of Airbnb property. You need to take several factors into account in order to fix the correct price. First of all, as stated, is what kind of services you are providing. Naturally, for something that you don't sell, you do not charge. Look at experience instead, what distinctive points of selling you may give, and set rate accordingly. The local economy and what the other rental property (short-term) managers in the area charge, the seasonal demands, also current events, you will need to remember. Ultimately, you need to set a fair price which you are sure will be getting you back that your service is worth.

3.7 How an Airbnb Business Works

Nearly everyone has listened to Airbnb or has used it. It is the platform for online home rentals that helps hosts renting vacant private short-term accommodation from a single room to whole homes. Airbnb launched in 2007 & has expanded exponentially to have listings in further than 65 thousand cities in the world with more than three million available properties. Here is how to start a sustainable Airbnb company if you have sufficient rental space and are searching for additional revenue. Through uploading photographs and details of the room for rent, the first move is to be a host on Airbnb and register the home. When an Airbnb property's listed, travelers searching for a room in the host area will access it. Guests may use a number of requirements to check for Airbnb listings, like:

- Availability dates

- Destination

- No. Of rooms, such as bedrooms and washrooms

- Price

- Host language

- Amenities such as hot tub, breakfast, pets allowed, and etc.

- Facilities like air conditioning, parking,etc.

Prior to booking the chosen space through the Airbnb guest may establish a contact with hosts directly for gathering additional information through the Airbnb service of messaging.

Access

Along with browser access, Airbnb offers mobile applications for Android and Apple IOS devices.

Security

For security purposes, the hosts are expected to provide Airbnb with appropriate identification. Travelers should post the reviews of hotels to create a trustworthy group (and the hosts may review the guests). The Reviews aren't anonymous.

Guest Services

Airbnb offers a stable payment platform for the guest's calmness of mind, and fees to the hosts are deferred until 24 hr after the arrival of the guest. In the event that any difficulties are faced during the renting time, Airbnb has a 24-hour hotline for the guest.

Fees

Host sets the price for lodging. Moreover, Airbnb charges under-mentioned fees:

Host: Three % transaction payment fee

Guest: six to twelve % booking fee

The Hosts can also ask for a security deposit & could well charge a cleaning fee.

Taxes

Airbnb could apply provincial, state, or city taxes for guest bookings depending on the jurisdiction.

Travelers Prefer Airbnb Rentals

One of the best things about operating an Airbnb company is that, for several reasons, travelers choose Airbnb over motels, hotels, or hostels:

Cost: Usually, Airbnb rent is much inexpensive than a similar hotel room. In certain instances, an entire house may be rented through Airbnb for the cost of a single suite of the hotel, depending on the location.

Living locally: Living the life of a local person is the key advantage of the Airbnb service. Most guests of Airbnb choose to stay inside the community and explore the destination way the locals do, instead of renting a generic hotel room.

Privacy: customers of Airbnb are not continuously surrounded by visitors and workers at the hotel.

Peace & quiet: the Airbnb rents are usually more secure and do not suffer from loud hotel events, such as guest exits early in the morning, young children, maid service, and traffic.

Witness what you get already: Unlike a hotel where you can see a snapshot of similar rooms on their Airbnb page at best, you get full images and explanations of the real premises.

Diversity: From yachts and boathouses to castles and lighthouses, Airbnb has an immense variety of available accommodations.

Home comforts: Airbnb has a homey atmosphere of a real living space instead of generic hotel spaces (few have resident pets even). Kitchens allow the guests to cook their own food if they desire to save money on outside dining or have dietary issues.

Friends or Family: Through Airbnb, you may save a lot of money by renting a whole apartment/ house/condo rather than the multiple rooms of a hotel for family and friends.

Is Renting Your Space Permissible or Advisable?

Ensure you're legally permitted to be an Airbnb host into jurisdiction before you plan to start an Airbnb business, & you're prepared to respect local laws & regulations. Depending on the state/ city or regional rules, municipal laws governing the hosting of paid visitors will vary greatly; they are absolutely banned in some areas whilst they're subject to occupancy tax in others if space is condominium or apartment, check to view if it is allowed to sub-let the premises. There are also regulations in place for apartment landlords & condominium societies to prohibit an owner from renting the units out as Airbnb rooms. Renting your apartment out without the knowledge of your landlord will have you evicted. Neighborhood ties are also a significant concern. In the area, a few inconsiderate or loud Airbnb guests will easily turn you in a pariah. If none of the challenges are insurmountable, it could be an outstanding opportunity of home-found business to become an Airbnb host.

Are You Committed to Becoming a Host

There are a variety of additional concerns to remember prior to making a definitive decision to host Airbnb:

Would you like to start a business? Then Starting an Airbnb company is like establishing any business- that you need enthusiasm, entrepreneurial spirit, & the ability to make the required effort, starting off with doing relevant background analysis and developing business plans.

Do you've energy? It could take a great amount of time to be a landlord, particularly for the short-term rents. You'll have to:

- Manage reservations and reply to interactions with prospective tenants.
- Plan to meet the guests to give out or receive keys
- ensure the property, including fresh linen, breakfast supplies, is cleaned properly and ready for the arrival of the guest (if applicable)
- Fix some property maintenance problems such as plumbing and pest control, electrical & appliance repair
- Be accessible to the visitors on a 24 into 7 basis if the property has any problems.

Demand: The deciding factor in the popularity & price of rented accommodation is visitor demand. The highest places for rental returns are:

 sought-after tourist destinations with high hotel rates (famous neighborhood ranks higher on the Airbnb searches)

situated Centrally, close to visitor attractions, shops & public transport,

Featuring panoramic views and facilities like parking, balconies, etc.

Seasonality: Demand for the property in the northern hemisphere will definitely drop drastically in winters (unless you're renting a ski chalet). In comparison, rental accommodation demand in colder southern locations (like Arizona) decreases dramatically in summers.

What are the marketing aims? Are you trying to earn a little cash or create a stable income on the side? The financial portion of the business plan must show target market analysis and reasonable forecasts of your property's future rental income. The income from the Airbnb contract depends upon:

Before you start thinking about leaving your job & making a living through running an Airbnb company, make sure that by seeing rental prices & booking regularity for comparing Airbnb listings of your area, you carefully examine the revenue potential of your property.

Extra costs: In addition to booking fees paid by Airbnb, there are extra costs involved with Airbnb hosting, including:

Insurance: Standard insurance plans for homeowners do not include the use of the property for commercial uses, including renting on Airbnb. Airbnb has a free host compensation insurance policy in Canada, U.K., U.S., and many other nations, offering up to 1 million dollars in guarantees against personal harm or property loss. If your place is not protected by Airbnb policies, please contact your insurance provider to see if there is sufficient coverage.

Business Licenses: Airbnb hosts are being required by more & more cities to hold a business license.

Repair and Cleaning: You want to keep rental properties in top condition all the time in order to keep your Airbnb host ranking at a high standard, which includes extensive cleaning during guest stays and daily repairs. The charges will contribute to your expenses if you have to sub-contract cleaning and repair duties.

Listing and Pricing Your Property on Airbnb

Accurately describe the place and make this stand out. Note that Airbnb is an online marketplace & you have to be thinking like a realtor to make listing stick out from the competition in order to optimize guest interest in your house. Start by looking at the same Airbnb listings inside the region and consider the amenities/features and prices listed. If this works, make a spreadsheet. The definition of your listing must be precise, comprehensive, complete, and highlight, which makes it special. Comprehensively define the facilities and functionality of your room also as any regulations or preferences of visitors. Providing high-quality photographs of the room is incredibly necessary. Airbnb has specialist availability of photography service in certain places if you are unable to do this yourself.. You don't want visitors to be upset because the room isn't as advertised or you've exaggerated amenities. Note that the guest rankings would be partially dependent on the accuracy of your listing description.

Price Your Listing Competitively

You should also get an idea of how to market your listing from your analysis of similar listings. It needs to be competitively priced to keep the property consistently booked (and increase profits).

Improving Your Host Ranking

Higher the property pops up in rankings, the more probable it's to be chosen by visitors, so having good rankings of Airbnb is crucial to the success of Airbnb business. Airbnb rankings are like internet search rankings. And by building confidence and offering a fantastic experience to your visitors, you will boost your rankings.

Build Trust

Airbnb community's based on trust and guests would be searching for hosts with contact information, credentials, and favorable feedback.

Verification

For the new hosts, verification is highly essential: change your profile and include other details like the email address, phone number, Facebook profile, and etc. For giving prospective visitors some confidence that you're a reliable host.

References

You should post the references from colleagues, co-workers, relatives, business partners, etc., to build more trust. For the other Airbnb users, you may even write references.

Provide Great Customer Service

Like any entrepreneur would tell you, the cornerstone of any successful business is customer care, and becoming an Airbnb host has no difference. Positive ratings, better search scores, and more bookings reward hosts of Airbnb who have the best experience of the guest. The hosts with the most popular are:

Responsive

The Hosts that can not be bothered for responding in a timely manner (or at some) to inquiries are a big turnoff for visitors. In reality, Airbnb keeps track and rates your replies to guests accordingly. With higher search rankings and improved bookings, the host who has the highest ratings of response is awarded. At all times, Airbnb mobile application will help you to keep connected. All the time when visitors are present, be available through phone and check up with them on extended trips and see if there's something more you may do to maximize the services.

Update Their Calendars Regularly

Keeping your calendar current, also enhancing the guest experience, boosts the Airbnb rankings of search.

Fix All Problems quickly

When a guest mentions problems like leaky taps or a burned-out lightbulb, it should be repaired promptly and render an apology to the guest. Sure ways to boost the guest rankings is to provide five-star service.

Act on Their Reviews

Fix the issue and benefit from the failures if a visitor writes a critical review. React to complaints all the time in a respectful way.

3.8 The Bottom Line

In real estate, there are many ways of earning profits. The growing success in the U.S. housing sector of Airbnb and other short-term rentals has created opportunities not just for real estate developers but also for property managers. Today, there is a great demand for vacation rental managers, and industry analysts expect that over the coming years, there will be national growth. Therefore, imagine being an Airbnb property manager if you're looking for a profitable means of generating passive income.

Conclusion

In a nutshell, passive income is money that comes at regular intervals without having to invest a large amount of work into generating it. By blogging, one method of producing passive income may be achieved. If you've figured out how to produce content that attracts sufficient traffic to the host advertising, you can make a product that your customers would want to purchase. From a basic e-book to a sophisticated app that produces sales for several years after it is released, passive income could be anything. Similarly, people have a lot of things, and they still look for cheap places to store this. What might be simpler than asking people to pay you for storing their things? An investment on a large-scale in purchasing storage facilities (with the cash) or anything simple like offering the basement or the shed might entail creating passive income by offering storage. All you'll need is to make sure their goods are clean and stable. You will make money by selling them to others against such charges if you've any things that you don't use at all times, which others will love to borrow. As rental items, useful items such as a tractor, trailer, kayak, trampoline, or your own lawn even may give you passive income. With the support of platforms like Airbnb, this also involves renting spare rooms out in your home. Upload the pictures of items, fix a date, and tell the world they're ready for the rent on your favorite social networking site. The reason why it is necessary to have passive income is that it will help increase your financial consistency. The more passive income you make, the easier it becomes to be consistent with your financial life, from consistently saving to consistently spending to consistently donating. One of the strongest and most relevant aspects of a sound financial condition is passive income. It is beneficial for you in several ways, from enhancing your financial health to reducing your financial burden.

The 9+1 Best Home-Based Business Model of 2021

Find Out how Millennials Have Built Millionaire Businesses from Home with Soap and Candle Making, Natural Cosmetics and much more

By

Iruka Nakamoto

Table of Contents

Introduction...425

CHAPTER 1: The Nirma Washing Powder's Success Story..........429

1.1 Invention of Nirma detergent?..429

1.2 Karsanbhai Patel's sale policy for Nirma detergent..............432

1.3 Invest In Research and Development....................................434

1.4 No Higher Costs...435

1.5 Be Proactive in your approach as it is beneficial for the business...437

1.6 Provide Customers with 'Value for Money'..........................437

1.7 Define Your Segment...438

1.8 Focus on Building a Brand..439

1.9 Astutely Manage the Brand Wars..440

1.10 Diversify the Portfolio...443

1.11 Conclusion..444

1.12 What Karsanbhai Patel and Nirma detergent did for the Indian Economy...445

1.13 Karsanbhai Patel's ventures other than the Nirma detergent 446

CHAPTER 2: Start a Profitable Soap Making Business 448

2.1 What will you name your business? 454

2.2 Form a legal entity 455

2.3 Small Business Taxes 456

2.4 Open a business bank account & credit card 456

2.5 Open a business bank account 456

2.6 Get a business credit card 457

2.7 Obtain necessary permits and licenses 457

2.8 State & Local Business Licensing Requirements 458

2.9 Labor safety requirements 458

2.10 Certificate of Occupancy 458

2.11 Trademark & Copyright Protection 459

2.12 Get business insurance 460

2.13 Learn more about General Liability Insurance 460

2.14 Define your brand 460

2.15 Soap Making Plan 462

2.16 Soap selling process...472

2.17 Soap making supplies 474

2.18 Marketing area for soap...474

2.19 Total investment 475

2.20 Selling price 476

2.21 Profit margin 476

2.22 Precaution 477

2.23 Risk...477

2.24 Conclusion 478

2.25 Advantage of starting a soap making business at home.....478

2.26 How Much Money Can You Make Making Soap?...............479

CHAPTER 3: Start a Profitable Candle Making Business..............480

3.1 Steps for starting a candle making business 480

3.2 How much can you charge customers? 485

3.3 Benefits of candle making business 497

Conclusion 499

Introduction

Karsanbhai Patel (Patel), the chemist at Mines and Geology Department of the Gujarat Government, produced synthetic powder of detergent phosphate-free in 1969 and began selling this locally. He priced the new yellow powder at 3.50rs per kg. It was at one time when Rs 15 was being charged for Hindustan Lever Limited (HLL) Surf. Soon, in Kishnapur (Gujarat), Patel's hometown, there was a big demand for Nirma. In 10x12 feet space in his home, he began preparing the formula. He had named powder after his daughter's name-Nirupama. On the way to the office by bicycle, about 15 kilometers away, Patel was able to sell around 15-20 packets a day. Thus, the new journey began. Hindustan Lever Limited (HLL) responded in a manner characteristic of many global corporations in the early 1970s, when washing powder Nirma was launched into the market of low-income. "That isn't our business," senior executives said of the new offering. "We don't have to be worried." However very soon, Hindustan Lever Limited (HLL) was persuaded by Nirma's performance in the detergent sector that this wanted to take a closer gaze at the less income market. Low-cost detergents & toilet soaps are almost synonymous with the brand name. Nirma, on the other hand, found that it would've to launch goods targeted at the higher end of the market to maintain the middle-class buyers as they moved up the market. For the luxury market, the firm introduced bathroom soaps. Analysts, on the other hand, claimed Nirma wouldn't be capable of duplicate its performance in the premium market. In the year 2000, the Nirma had a 15 percent share of the toilet soap market and a 30% share of the detergent market. Nirma's revenue for the year ended in March 2000 grew by 17 percent over the previous fiscal year, to 17.17rs. bn, backed by volume development and commissioning of backward integration projects. By 1985, in many areas of the world, washing powder Nirma became one of the most common detergent brands. Nirma was a global consumer company by 1999, with a wide variety of soaps, detergents, & personal care items. Nirma has brought in the latest technologies for the manufacturing facilities in six locations across India, in line with its ideology of delivering premium goods at the best possible costs. The success of Nirma in the intensely competitive market for soaps & detergents was due to its efforts to support the brand, which had been complemented by the sales scope & market penetration. The network of Nirma spread across the country, with over two million outlets of retail and 400 distributors. Nirma was able to reach out to even the smallest villages due to its vast network. Nirma spread to the markets overseas in 1999 after establishing itself in India. Via a joint venture called Commerces Overseas Limited, it made its first foray into Bangladesh. Within a year, the company had risen to the top of Bangladesh's detergent market. Other areas such as Middle East, Russia, China, Africa & additional Asian countries were also intended for the entry of the organization. Nirma became a 17 billion Rs company in 3 decades, beginning as a single-product single-man article of clothing in 1969. Under the umbrella name Nirma, the company had several production plants and a large product range. The mission of the organization to have "Better Product, Better Values and Better Living" added much to its growth. Nirma was able to outshine Hindustan Levers Limited (then HLL) and carve out a niche for oneself in the lower-ends of detergent & market toilet soap. HLL's Surf was the first to be used as a detergent powder in India in 1959. But by the 1970s, merely by making the product available at a reasonable price, Nirma led the demand for detergent powder. Nirma launched its Nirma Beauty soaps to the Indian toilet soap industry in 1990. Nirma had gained a 15% share of 530,000 tons per annum toilet soap industry by 1999, making it India's second-largest producer. Although it was way behind HLL's 65 percent share, the success of Nirma was impressive compared to Godrej, which had an 8 percent share. By 1999-2000, Nirma had already acquired a 38 percent share of India's detergent market of 2.4 million tonnes. For the same period, HLL's market share was 31%. In this book, we will study and analyze the case of Nirma and its rise to the top detergent companies of India. Besides, we will also give profitable ideas and options for starting a lucrative detergent soap, candle making, and natural cosmetics business.

CHAPTER 1: The Nirma Washing Powder's Success Story

The success story of the famous Nirma washing powder began in a small Gujarati farmer's house. We'll tell you about a billionaire father who lost his daughter in a car crash and later discovered a way to get her back to life. When she was alive, only a few people knew of her daughter, but it was the sheer persistence and willpower of this man that made his daughter famous in the world, even though she was no more. This is the story of a man who was born into a poor farming family and turned his daughter's nickname into India's leading detergent, soda ash, and education brand. A man of valor and passion who showed that nothing will hinder you if you have the willpower. Here is the story of **"Sabki Pasand Nirma, Washing Powder Nirma."**

1.1 Invention of Nirma detergent?

Karsanbhai was born in Ruppur, Gujarat, to a farmer's family in 1945. He had earned a bachelor's degree in chemistry by the age of 21. He attempted to do a normal job like his colleagues at first. He served as a lab technician for the Lalbhai Group's New Cotton Mills, which is credited with launching the Indian jeans movement. He also took up a position at the Geology and Mining Department of the Gujarat government after this short stint. The year 1969 marked the start of a turning point in the career trajectory of Karsanbhai. It was at this time that Hindustan Lever Ltd (now Hindustan Unilever) formed a full monopoly on the Indian detergent market under the brand name "Surf." A Surf Pack was sold somewhere from Rs 10-15 back then. The USP was that, unlike normal washing soap bars, it eliminated stains from your clothes and didn't irritate your skin. However, for middle-class families, which had no other choice than to return to the old bar soap, this price point was not affordable. The tycoon in Karsanbhai noticed the issue and devised a plan. A young Karsanbhai will come home from work and dedicate all his time and energy to making a phosphate-free detergent in his yard. He wanted to bear in mind that he needed to produce a detergent with a low manufacturing cost so that everybody could afford it. Karsanbhai utilized a recipe for a yellow-colored detergent powder that could be marketed for a mere Rs 3 after several trials and failures. He chose to name the invention after Nirupama, his daughter. He finally got the formula right one day, and as an after-work business, he began making detergents in his 100-square-foot backyard. He will cycle around the neighborhoods, selling door-to-door homemade detergent packages. Patel set the price of his detergent at Rs. 3, almost a third less than Hindustan Unilever's well-known brand "Surf." The product's high quality and low price made it a success, and it was well-received by many who saw great benefit in purchasing it. Because of the business's high promise, Karsanbhai quit his government job three years later to pursue it full-time. Karsanbhai was so fond of the commodity that he called it Nirma, after his daughter Nirupama's nickname. To make sure that everybody remembers her, he used her picture (the girl in the white frock) on the pack and in TV advertisements. Such was a father's love for his daughter. While Karsanbhai Patel himself was not an MBA graduate, the techniques he adopted to expand his company left marketers bewildered and amazed. 'Nirma' was not only a game-changer but also a trendsetter for several small companies. Here are a couple of 'Washing Powder Nirma's' management lessons.

1.2 Karsanbhai Patel's sale policy for Nirma detergent

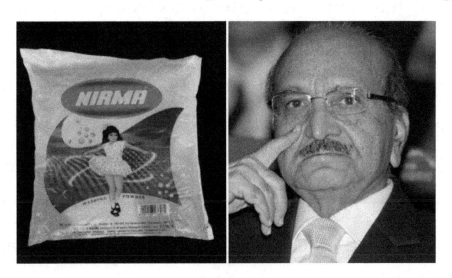

Karsanbhai Patel agreed to start marketing it once the product had a strong formula. On his cycle, he used to go door-to-door and neighborhood-to-neighborhood every day for three years, pitching the detergent. As it was a brand new product, if they found the product poor, he gave his consumers a money-back guarantee. Nirma has been the cheapest detergent in Ahmedabad at the time. As a result, Karsanbhai's product was an immediate hit. He left his government job three years later and set up a store in Ahmedabad to carry out this full-time enterprise. In some areas of Gujarat, his brand was doing very well, but there was a need to expand its scope. At the time, the standard was to offer the product to retailers on credit. This was a huge gamble because if the product didn't sell, Karsanbhai would have had to close down the company. At that time, he chose to try something different. He planned to spend a little money on advertising. These commercials, with their catchy jingles, were directed at housewives. And this bet paid off well. Nirma became a famous household brand and it had to be purchased by people. He did, however, remove 90% of the stock from the market at this time. Potential buyers had asked for the detergent at their local retailers for about a full month but would have to return empty-handed. During this time, retail store owners flocked to Karsanbhai, demanding that the detergent supply be increased. After another month, he eventually decided. Nirma was able to take over the sales and even beat Surf at their own game due to this approach. It went on to become the country's highest-selling detergent. It remained India's largest-selling detergent even after a decade,

1.3 Invest In Research and Development

Karsanbhai Patel had little means and was not a man born with a silver spoon in his mouth. Karsanbhai loved experimenting with chemicals after completing a B.Sc. in Chemistry at the age of 21 and then working as a laboratory technician. He noticed that only MNCs in India were selling detergents and there was no economy brand detergent for the country. His excitement about bridging the distance grew, sensing a massive opening, and Karsanbhai began experimenting with chemicals. He quickly succeeded in manufacturing a detergent of high quality at a much cheaper price, which was an immediate success in the industry. Every good product needs a substantial expenditure in time, resources, and commitment in research and development.

1.4 No Higher Costs

Nirma had rewritten the rules of the game within a short time, by delivering high-quality goods at an unprecedentedly low price. Nirma's success was due to its cost-cutting policy. Patel had concentrated from the very beginning on delivering high-value goods at the lowest price possible. The corporation sought to keep improving efficiency while reducing prices. Nirma sought out captive processing plants for raw materials to keep production costs to a minimum. This led to the backward integration initiative, as part of which, at Baroda and Bhavnagar, which became operational in 2000, two state-of-the-art plants were established. This also led to a reduction in raw-material prices. Ahead of time and at a much smaller cost than anticipated, the two new plants were completed. The Baroda plant's second phase was finished 6 months ahead of schedule and at a cost of Rs.2.5 billion compared to the initial projected cost of Rs. 2.8 billion. Compared to the initial projected cost of Rs. 10.36 billion, the Bhavnagar plant was finished in a record period of 2 years at a cost of Rs.9.86 billion. This plant had a workforce of just 500 employees. Concerning Nirma's plant, Tata Chemical's plant, which had around twice the amount, employed ten times the number of workers. Almost 65000 tpa of N-Paraffin was produced by the Baroda plant for Linear Alkyl Benzene (LAB) and Synthetic detergents. Similarly, almost 4.20,000 tpa of soda ash could be produced by the Bhavnagar facility. Akzo Nobel Engineering in Holland produced the Akzo Dry Lime technology used in this factory. The plant had 108 kilometers of salt bunds, which would assist in the potential development of vacuum iodized salt. Patel said, "We have a processing potential of three lakh tons of pure salt. No one in the world had a related plant, but Tata Salt." Nirma had reduced its distribution costs by obviating the need for middlemen. The item went to the dealer straight from the manufacturer. Hiren K Patel (Hiren), CMD, explained to Nirma Customer Care Ltd., "An order is placed and the truck immediately leaves. It's similar to a bank account. We're sending stock, they're sending money." In states like Tamil Nadu, Andhra Pradesh, and southern Karnataka, the company-maintained depots, as it was often difficult to bring stocks to these regions. Stocks were shipped directly from the plants in states like Madhya Pradesh and Uttar Pradesh. In March 2000, Nirma opted for in-house packaging and printing by obtaining Kisan Factories at Moriya, near Ahmedabad, in a further cost-cutting exercise. Nirma hoped that this would increase the packaging's quality.

1.5 Be Proactive in your approach as it is beneficial for the business

Karsanbhai Patel was the only person who started this business and starting selling Nirma. He was educated and had a government career, but he was never afraid of selling door-to-door detergent. He was diligent in doing something and knew that the company was tiny and bootstrapping, so he had to consider everything and anything about his business that could be fruitful. There is no such thing as a small or large undertaking. And if you are the CEO, you should embrace the obligations that are valuable to the company without guilt.

1.6 Provide Customers with 'Value for Money'

Customers noticed the advantages of purchasing Nirma, and it became an immediate success. They considered the standard to be at par with the giant Surf brand, but to take advantage of the same perks, they just had to pay one-third of the amount. Customers would only appreciate the product if you show them the advantages and give them decent value for their money.

1.7 Define Your Segment

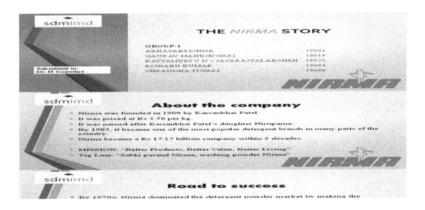

Karsanbhai Patel identified the target segment for his detergent almost as soon as he found the magical formula. He realized that a luxury brand sold in tier 1 cities was the alternative Surf brand, so he concentrated on marketing his brand in tier 2-3 cities. He priced his detergent low and made it a mass brand to get more consumer traction. People from the lower middle class and middle class quickly adopted the product, and it quickly rose in popularity. Where most firms adopted the conventional top-down strategy, i.e., spreading from metro towns to rural cities, Nirma did the reverse and changed the whole game. It is really important to evaluate the competitors for every company and define the most lucrative segment.

1.8 Focus on Building a Brand

It was failing to find vendors outside the city in the early 80s, although the commodity was approved on a small scale in Ahmedabad. Since clients were unaware of its presence, retailers were wary of keeping the detergent in their stores. It resulted in overdue payments, return on inventory, and large business losses. Karsanbhai Patel came up with a good publicity approach to handle the situation and launched a TV advertisement campaign. The popular "Washing powder Nirma, detergent tikiya Nirma" jingle became an anthem for the company and customers began to equate Nirma as a strong brand. The demand for Nirma soon peaked, and with his products, Patel flooded the retail stores. A good brand decreases a buyer's potential risk and increases the company's bargaining power.

1.9 Astutely Manage the Brand Wars

Nirma also had innovative marketing campaigns. Nirma successfully spread the name to other product segments in the mid-nineties, such as premium detergents (Nirma Mega Detergent Cake and Washing Powder), premium toilet soaps, and (Nirma Sandal, Nima Premium, Nirma Lime Fresh). In both the economy and luxury markets, it maintained its initial pricing and marketing plans. In 2000, with Nirma Beauty Shampoo, Nirma Shikakai, and Toothpaste, the firm entered the hair care market. Soaps, unlike detergents, were a private-care commodity. Many consumers had strong emotional attachments with their soap products. Furthermore, HLL segmented the market by price, fragrance appeal, and brand personality. So, against Lifebuoy, Nirma put Nirma Wash, Nirma Beauty Soap against Lux, Nima Rose against

Breeze7, and Nima Lime against Jai Lime. Explaining how Nirma hoped to win this match, playing by the rules of HLL, Hiren said"Worldwide, there are only four or five channels that account for most of the soaps sold: floral, fashion, fitness, freshness." With the relevant scents, Nirma manufactured high-fatty-matter soaps and priced them much lower than other brands. As a result, the 'sub-premium' section was born. The game of controlling the geographical variety of market desires was also perfected by Nirma. The North, for instance, favored pink soaps, and green ones were favored by the South. In the South, sandal soaps were more common. Initially, the company's promotional budget, relative to other FMCG firms, was very poor. In contrast to the usual 6-10 percent, Nirma spent just 1.25-2 percent of its sales on ads. The firm used starlets such as Sangeeta Bijlani, Sonali Bendre, and Riya Sen, who were comparatively unknown at the time, to endorse soaps. The promotional messages were both transparent and centered on the product's benefits. Nirma still chose to first put the item on the shelf, get reviews, and then create a lasting ad campaign. Nirma used its tried-and-true tool, price, to introduce toilet soaps and detergents in the premium market. In these divisions, the company intended to rely on quantities as well. However, the margins granted to retailers had shifted. Unlike economic goods, where the cost advantages were passed on to customers, this advantage was passed on to retailers by Nirma. It provided them with massive profit margins. For instance, it offered 52 percent for Nirma premium soap and an incredible margin of 140 percent for Nirma shampoo. In the luxury segment of the soap industry, observers were pessimistic about Nirma's chances of success.

Unlike detergents, the demand for soaps and shampoos was incredibly fragmented. There were only 15-20 brands, and it was hard to get a considerable market share for any soap. This market was also less price sensitive. So, it was hard for any enterprise to support itself on price alone. Analysts thought that shifting the brand value of Nirma would take years. According to a survey conducted by Nirma's marketing agency, Samsika Marketing Consultancy, Nirma was viewed as a low-cost brand. Many people were almost afraid to say they used it. Nirma published corporate advertisements worth Rs 10 bn in India in the late nineties to shed this image. Analysts claim that the fast-growing shampoo market is a safer investment than luxury soaps. Just 30% of the population in India used shampoo, with more than 70% of this group living in urban areas. However, according to some researchers, while the rural market's presumed potential was very high, it was difficult to convince rural folk to use shampoos in actual practice. A further concern faced by Nirma was that of insufficient facilities. While it had a good presence in the smaller towns and villages, it lacked the requisite network for urban centers to penetrate. As a result, Nirma's foray into high-end soaps and shampoos proved to be a flop.

1.10 Diversify the Portfolio

For low-income groups, Nirma began with a low-cost detergent, but later introduced products for higher-income groups, such as Nirma Sandal soap, Nirma Beauty soap, etc.

Not just that, but in 2003, Karsanbhai Patel formed Nirma University to diversify the company's brand portfolio. The brand is currently exploring its options in the cement industry to grow its market. Diversifying the portfolio decreases the company's potential risk of loss while still allowing it to serve a broader variety of consumers.

1.11 Conclusion

While Nirma was best known as a manufacturer of goods for the low-cost economy, it was popular in the middle and upmarket segments. Yet rivalry was also growing at the same time. Although HLL continued to be a major threat, offensive initiatives were also introduced by P&G and Henkel SPIC. In the detergent and washing powder market, participants from the unorganized field were also introduced to the rivalry. Patel was confident of tackling the rivalry, though. "He added, "We keep the price line and the happy customer returns to us normally. Based on its growth strategy, the company has risen in demand and volume in the last three decades: "A buyer is not looking for one-time frills or feel-good variables. The landlord, on the other hand, is searching for a long-term solution to his or her issues." Karsanbhai Patel, who began with a vision of making his daughter famous through his brand and ended up being one of the greatest entrepreneurs of all time, exemplifies the relevance of this quotation. He began with an aim of creating his daughter famous through his brand and ended up becoming one of the greatest entrepreneurs of all time. His name not only gained tremendous respect but also became a trendsetter for many new firms. The brand has taught young entrepreneurs many useful lessons and has proven to be a valuable resource for the region. Karsanbhai Patel has shown that no goal is too lofty if you have the ambition and zeal to achieve it.

1.12 What Karsanbhai Patel and Nirma detergent did for the Indian Economy

Nirma's meteoric growth in prominence culminated in the introduction of a new economic market for detergent powder. It was of good quality and was inexpensive. Plus, contrary to the others, the fact that it was manufactured without phosphates made it the most environmentally-friendly detergent. In comparison, a labor-consuming process was the process of producing the detergent. And thus, Nirma went on to hire more than 14,000 workers and became the country's leading employer.

1.13 Karsanbhai Patel's ventures other than the Nirma detergent

Karsanbhai wanted to grow his FMCG business after Nirma dominated the detergent industry. Nirma launched its line of toilet soaps, beauty soaps, and even shampoos in the premium market. While the latter venture failed, one of their products, edible salt Shudh, is still available and doing well. Overall, Nirma has a 20 percent market share in soap cakes and a 35 percent market share in detergents. That isn't it, however. In 1995, Karsanbhai Patel founded the Nirma Institute of Technology in Ahmedabad. Later, it became one of Gujarat's most prestigious engineering schools. After that, the whole structure was merged under the Nirma University of Science and Technology, which is supervised by the Nirma Education and Research Foundation, and in 2003, the entire structure was unified under the Nirma University of Science and Technology. This is overseen by the Nirma Education and Research Foundation. Since 2004, Karsanbhai's CSR initiative,

Nirmalabs education, has aimed to train and incubate entrepreneurs. Karsanbhai Patel has now turned over the reins of his profitable company to his two sons. Pratibha Patil, the then-President of India, bestowed the Padma Shri on him in 2010. Nirma is now the world's biggest manufacturer of soda ash, and the company has been privately owned since 2012. Karsanbhai Patel invested his huge fortune on a six-seat chopper in 2013, which cost Rs 40 crore. After Gautam Adani (Adani Group) and Pankaj Patel (Zydus Group), he became the third Ahmedabad-based industrialist to purchase a helicopter. Nirma, on the other hand, is still one of India's most popular detergents. And the jingles will live on forever.

CHAPTER 2: Start a Profitable Soap Making Business

As a soap manufacturer, you'll create your recipes for soaps and probably other personal cleaning and beauty products. Ecommerce, farmers markets, arts events, wholesale positioning in spas and boutiques, and even door-to-door sales are all options for selling the goods. You'll test several solutions and see if you can find a steady stream of clients. Learn how to launch a soap-making company of your own.

Steps for starting a soap making business

You've uncovered the ideal market opportunity and are now prepared to take the next step. There's more to launching a company than simply filing papers with the government. We've put together a list of steps to help you get started with your soap-making business. These measures will ensure that the new company is well-planned, legally compliant, and properly registered.

Plan your business

As an entrepreneur, you must have a well-thought-out strategy. It will assist you in figuring out the additional data of your organization and uncovering any unknowns. Given below are some key points to consider:

What are the startup and recurring costs?

Who is the targeted audience?

What is the maximum price you will charge from the customers?

What would you name your company?

What are the costs involved in opening a soap-making business?

You've got a good start if you have a kitchen or workspace as well as a few simple kitchen utensils. Making soap isn't an expensive business to undertake, but you would need to invest in some basic equipment. Ingredients cost at least $200. Lye and fats or oils are used to make soap. That's a good start, but it'll be your special formula that sets you apart. For superior feel, fragrance, and lather, you can use coconut oil, olive oil, almond oil, and several fragrance oils, extracts, and natural additives. To keep materials costs down and simplify production, you could start with only one or two simple recipes. Equipment for producing soap will cost around $300. Your equipment specifications will be determined by the type of soap-making you do. Hot process, cold process, rebatching, and melt and pour are the four basic forms of processing, and each needs different equipment. But, regardless of the route you take, you'll almost definitely need soap molds, packing, and shipping items. You can get your basic ingredients, additives, equipment, and supplies from several online retailers. Marketing software will cost up to $750. A professional-looking website with enticing product images is key to the company's growth. Since your online consumers can't touch or smell your goods, they must be able to judge the good quality of what they see. That means recruiting a graphic designer and web developer to help you make the best out of your logo and online presence is a smart investment. To express your love and dedication to product quality, your visual imagery will be carried through in your labeling and branding. Skilled services will cost up to $200. Is it legal in your state and society for you to run this sort of business from home? Before you put up your shingle, meet with a lawyer for a quick consultation. The Handcrafted Soap & Cosmetics Guild charges a membership fee of $100 per year (HSCG). Small-batch soap makers will benefit from this organization's preparation, funding, and useful networking opportunities. Insurance for general liability and product liability would cost $265-$375 a year. This is also accessible via the HSCG.

What are the ongoing expenses for a soap-making business?

The consumable commodity materials you'll need for ongoing development would be your greatest ongoing expense. Your increasing variable expenses would be more than offset by a rise in revenue if you've priced your offering correctly.

Who is the target market?

While women make up the majority of the demand for homemade soaps, some firms have had success selling male-oriented soap scents. You may approach consumers who admire your product's consistency and luxury, or those who only purchase organic or vegan goods. Customers will note the difference in quality among your soaps and those sold on the shelves of a traditional supermarket.

How does a soap-making business make money?

In the majority of the cases, all of your revenue shall be derived from the products you make or sell.

How much can you charge customers?

Your goods could be sold for $5 or $6 a bar. This is more than your consumers are likely to spend for mass-produced retail soaps, but your product has a high perceived value. Other price points can be met by providing discounts on multiple orders, marketing multi-bar bundles, and extending the product range. Look at local rivals' websites to see what they're costing and how that would impact the pricing. Will you charge more to suggest a higher-end product range, or will you charge less to compensate for the lower per-unit sales margin with higher volume?

How much profit can a soap-making business make?

There are a few well-known soap makers who began their careers in the same way you did. Take, for example, Burt's Bees. Others in your business run it as a side venture, something between a crafts hobby and a modestly profitable business. You will go as far as your dedication, imagination, promotional skills, and hard work can take you, as with many home-based companies.

How can you make your business more profitable?

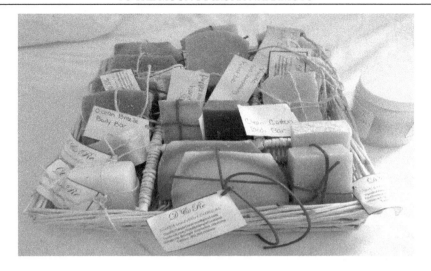

Many soap makers diversify their product range to include more exotic soaps (goat's milk soap is one example) or complementary goods. Making candles is a natural progression for soap makers who still use a hot process. Others are involved in home fragrances, lip balms, hair care, and even pet products. Focus on what else will cater to the consumer base when speaking about expanding your product mix. Many companies aim to maximize their net income by lowering the cost of goods produced. Growing the earnings by issuing bigger batches at a time is a cost-effective technique.

2.1 What will you name your business?

Choosing the correct name is vital and daunting. If you own a sole proprietorship, you should start using a separate company name from your own. We suggest reviewing the following references before filing a company name:

The state's business records

Federal and state trademark records

Social media sites

Web domain availability

It's important to have your domain name registered before anyone else does.

2.2 Form a legal entity

The sole proprietorship, partnership, limited liability company (LLC), and corporation are the most traditional corporate structures. If your soap manufacturing company is used, creating a legitimate business entity such as an LLC or corporation prevents you from being found legally accountable.

Register for taxes

Before you can start doing business, you'll need to apply for several state and federal taxes. You would need to apply for an EIN to pay for taxation. It's very basic and free.

2.3 Small Business Taxes

Depending on which business arrangement you select, you can have various taxation choices for your corporation. There could be state-specific taxes that apply to your business. In the state sales tax guides, you can read more about state sales taxes and franchise taxes.

2.4 Open a business bank account & credit card

Personal wealth security necessitates the use of dedicated company banking and credit accounts. If your personal and corporate accounts are combined, your personal properties (such as your house, vehicle, and other valuables) are put at risk if your company-issued. This is referred to as piercing the corporate veil in business law. Furthermore, learning how to create company credit will help you receive credit cards and other borrowings under your business's name (rather than your own), lower interest rates, and more credit lines, among other advantages.

2.5 Open a business bank account

This protects your assets from those of your business, which is essential for personal wealth security, as well as making accounting and tax reporting simpler.

2.6 Get a business credit card

It will help you achieve the following benefits:

It builds the company's credit background and will be beneficial for raising capital and profit later on.

It lets you differentiate personal and business expenditures by placing all of your business's costs under one account.

Set up business accounting

Understanding your business's financial results includes keeping track of your different costs and sources of revenue. Maintaining correct and comprehensive reports also makes annual tax filing even simpler.

2.7 Obtain necessary permits and licenses

Failure to obtain required permits and licenses will result in hefty fines or even the closure of your company. If you intend to market homemade soaps, you must first acquire a business license.

2.8 State & Local Business Licensing Requirements

Operating a handmade soap company can necessitate the procurement of some state permits and licenses. Furthermore, several states have varying laws governing the manufacturing of cosmetics and other body care goods. Visit the SBA's guide to state licenses and permits to read more about your state's licensing criteria.

2.9 Labor safety requirements

It is essential to comply with all Occupational Safety and Health Administration protocols. Pertinent requirements include:

Employee injury report

Safety signage

2.10 Certificate of Occupancy

A Certificate of Occupancy is normally required for businesses that operate out of a specific location (CO). All requirements concerning building codes, zoning rules, and local requirements have been followed, according to a CO. If you're thinking about renting a space, keep the following in mind:

Securing a CO is normally the landlord's duty.

Before signing a contract, make sure your landlord has or can get a legitimate CO for a soap-making operation.

A new CO is often needed after a significant renovation. If your company will be renovated before opening, add wording in your lease agreement that specifies that lease payments will not begin before a valid CO is issued.

If you intend to buy or build a place:

You would be responsible for securing a legal CO from a local government body.

Review all building codes and zoning standards for your soap-making business's place to ensure that you'll comply and eligible to get a CO.

2.11 Trademark & Copyright Protection

It is wise to protect your interests by applying for the required trademarks and copyrights if you are creating a new product, idea, brand, or design. The essence of legal standards in distance education is continually evolving, especially when it comes to copyright laws. This is a regularly revised database that can assist you with keeping on top of legal specifications.

2.12 Get business insurance

Insurance, including licenses and permits, are necessary for your company to run safely and legally. In the case of a covered loss, corporate insurance covers your company's financial well-being. There are several insurance schemes tailored for diverse types of companies with various risks. If you're not sure what kinds of risks your company might face, start with General Liability Insurance. This is the most popular form of coverage required by small companies, so it's a good place to start.

2.13 Learn more about General Liability Insurance

Workers' Compensation Insurance is another essential insurance scheme that many companies need. When your company hires staff, your state may mandate you to carry the Workers' Benefits Package.

2.14 Define your brand

Your company's brand is what it stands for, as well as how the general public perceives it. A good name would set the company apart from the market.

How to promote & market a soap making business

Look for areas where you can stand out. Try having a larger-than-usual bar of soap or one that is formulated to last longer. Perhaps you should market a six-pack of sampler soaps in smaller sizes so that your customers can check out your whole product range and pick their preferences. Consider an uncommon fragrance or texture additive for applying to your soaps to make them stand out. When you've found a winning design, publicize it on your website and social media. Also, if you're showing your soaps at an exhibition, bring some unwrapped samples of your entire product line so consumers can touch them, see what they're made of, feel their textures, and experience the various scents.

How to keep customers coming back

bear in mind that you're offering an aesthetic experience. Make sure your logo, labels and packages, and the name of your product line all cater to consumers looking for a low-cost luxury experience. One benefit is that the more your consumers like your stuff, the faster they can consume it and require more. Ensure that you retain contact with your clients and that they are aware of how to contact you. Request email addresses from all of your clients to obtain their approval to send out a monthly e-newsletter or catalog. It's important not to bother someone with so many promotional newsletters, but a monthly newsletter will keep consumers updated on all of the new items you have to sell. You might want to add a toll-free phone number for orders as your company expands.

Establish your web presence

Customers can learn more about your business and the goods or services you deliver by visiting your website. One of the most successful ways to build your web presence is through press releases and social media.

2.15 Soap Making Plan

If you live in the jungle and love your body odor, you would not need soap. It is a regular need and one of the common goods. As a result, soap has a huge demand. There are various varieties of soaps available due to the wide range of skin types. Soaps are manufactured in a multitude of ways to suit the needs of all. One of the most promising FMCGs is soap production. Perhaps this is why so many people are drawn to this sector year after year. Every day, in a country like India, there is a massive demand for soap. However, there are only a few competitors in the business. We have a few ideas for you if you want to launch your own soap company. Let's get this started.

Tips for soap making using the cold process method

Soap making is easy at the most fundamental level. The cold process approach is the most common way to produce soap. It's "cold" because the ingredients aren't heated before being combined. Using the "hot process" technique, you can make soap with heat. We will use the cold process. Soap is made by mixing fats and oils with a lye and water solution in the most basic form. Soap is made from a combination of water, lye, fats, and oils. The fun starts as you change the components and quantities of the various materials. But, to keep things simple, note that soap is essentially a solution of fats and oils, lye, and water. It's as plain as that.

Is making soap without lye possible?

Is it possible to produce soap without lye? Not at all. Soap bases that can be heated and poured into molds can be purchased. You didn't have to use lye to make the base as everyone else did. However, you have no idea what's in those bases. Sodium hydroxide is the lye used to produce bar soap. Soft soaps are made of potassium hydroxide. Leaching lye from wood ashes is an easy way to create it. This form of lye results in a smoother soap. Unless you have access to a chemical supply house, lye is typically difficult to come by locally. It is, however, simple to put an order. Lye is highly caustic, and it can sear the skin and strip color from whatever surface it comes into contact with. If it gets into your eyes, it will blind you. This is a toxic drug and can never be used in a place where children may reach it. Adults, on the other hand, would have no trouble with the lye if they take simple precautions. When dealing with lye, please wear safety goggles. Long sleeves and protective gloves are also recommended. Leave lye or lye mixtures unattended at all times. Uncured soap should be used similarly to lye.

Fats and oils required for making the cold process soap

Another fundamental to producing soap can be found here. To turn oils and fats into soap, different quantities of lye are needed. Every fat that is likely to be used in soap making has a known amount of time it takes to turn oil or fat into soap. Simply look up the amount of lye needed to produce soap from a certain oil in a table. The volume of lye used in each recipe is then determined based on the oils used. Using a little less lye than is needed to transform all of the oils into soap. This is achieved as a precautionary step to ensure that all of the lye is absorbed during the process. The lye discount is the volume of lye used that is reduced. It's normal to use around 5% less lye than is needed to completely transform the oils into soap. Coconut, palm, and olive oils are the most common oils used in soap making. If you just use those three oils to make soap, you will make amazing results. Each of these oils has its collection of characteristics that make it useful as a soaping oil. You can produce a soap with only one of the oils, but the results won't be as strong as if you used all three. This is why. If you want a lot of bubbles in your soap, coconut oil is the way to go. It's the root of a slew of big, light bubbles. However, soap made entirely of coconut oil cleans so well that it extracts much of the oil from the skin, leaving it dry. This is why it can only account for about 30% of the soap oils. Palm oil is important for hard, long-lasting bars, but it isn't as clean or bubbly as coconut oil.

This fat is often referred to as "vegetable tallow," but it is similar to beef tallow in any way. If you don't want to eat meat fats, use them instead of beef fat. Then you should ask about olive oil. Just olive oil is used to produce castile soap conventionally. If you've ever used this form of soap, you know how good it is as a skin conditioner. It's amazing. However, if olive oil is the only oil used in the soap, the effect is tiny little bubbles and bars that fade away quicker than you'd like. As a result, this type of oil is only used to make up about 40% of the oils in a recipe. Granted, soap can be made from almost any form of fat or oil, and there are several alternatives.

Adding ingredients for premium luxury results

If you choose to use other oils, just apply a small amount during the final stages of the soap-making process. you'll find that you can use almond oil in your example recipe. Simply raise the amount of olive oil in the formula and leave out the almond oil. It was chosen because it brings a little more to the bar's feel and quality. Soap can be used for a lot more than just producing pure soap. All of the additives are what make soap production so exciting. Clays, natural oils, medicinal products, colors, patterns, and a slew of other alternatives are available as additives. The first step to perfect soap is to get the fundamentals correctly, which can be achieved fast and effectively. After learning the fundamentals of soap manufacturing, the soap manufacturer progresses to using a range of exotic ingredients.

How to make soap?

We'll go into the fundamentals of how the soap is made. Bear in mind that this is just the first step. Following that, you may need additional materials and a special recipe to distinguish the product from competitors.

Ingredients

Given below are the following ingredients that would be required for preparing soap:

Take 2/3 cup of coconut oil (that will create lather) and the same amount of olive oil. Moreover, 2/3 cup almond, safflower oil, or grape seed will also be needed.

Then you'll need a quarter cup of lye, which is sodium hydroxide in its purest form. Finally, you'll require 3/4 cup of cool water that is distilled or pure.

You'll also need oatmeal, aloe vera gel, cornmeal, clay, salt, and any other items you choose to use.

Instructions

Listed below are the step-by-step directions that you must follow in the preparation of soap:

Put on your gloves and pour lye and water into a canning jar. Allow them to sit for a few minutes after they've been stirred gently and the water has begun to clear.

Now pour in the oil from the pint jar. Then Stir well, then put the jar in a warm pan of the water that is bubbling (and/or you may microwave it, when you do, place temperature to one hundred and twenty degrees F).

Remove the lye after that is finished. Allow the lye to cool. Remove pint jar & allow your oil to cool as well. Both can achieve a temperature of 95 to 105 degrees Fahrenheit. If the temperature drops below 95 degrees F, the soap will begin to crumble.

Pour them into a mixing bowl until they've hit the ideal temperature and whisk until fully combined. After stirring for five minutes, mix it with an immersion blender.

Then, to make the soap special, apply herbs, essential oils, & any other things that go with it. They can be thoroughly combined so they appear coarse. Place them in molds & cover with a towel.

After a day check the soap and let it stay for an additional 12 to 24 hours if it's either warm or soft.

When the soaps are fully cured, wrap them in the paper wax & lock them in an airtight jar for a week. Since this soap contains oil on its own, we'll need an airtight jar. As a consequence, interaction with air will cause it to pick up debris and dust.

Soap making machine and price

fiber covered mixing machine will cost you at least about US$ 1000. This price includes a fiber-covered mixing machine capable of producing 200 kilograms of detergent powder.

Where to get soap making machine?

Online, you can buy a soap-manufacturing machine. Soap manufacturing machines are available from several online retailers. These websites sell the requisite appliances, including the microwave, blender, wrapper, mold, and labeler, also the main device. A soap-making unit, for example, can be bought for the US

$ 5000. This item can be used to produce toilet soaps and detergent cakes. If you're searching for something less costly, say under the US $ 1500 apiece, you can easily find it on the market. It can be used to produce soap for bathing purposes. There are also other products of varying price points. However, the budget may start at one dollar an item. You'll get a good detergent maker for this amount.

Soap making raw material and price

The Soap-making ingredients may be bought for a very cheap price. It is much less costly if you buy them in bulk. If you may get the price correct upfront, the rest of the company will be a breeze later on. As a consequence, we prefer bulk raw materials. Alkali and fat are the two main raw materials used to produce soap. the raw material which is most commonly used in soap manufacture is sodium hydroxide. Potassium hydroxide, on the other hand, maybe used. The latter makes a soap that is more soluble in water. As a result, potassium hydroxide creates "warm soap." Locally, raw products are available at a reduced quality. You can discover raw materials for manufacturing soaps online or in your neighborhood with a fast Google search. People typically buy this locally so it cuts the price even further. Rest assured that rates can differ depending on your needs. It depends solely on how much you're making & how much of the raw material you'll need. Caustic soda costs about US $ 150-250 per metric ton on the market. The price of 1000 grams of laundry soap ranges between US$1 and $1.25.

Soap making formulae

legitimate chemical formulae for the soap's $C_{17}H_{35}COONa$. Its chemical name is thus sodium stearate. However, it is important to note that it's for the common soap that is used for personal purposes only. For the detergents, there are normally long chains of carboxylic acid as well as sulfonate salts or ammonium salt.

2.16 Soap selling process

Let us now go through the packaging, distribution, marketing, and promotion processes.

Colorful wrappings

Choose a bright & eye-catching label that will guarantee that the product is noticed. To set it apart from the competition, style it & use the proper design.

Branding

Make the most of this opportunity to build your brand through packaging. Choose a design that you think best reflects your business.

Go simple

Today's entrepreneurs aim for simplicity. Examine the performance of POP displays as well. If they don't live up to your standards, it's time to make a change.

Soap marketing strategy

You can use the following strategies for marketing soap:

Email marketing

And the ones who also sign up for your offer are truly interested in the soaps, email marketing is the perfect way to market. It's also becoming highly customizable and cost-efficient these days.

Blogging

The next logical move is to start blogging. You'll need to hunt down some prominent bloggers who may help you spread the word about the business. You may even invite them to write a review on their blog about a sample of the product.

Social media

Due to availability of the social media, it is now easier to create a brand. Furthermore, guess what? It's the shortest and least expensive alternative. The secret is to make something go viral. this could be the merchandise, online presence, or your ads.

2.17 Soap making supplies

To make it function properly, you'll need some modernized tools equipment, as well as a lot of the space. You will need to find rental space to make the soap. Some of the typical things you'll need to get started include cyclone, mixing vessels, perfumers, blowers, reactors, furnaces, weighing scales, and blenders.

2.18 Marketing area for soap

The marketing region you select will be decided by the audience you're targeting. You would be able to segment your customers depending on age and demographic in social media marketing. Your marketing field can be decided by the type of soap you sell. If you're selling detergent cakes, for example, they're mainly aimed at homemakers of different ages. As a consequence, you will show the commercial depending on age & gender. Marketing is successful on a variety of measures. It simply depends upon whether you've online or a physical company. In any case, it's better to entrust this to a practitioner.

2.19 Total investment

The Investment isn't based on raw materials. Just As mentioned above, different raw materials are used for personal and detergent soaps. Therefore investment will be different for each category.

You must take into consideration the size and place of the business for starting the business. So You need minimum money of US $ 20,000to purchase the machinery along with primary raw materials –if you decide to start with little.

Raw materials shall cost the US $ 2500 per month. Moreover, making unit rentals would charge not less than the US $ 1000 per month. In addition to the above-mentioned costs, the salary of the plant manager is expected to be around the US $ 500. Equipment shall cost around the US $ 10,000 or more.

In addition to the above prices, you need the US $ 500 for license & registration. Moreover, you will need another US $ 800 to cover the accidental coverage. the Marketing might cost you approximately US $ 500 per month.

2.20 Selling price

Supply, materials, brand, packaging, and other factors impact soap pricing. When you're only starting, keep the rates comparable to those of your rivals.

Prices are determined by several factors. A lower-cost soap is generally assumed to be of lower quality. As a result, we won't keep prices very low about market prices.

Additionally, too high prices could decrease overall demand. As a consequence, we will arrive at the golden middle & retain it just marginally, so at all, below current levels.

2.21 Profit margin

Measure profit margins through factoring in your annual manufacturing expenses. You must also remember manpower, raw materials, utilities, and maintenance costs.

This business has a high-profit margin, but it also has a lot of competition from well-known brands. As a result, profit margins would be dictated by the price of the goods.

Know more about your rivals' prices and, as a result, determine which would give the greatest return – find the "golden value point" for the sales.

2.22 Precaution

It is important to obtain insurance. it is why, in addition to other necessities, insurance must still be part of the investment.

Another crucial step's to understand the company's legal framework. Obtain both the "consent to establish" and "consent to operate."

2.23 Risk

In the soap industry, the risk is not creating a large enough brand to compete with the rivals. There are a lot of competitors in the business, so making a name for your company can be challenging.

Another danger is that the company will collapse due to a lack of consumer awareness. To run a good soap company, you must first select the right market.

2.24 Conclusion

Soap production, as satisfying as this is, necessitates thorough study and measured risk-taking. Seeking your niche and launching a company are just simple activities. However, careful preparation and intervention are necessary to make this a success. Make sure you don't undersell yourself & that you also stand out.

2.25 Advantage of starting a soap making business at home

Soap making requires little investment to start with

The supplies needed to make soap can be easily acquired

Equipment required can also be easily acquired

It is comparatively much easier to learn the making of soap

There is already good demand for handmade soap and people are willing to purchase handmade soap,

You can easily specialize in your particular field

It's rather easier to make soap that is both distinctive and different from the existing ones

You can create other products that can gel in with your existing products

You can generate handsome profits by selling soap

It is very easy to locate a market for the soaps

2.26 How Much Money Can You Make Making Soap?

That's a tough question to answer because so much depends on you. And, just to be clear, producing soap is not lucrative. Of course, the money is in the soap sales. To make money selling a product, much as with any other business endeavor takes a lot of time and commitment.

CHAPTER 3: Start a Profitable Candle Making Business

Candlemakers are extremely professional artisans who pay particular attention to the sensory aesthetics of their products and experienced business people who know how to entice consumers with innovative marketing tactics. Learn how to launch a candle-making company of your own.

3.1 Steps for starting a candle making business

You've uncovered the ideal market opportunity and are now prepared to take the next step. There's more to launching a company than simply filing papers with the government. We've put together a list of steps to help you get started with your candle-making business. These measures will ensure that the new company is well-planned, legally compliant, and properly registered.

Plan your business

As an entrepreneur, you must have a well-thought-out strategy. It will assist you in figuring out the additional data of your organization and uncovering any unknowns. Given below are some key points to consider:

What are the startup and recurring costs?

Who is the targeted audience?

What is the maximum price you will charge from the customers?

What would you name your company?

What are the costs involved in opening a candle-making business?

You will be able to start your business at home, based on local zoning rules, making use of your kitchen heat source as well as utensils. Many online retailers, including Candle Science and CandleChem, offer a starter kit of items. To start, your candle materials shouldn't cost more than a few hundred dollars. This includes:

Paraffin, gel, soy, beeswax, or other wax

Wicks

Jars, tins, or other containers (though bear in mind that if you're just selling pillar candles, you won't need containers)

Fragrance oils

Coloring agents

Packaging materials

Transportation costs of raw goods in and finished products out

Web growth, which can cost anywhere from nothing to a few hundred dollars based on the expertise in the industry and at least properly contributes to some other start-up costs. A booth will cost $100 per day if you intend to showcase your goods at different exhibits and festivals, plus you'll have to pay for fuel and other travel expenses. You can also contact an insurance provider first. Since there is a chance of a fire accident, you can ensure that your company is fire-proofed and that you have a fire extinguisher onboard. You can also have an initial consultation with a lawyer to decide what licenses or permits are required in your region.

What are the ongoing expenses for a candle-making business?

The majority of the business revolves around different varieties of wax, your containers, and paint and scent additives. You can purchase these goods in bulk at lower per-unit prices once you've established your business model is viable. Wax, for example, can be ordered in 25-pound sizes for as little as a dollar per pound. Wicks are sold in 100-foot spools. Bulk amounts of containers, such as glass pots, mason jars, and tins, are also available.

Who is the target market?

Anyone who needs candles is your end customer. Some may have specific concerns, such as lights in the case of a power outage, and others are searching for a more sensory experience. Churches that use candles to decorate prayer offerings or stores that wish to bring a dramatic effect to their showrooms are often fantastic consumers. You may also approach resellers that can order the goods in vast quantities. Shop owners from the neighborhood and beyond will be among them. Customers like these are usually seen at arts and crafts shows. Try renting stalls at arts and crafts shows, flea markets, festivals and fairs, and other similar venues if you love seeing your customers face to face in an atmosphere where they can truly appreciate the aesthetics of your goods.

How does a candle-making business make money?

Candlemakers market candles to customers directly or indirectly through resellers such as boutiques, gift stores, and other arts and crafts shopping outlets. Since candle making is such a wide field, differentiate yourself by the types of candles you sell (pillar, floating, votive, tea, etc.) or the quality of your offering. Experiment with scents, textures, and molds to come up with something unique that is worth premium pricing. Furthermore, for optimum profit margins on your sales, you can still be on the lookout for low-cost raw material suppliers. To widen your target audience, think of related products or candle styles.

3.2 How much can you charge customers?

Your goods could sell for as little as a few bucks or as much as $20 or more per unit. Pricing will be dictated by the nature and reach of your product line, as well as your target market, marketing plan, and competitiveness. If you want to be the lowest vendor, make sure you're buying your raw materials at a discount and that you're still aware of what your rivals are charging. To save the most cost per unit, you'll want to buy wax, wicks, coloring agents, scents, and other products in bulk. If your goal is to market a higher-end product line, price is less important as long as your goods are visually pleasing. If you find a retail reseller that can move a lot of your product, you might want to consider giving deep discounts on prices.

How much profit can a candle-making business make?

Profit margins of 50% or more are not out of the question. While the cost of materials is not especially high, make sure you have the resources to devote to making your company profitable.

How can you make your business more profitable?

Consider expanding the product offerings once you've perfected the principles of candle-making. For example, learning how to mold or carve candles into any shape will improve the cost and revenue potential. Alternatively, you might start selling fancy oil lamps made from liquid candles. Find scented soaps and incense as well as other sensory items. You might be able to learn how to make these additions to your expanding product line, or you might be able to figure out where to purchase them for resale. Consider offering candle-making lessons if you have the requisite space in your workshop. You might contact the local community center or community college in this effort and see if they'd be involved in adding your class to their program. Finally, is the company prosperous enough that you might consider franchising it? You have to give this important factor a thorough consideration if you want to enhance your profits.

What will you name your business?

Choosing the correct name is vital and daunting. If you own a sole proprietorship, you should start using a separate company name from your own. We suggest reviewing the following references before filing a company name:

The state's business records

Federal and state trademark records

Social media sites

Web domain availability

It's important to get your domain name registered before anyone else. After registering a domain name, you should consider setting up a professional email account (@yourcompany.com).

Form a legal entity

The sole proprietorship, partnership, limited liability company (LLC), and corporation are the most traditional corporate structures. If your candle manufacturing company is used, creating a legitimate business entity such as an LLC or corporation prevents you from being found legally accountable.

Register for taxes

Before you can start doing business, you'll need to apply for several state and federal taxes. You would need to apply for an EIN to pay for taxation. It's very basic and free.

Small Business Taxes

Depending on which business arrangement you select, you can have various taxation choices for your corporation. There could be state-specific taxes that apply to your business. In the state sales tax guides, you can read more about state sales taxes and franchise taxes.

Open a business bank account & credit card

Personal wealth security necessitates the use of dedicated company banking and credit accounts. If your personal and corporate accounts are combined, your personal properties (such as your house, vehicle, and other valuables) are put at risk if your company-issued. This is referred to as piercing the corporate veil in business law. Furthermore, learning how to create company credit will help you receive credit cards and another borrowing under your business's name (rather than your own), lower interest rates, and more credit lines, among other advantages.

Open a business bank account

This protects your assets from those of your business, which is essential for personal wealth security, as well as making accounting and tax reporting simpler.

Get a business credit card

It will help you achieve the following benefits:

It builds the company's credit background and will be beneficial for raising capital and profit later on.

It lets you differentiate personal and business expenditures by placing all of your business's costs under one account.

Set up business accounting

Understanding your business's financial results includes keeping track of your different costs and sources of revenue. Maintaining correct and comprehensive reports also makes annual tax filing even simpler.

Labor safety requirements

It is essential to comply with all Occupational Safety and Health Administration protocols. Pertinent requirements include:

Employee injury report

Safety signage

Certificate of Occupancy

A Certificate of Occupancy is normally required for businesses that operate out of a specific location (CO). All requirements concerning building codes, zoning rules, and local requirements have been followed, according to a CO. If you're thinking about renting a space, keep the following in mind:

Securing a CO is normally the landlord's duty.

Before signing a contract, make sure your landlord has or can get a legitimate CO for a soap-making operation.

A new CO is often needed after a significant renovation. If your company will be renovated before opening, add wording in your lease agreement that specifies that lease payments will not begin before a valid CO is issued.

If you intend to buy or build a place:

You would be responsible for securing a legal CO from a local government body.

Review all building codes and zoning standards for your candle-making business's place to ensure that you'll comply and eligible to get a CO.

Trademark & Copyright Protection

It is wise to protect your interests by applying for the required trademarks and copyrights if you are creating a new product, idea, brand, or design. The essence of legal standards in distance education is continually evolving, especially when it comes to copyright laws. This is a regularly revised database that can assist you with keeping on top of legal specifications.

Get business insurance

Insurance, including licenses and permits, are necessary for your company to run safely and legally. In the case of a covered loss, corporate insurance covers your company's financial well-being. There are several insurance schemes tailored for diverse types of companies with various risks. If you're not sure what kinds of risks your company might face, start with General Liability Insurance.

This is the most popular form of coverage required by small companies, so it's a good place to start.

Define your brand

Your company's brand is what it stands for, as well as how the general public perceives it. A good name would set the company apart from the market.

How to promote & market a candle making business

The first and most crucial step is to decide who you intend to reach. Is your average customer a cost-conscious shopper, or is she more concerned with the sensory experience? If your target market is the former, you should be able to deliver fair prices. If it's the latter, make sure your product range is well-presented and that your color and scent options are pleasing. Try building an online presence on sites including eBay, Amazon, and Etsy. Since these platforms have a lot of competition, keep the costs as low as possible. There is a slew of other arts and crafts marketplaces, but they aren't as well-known as Etsy (and therefore potentially less populated with competitors). Among them are ArtFire, Big Cartel, and Craft Is Art, to name a few.

How to keep customers coming back

You aim to not only retain buyers but to keep them coming back. Since candles are consumable goods that must be replaced daily, the current consumer partnerships may become profitable over time. As a result, make sure you fulfill their needs so that they appreciate the quality of your goods and know-how to reach you if stocks run out. As a consequence, any order must provide easy-to-find contact information, such as your website, email address, or phone number (or all three). As part of the packaging, you could add a business card or sticker with this detail. Make sure shoppers and passers-by alike get your business card when approaching clients in people, such as at art shows or flea markets. Often, get their names and permission to connect them to an email list you give out, maybe before peak candle-buying seasons like the holidays or Mother's Day.

Establish your web presence

Customers can learn more about your business and the goods or services you deliver by visiting your website. One of the most successful ways to build your online presence is through press releases and social media.

Top of Form

Bottom of Form

Is this Business Right For You?

The perfect candle maker is passionate about the craft and has experience in sales and promotion. Candlemakers may start small, with a minimal budget and inventory, in the kitchen and storage room of their home or apartment. Since candles are always thought of as commodity products, you must continually search for ways to brand your line to set yourself apart from the competition. Excellent image photography, a solid web presence, and savvy sales expertise can help you highlight your product line attractively.

What are some skills and experiences that will help you build a successful candle-making business?

The bulk of people get into this business as hobby candle builders. You should appreciate the aesthetics of making candles and related products and have a clear understanding of how to mark your business. You should be familiar with the principles of eCommerce and how to build an online presence. If you sell from a booth at a fair, your display presentation skills are relevant both online (in the quality of your images and written product descriptions) and in physical displays. If you plan to market your product line in person, either to consumers personally or to resellers, personal sales skill is important. You must trust in the goods and be able to convince people to do so as well.

What is the growth potential for a candle-making business?

A good full-time candle maker could earn between $25,000 and $50,000 per year. However, if you sell to a big reseller, you might make more money. Consider franchising your organization once it has become popular enough for others to choose to follow in your footsteps. Candle making is an easy business to launch on your own. However, your ambition likely is to become so well-known that you'll need assistance with crafting, selling, and/or shipping your merchandise. Begin by enlisting the support of friends or family members if required, such as to match seasonal revenue spikes. Don't recruit permanent full-time support once you've been through ample revenue periods to realize that you'll be able to easily reach payroll over the year. Also, contact the accountant to hear about all the hidden expenses.

Candles Pricing

From a business standpoint, you'll need to find out how much you need/want to receive every hour and how many candles you can make in that time. Divide the hourly wage by the number of units (candles) generated to get a figure to add to the basic cost of the supplies used to manufacture each candle until you have these two numbers. Consider the following scenario: You pay $50 on ingredients (not equipment) and can make 20 candles from them. For the supplies, you paid $2.50 per candle. Making candles is a way for you to earn $20 per hour. Since the 20 candles you made took two hours to make, the overall cost is two times $20, or $40. Then you divide $40 by 20 to get a $2 per candle labor rate. When you apply the $2 labor cost to the $2.50 content cost, you get $4.50 per candle. This isn't a great example because you'll need to pay for other expenses like the additional utilities needed to produce the candles and the expense of importing supplies like boilers, pots, and jugs.

How much should you charge for candles?

This is based on the sort of brand you choose to be affiliated with. If you intend to sell bulk candles at a low price, you should expect your company to turn out a huge amount of low-cost candles with a slight but steady profit per candle. Votive candles are cheap and can be ordered for as little as $0.50 each. This approach can be very successful, particularly when several cheap candles are purchased in bulk, resulting in several sales for each customer. The drawback is that you would have to bring in a lot of money to make a big profit. You'll almost definitely need to expand, recruiting someone to help you achieve your broad production goals. Another choice is to create your brand. This means catering to a more discerning public able to pay a premium price for a candle. Some high-end artisanal candles will cost upwards of $200 each. For a brand, you'd have to worry about the packaging theme and what you're encouraging your clients to do with their candles.

3.3 Benefits of candle making business

If you've ever visited a big shopping center, you've probably seen a variety of candle shops. There are whole areas devoted to candles in several major department stores. To give you an example of how strong the candle business is, over 1 million pounds of wax are used to produce candles for the US market alone every year. The candle industry is worth around $2.3 billion a year without additional products such as candlesticks, ceramic pots, and so on. Who makes the most candle purchases? Seasonal holidays account for just 35% of overall sales, making them an outstanding all-year-round investment. Outside of these days, candles are purchased for 65 percent of the year. The most popular motives for buying a candle as a present include a seasonal gift, a housewarming gift, a dinner party gift, a thank you gift, and adult birthday presents. People nowadays believe fragrance to be the most important consideration when buying a candle. Make sure the candles you're thinking of selling have high-quality scents since this can be the difference between success and failure in the candle industry.

Conclusion

In 1969, in a period when India's domestic detergent industry had very few competitors, predominantly multi-national firms, which targeted the affluent of India, Karsanbhai launched Nirma. The detergents were not affordable for most middle-class and poor citizens. Karsanbhai began producing detergent powder in the backyard of his home in Khokra, near Ahmedabad and selling it door to door for Rs 3 per kg, while other brands were charging Rs 13 per kg. Business Standard reported how Karsanbhai came up with a genius idea during the early 1980s, when the Nirma was still struggling with the sales, for drying out market of the goods collecting all the due credits. This was accompanied by a huge ad campaign featuring his daughter singing the iconic Nirma jingle in a white frock. Customers were flocking to markets, only to return empty-handed. Karsanbhai flooded the industry with his goods as the demand for Nirma peaked, leading to huge sales. Nirma's sales peaked that year, making it the most successful detergent, well outselling its closest competitor, Hindustan Unilever's Surf. As Karsanbhai purchased the cement firm LafargeHolcim for 1.4 billion dollars that year, he showed once again that the business appetite is away from over. Mint reported how the deal in Rajasthan and the surrounding area would help Nirma achieve a stronger grip. While a media-shy guy, Karsanbhai, an entrepreneur in the truest sense, has a sharp eye for nation-building. In 1995, he founded the Nirma Institute of Technology, which was followed by the Nirma University of Science and Technology, which was founded in 2003 and is supervised by the Nirma Education and Research Foundation. He initiated the education project Nirmalabs in 2004, aimed at educating and incubating entrepreneurs in India. Karsanbhai Patel received the Padma Shri award in 2010. Just like Nirma, you can also transform your soap and candle-making business into large corporate businesses with the help of your ingenious marketing and creative skills, dedication, perseverance, and unfearfulness of new and challenging situations.

Bookkeeping and QuickBooks Made Easy

A Comprehensive Guide of 87 Useful Tricks to Hack QuickBooks and Organize Bookkeeping as a Silicon Valley Company

By

Iruka Nakamoto

Table of Contents

Introduction 509

Chapter 1. Bookkeeping 515

1.1. What is Bookkeeping? 515

1.2. Who is A bookkeeper? 516

1.3. Importance of Bookkeeping 518

1.4. Type of Accounting Method 519

1.5. What do the bookkeepers do? 520

1.5.1. Record the Transactions Each Day 521

1.5.2. Sending Invoices to Clients 521

1.5.3. Keep Track of Payments 522

1.5.4. Being Responsible for the Payable Ledger 522

1.5.5. Responsible for Managing the Cash Flow 522

1.5.6. Compile All Accounts 523

1.6. How can a Bookkeeper be Beneficial for Business? 523

1.6.1. Let you Focus on Your Business Strategy 524

1.6.2. The Accounting Cost can be Saved. 524

1.6.3. Double Check Your Cashflow 525

1.6.4. Be Informed of Current Financial Situation: 525

1.6.5. The Financial Data is Organized 525

Chapter 2. QuickBooks Explained 527

1.7. 2.1. What is QuickBooks? 527

2.1.1. QuickBooks 528

2.1.2. The History of QuickBooks 529

1.8. 2.2. QuickBooks Features 529

2.2.1. user Friendly 530

2.2.2. Data Migration 530

2.2.3 Smooth Navigation 530

2.2.4. Smooth Transactions 531

2.2.5. Invoices 531

2.2.6. Calculate Tax...531

2.2.7. Projections 532

1.9. 2.3. Set-up QuickBooks 532

2.3.1. Start 533

2.3.2. setup 533

2.3.3. Vendor Setup 534

2.3.4. Setup Employee Accounts 534

2.3.5. Set Up Customer Account 535

2.3.6. Setup Report Generation 535

1.10. 2.4. Using QuickBooks 536

2.4.1. Chart of Accounts 536

2.4.2. Other Lists 537

2.4.3. The Reports 538

2.4.4. payroll 539

1.11. 2.5. QuickBooks Versions 539

Chapter 3. Choosing the Best Version of QuickBooks...................541

1.12. 3.1. QuickBooks for Self-Employed 545

3.1.1. QuickBooks Self Employed Package 546

3.1.2. QuickBooks for Self-Employed Tax Bundle 546

3.1.3. QuickBooks for Self-Employed Live Tax Bundle 547

3.1.4. Benefit 547

3.1.5. Drawback 547

1.13. 3.2. QuickBooks Online.......................................548

3.2.1. Common Features 549

3.2.2. QuickBooks Online Simple Start 550

3.2.3. QuickBooks Online Essentials 550

3.2.4. QuickBooks Online Plus 550

3.2.5. QuickBooks Online Advanced...............................551

3.2.6. Benefits...............................551

3.2.7. Drawbacks...............................551

1.14.   3.3. QuickBooks Desktop 552

3.3.1. QuickBooks Desktop Pro:...............................552

3.3.2. QuickBooks Desktop Premier:...............................553

3.3.3. QuickBooks Desktop Enterprise:...............................553

3.3.4. QuickBooks Desktop Plus and QuickBooks Desktop Pro 554

3.3.5. QuickBooks for Mac 554

1.15.   3.4. QuickBooks Apps 555

3.4.1. QuickBooks Payments...............................555

3.4.2. QuickBooks Point of Sale...............................555

3.4.3. QuickBooks Payroll 556

1.16.   3.5. Find the Best Version for You 556

3.5.1. Read Reviews..557

3.5.2. Take an Online Survey 557

3.5.3. Talk to an Expert. 557

Chapter 4. The Best Way to Make Money In 2021 558

1.17.   4.1. Salary of Part-Time QuickBooks Bookkeepers 559

1.18.   4.2. The Top 10 Highest Paying Cities for Bookkeepers in the USA..562

1.19.   4.3. Best Paying QuickBooks Bookkeeping Jobs in the USA 565

4.3.1. CPA Firm Bookkeeper................................566

4.3.2. QuickBooks Remote Bookkeeper 567

4.3.3. Telecommute Bookkeeper 567

4.3.4. At Home Bookkeeper 567

4.3.5. QuickBooks Consultant 568

Chapter 5. Becoming a QuickBooks Bookkeeper 568

1.20.   5.1. The Type of Investment Required for Certification...570

1.21.   5.2. The Different Courses Offered 571

1.22.   5.3. Information About QuickBooks Certification...........571

1.23. 5.4. Why Should You Invest 573

1.24. 5.5. The Certification Fee 574

1.25. 5.6. The Length of Courses 575

Chapter 6. Hacks and Tricks for QuickBooks 578

1.26. 6.1. Cash Receipts Should be Created...579

1.27. 6.2. Use Attachments 580

1.28. 6.3. Use Keyboard Shortcuts 582

1.29. 6.4. Automate the emails. 583

1.30. 6.5. Use the QuickBooks Online to Track Time 583

1.31. 6.6. Always use the Bank Rules 584

Chapter 7. QuickBooks Usage in Small Businesses 585

1.32. 7.1. Make and Track Invoices..586

1.33. 7.2. Monitor Expenses and Other Bills 586

1.34. 7.3. Generate Business Financial Statements 587

1.35. 7.4. Manage Payroll 587

1.36. 7.5. Do the Inventory. 588

1.37. 7.6. Simplify Taxes 588

1.38. 7.7. Online Payments...589

1.39. 7.8. Record Receipts..589

1.40. 7.9. Manage Mileage...589

Conclusion 590

Introduction

This book is your basic guide to bookkeeping and QuickBooks. If you are a bookkeeper and want to upgrade your skillset and learn more about the QuickBooks software, this book is just for you. You will find a comprehensive detail of all the considerations, the advantages, and the ways you can become a QuickBooks bookkeeper. If you are a beginner and managing finances interests you, you can equally benefit from this book.

In the following chapters, you will find a detailed explanation of bookkeeping and why proper bookkeeping is necessary to keep businesses afloat. With people starting their businesses by the minute, the need for accurate bookkeeping is ever in demand. Small business owners invest in good financial handling software and outsourcing their account management to bookkeepers as affording an accountant is sometimes not possible for a small business owner.

You might question that bookkeeping is not as lucrative but do not pay head to that. Yes, conventional bookkeeping is becoming outdated, but still, there is demand. Most small business owners in the US use the software QuickBooks for their financial recording. Though some business owners know how to use it and keep updated, most of them will require help with crunching numbers and outsource professional bookkeepers to do the job.

QuickBooks was launched in the year 2003 by the company Intuit. After its launch, the company has launched various versions of the software to cater to different business owners' requirements. QuickBooks usage dominates the small business market by 80%. The company provides desktop-based and cloud-based versions of the software. From 2014 onwards there is a shift in trend. Before 2014, the business owners preferred the desktop model, but after the year 2014, more and more business owners are shifting to the cloud-based versions.

A whole chapter is dedicated to explaining the QuickBooks software. We discuss in detail the entire software. The services it provides and how a small business owner can benefit from it. There is a step-by-step guide to set up and install QuickBooks into your computer or other devices. After installation, guidelines are given to set up your account and add the vendor and customer accounts. A detailed explanation about how to enter employee details and how some versions can also manage automated payroll tasks. Reading about all this will make you understand the software's entire system and objective and realize how easy it is to operate. Technology has made even the most difficult and complicated tasks simpler for us. Now, it is our job to use technology for our benefit.

After you have understood the basic functioning of the software, you might want to invest in one. But this is not as easy as just purchasing one online. There are different packages of software available for different individuals. There are four basic packages available:

- QuickBooks Online

- QuickBooks Self-Employed

- QuickBooks Desktop

- QuickBooks App

Choosing the correct package that suits your requirements is also an important and difficult decision. In this book, we give you an overview of all the available packages and their specific features. All this information will hopefully make your decision easy.

In the US, the small to mid-size business market is denominated by QuickBooks users, and the owners are always on the lookout for professional QuickBooks bookkeepers for the job. You do not have to do it full time; you can manage all the accounts as a side hustle because QuickBooks software makes everything easy. You have to setup your accounting needs in the software, and most of the work is done by the software. However, it is n0t as easy as it sounds. The software is user-friendly, but you still require basic accounting knowledge and correct usage of the program. You might consider becoming a certified QuickBooks bookkeeper.

In this book, we have also discussed how in 2021, QuickBooks bookkeepers who work online make good money. There is a whole chapter in which we discuss working part-time as a QuickBooks bookkeeper is becoming a high-paying job. The average income of a QuickBooks professional in the US is discussed along with the US's best cities where you can practice QuickBooks bookkeeping. The considerations you should keep in mind while moving base to become a bookkeeper. California is the best place to be because the money QuickBooks bookkeepers are making there is approximately $10000 more than the US average per year.

There is an entire chapter dedicated to the ways you can become a certified QuickBooks bookkeeper. Sometimes a person knows what he/she wants but is unable to do anything because of the lack of guidance. This book gives you just that, proper step-by-step guidance on how to qualify yourself to become a QuickBooks bookkeeper. It does take time and effort, but you have numerous possibilities and options once you are qualified. To become a bookkeeper, you will need a certification. There are commonly three types of certifications you can choose from:

- QuickBooks Online Certification: Basic

- QuickBooks Desktop Certification: Basic

- QuickBooks Desktop Certification: Advance

The certifications are not just a one-time feat. You must keep your certifications up to date. You will require recertification each year by taking the certification exam. These tests are expensive but worth it.

Finally, we discuss the tricks and hacks you can use to use QuickBooks efficiently and effectively. These trips and hacks make your work easier and quicker. You will have to put in fewer hours. It is always wise to use trips and hacks and make the most benefit of the latest technologies. Sometimes doing online courses and certifications enable you to learn these tricks and hacks. Therefore, it is always recommended to keep your knowledge latest and keep improving your skills. The process of learning never stops. You keep learning throughout life. In present times learning has become a necessity rather than a luxury. In the ever-changing world, you will be left behind if you do not keep your skillset updated.

We hope you are going to find this book informative and helpful for your future professional endeavors. If bookkeeping is your calling, you should pursue it. It is one of the most in-demand services in the small business and mid-size business sector.

Chapter 1. Bookkeeping

In this chapter, we will focus on the basics. We will discuss the concept of bookkeeping and how it is the one-stop solution to all your accounting needs. Before anything else, we will try to understand what bookkeeping is and its importance.

Bookkeeping is an essential part of financial management. Small business owners sometimes try to manage the bookkeeping themselves, which becomes a reason for their businesses to fail. People do not realize that bookkeeping is a full-time job. You cannot manage a business and run numbers simultaneously. For this purpose, it is always wise to hire professionals for your accounting and bookkeeping.

1.1. What is Bookkeeping?

You must have heard about the term accounting. Bookkeeping is just that; it is related to managing the accounts. This term is used for business. The management of the complete finances of a business is termed bookkeeping.

To be more specific, we say that bookkeeping involves recording all the financing situations of a business. Bookkeeping is about keeping a record of all financial transactions daily, the influx and efflux of cash, the Payroll, profits, loss, investments, return on investments, and all the decisions related to the business's finance aspect. Bookkeeping helps the business owners keep track of all the information regarding the financial transactions.

After learning about what bookkeeping is, one wonders how a business owner can do all that by themselves? Not all business owners are literate about managing their finances. So, how can a business owner manage their accounts and finances? The simple answer to this question is a bookkeeper.

1.2. Who is A bookkeeper?

Bookkeepers are professionals who are responsible for managing all the finances of a company. They keep the owners aware of their present financial situation, record all related financial data and the total transactions made.

Correct bookkeeping is important for the business owners as well as prospected investors as well. Bookkeeping information is beneficial for the government and financial institutions as well. It will give a clear overview of the economic impacts of that certain business. Big companies and individual investors tend to research before they invest their money somewhere. The best and most reliable source of this information can be found in the company books. Looking at the books, the investor will decide whether he/she wants to invest in a certain company or project. In this way, bookkeeping is important for the owners because it is like his business introduction to the investment world. The better and more accurate the bookkeeping, the more chances of investment.

(A typical Bookkeeper)

1.3. Importance of Bookkeeping

When people start a new business, they tend to neglect the importance of good bookkeeping. Finance must be taken charge from day one and cannot be neglected for a single day. Now, what does bookkeeping do? It gives the company a tangible indicator of its performance and current situation. With this information's help, it becomes easier for the owner to make proper decisions financially, revenue generated, the profits, the loss, the income goals, etc. Each transaction must be recorded; the cash influx, efflux, credits, assets, liabilities all need to be recorded.

Bookkeeping is essential to keep the business afloat. Bigger companies usually hire accountants for the financial department, but it is not always possible for small business owners. So, small business owners mostly rely on hiring a bookkeeper. There whole accounting companies from where you can outsource a bookkeeper. It is cheaper than employing a full-time accountant, and a bookkeeper can easily manage a small business account. Anyone who starts a new business should never ignore the importance of keeping a record of every dime they spent and earn. Everything should be recorded.

1.4. Type of Accounting Method

Each business model follows one of the two accounting methods.

- Cash Basis of Accounting

- Accrual Basis of Accounting

To implement the bookkeeping function properly, the business owner should decide which accounting method they will follow. There are two basic models for accounting which are mentioned above. Now, what is the difference between these two? We will try to explain:

Cash Basis of Accounting:

In this type of accounting, a transaction is only recorded when a payment or cash is received or spent.

For example, if you buy fifty units of a product and the payment will be done after two weeks. No transaction will be recorded. It will only be recorded after two weeks when the payment is made.

This type of accounting model is now considered outdated in present times.

Accrual Basis of Accounting:

In accrual accounting, the expenses and revenue are put down when the transaction is made rather than when the payment is made.

We use the same example of buying 50 units of a product and payment must be made after two weeks. The record will be entered as soon as the receipt is received and will be recorded as payables. This is the more modern model for accounting and is widely accepted.

1.5. What do the bookkeepers do?

Now that you have a basic idea of who a bookkeeper is let us move to the set of responsibilities and jobs the Bookkeeper carries out. Listed are the tasks carried out by bookkeepers that make it convenient for the business owner to systematically run the business and provide a clear picture of its financial position. The responsibilities of bookkeepers include:

- Recording transactions every day.

- Sending invoices to clients.

- Keep track of payments.

- Prepare and maintain the payable ledger.

- Manage the cash flow.

- Compile and maintain all accounts.

1.5.1.   Record the Transactions Each Day

One of the jobs of the Bookkeeper is to enter the transactions each day. These include bank transactions. Nowadays, most companies use software to manage accounts. Some software has a function to generate automated bank feeds, which makes the task easier. You must keep a check on the cash, and precious data entry time is saved.

1.5.2.   Sending Invoices to Clients

Another responsibility of the Bookkeeper is to make receipts and invoices on purchases and send them to the clients.

1.5.3. Keep Track of Payments

Once the invoice is sent out, keeping a record of the payments received is also the Bookkeeper's responsibility. To keep a follow-up to receive pending payments is also the responsibility of the Bookkeeper. This is also known as being responsible for the receivable ledger.

1.5.4. Being Responsible for the Payable Ledger

Up to a certain amount determined by the business owner, the Bookkeeper makes the payments made on the owner's behalf. The Bookkeeper keeps records of all the payments made by the business. These include the payments to the suppliers, the extra cash available, and the other business expenses. The Bookkeeper records all this information and checks it every day.

1.5.5. Responsible for Managing the Cash Flow

One of the most important business rules is that a certain amount of cash is always available. The responsibility of the Bookkeeper is to always maintain the balance. This can be done by keeping a record of the day-to-day expenses and revenues. There should always be cash available for the day-to-day expenses. If the Bookkeeper suspects that the balance might be disrupted, he/she can offer advice to the owner by telling them ways to control the outflow and increase the inflow. These devices are almost always short-term fixes.

1.5.6. Compile All Accounts

The most important job of the Bookkeeper is to maintain the account books. The account records should all be up to date. These include all the ledgers. This is necessary for further investments and business decisions. The owner or prospect investor looks at these accounts and makes decisions according to the financial situations mentioned in the books.

1.6. How can a Bookkeeper be Beneficial for Business?

When you have a smaller business setup, it makes sense to manage your account yourself. But when the business expands, it is always a good idea to hire someone to take care of the bookkeeping. In this way, you can concentrate on expanding the business, and your Bookkeeper can take care of your day-to-day expenses. Many people do not hire a bookkeeper to save money but lose a lot of precious time in managing their account that they could be using to innovate and expand their business. Bookkeeping is a time-consuming job, and it should be left to the ones who are professionally trained to do so. They might as well do the job better and take less time. Following are listed a few benefits of hiring a bookkeeper:

1.6.1. Let you Focus on Your Business Strategy

As explained earlier, bookkeeping is a time-consuming task and demands attention to detail. Hiring a bookkeeper will save you all that time, and you will have plenty of time to focus on your business.

1.6.2. The Accounting Cost can be Saved.

If you have a small business, it is a better idea to hire a bookkeeper. If you hire an accountant, it will cost you more money and will become a liability. All the recording and accounts can be easily managed by a bookkeeper as well, and it will cost you a lot less money.

1.6.3. Double Check Your Cashflow

As a business owner, it is wise to always keep your eyes on the cashflow. But sometimes, you can get caught up, and in that situation, your Bookkeeper is there to tell you when you need to manage your cash flow. The Bookkeeper can warn your earlier, and you will still have time to manage the situation.

1.6.4. Be Informed of Current Financial Situation:

As the Bookkeeper is working on a day-to-day basis, he/she will be aware of all the business's financial situations. If you require any help and advice in this department, you can advise your Bookkeeper to have the complete information and explain the clear picture to you.

1.6.5. The Financial Data is Organized

In case you get hold of good software like QuickBooks, the Bookkeeper will work on the same software. The data is kept organized and transparent using the software because the margin for mistakes is highly reduced. The accountant can analyze the same data if you wish to get advice regarding business expansion and investment.

All in all, bookkeeping is particularly useful for business owners and investors alike. If you are not a businessperson and are interested in managing accounts for other small businesses, bookkeeping could be a good profession for you. The possibilities are limitless.

Chapter 2. QuickBooks Explained

With a basic knowledge of bookkeeping and what it means for small businesses, we can now discuss bookkeeping solutions. 2021 is all about solutions. Bookkeeping is a difficult task. It can be made easy with the help of accounting software. In this chapter, we are going to discuss software known as QuickBooks.

1.7. 2.1. What is QuickBooks?

If you are a small business owner and you aim to reach the next level, you might want to start keeping track of your finances. Most people control their finances when they start with a business, but it becomes difficult once the business gains pace. If you wish to expand your business, you will have to become more proactive, take hold of your finances, plan your next financial moves, keep an eye on day-to-day transactions, and organize a cash inflow and outflow system. You should set up a payroll. All the administrative work should be organized. Reading all this must have given you a headache. You were thinking about making some money; how are you going to manage all the financial stuff?

It would be best if you were thankful for your stars that you live in the 21st Century and there is software available for everything. In this chapter, we are discussing accounting software that works like magic. The software is known as QuickBooks. QuickBooks is the perfect tool for your financial necessities.

2.1.1. QuickBooks

It is accounting software that has features to organize the financial aspects of small businesses. The functions of QuickBooks include:

- Recording everyday transactions

- Track and record revenue and expense.

- Report generation for planning

- Prepare bills.

- Preparation of Payroll

The software is targeted towards small to medium-sized business setups. The QuickBooks software has features that make it possible for you to manage report generation, sales, cash flow, billing, revenue, taxes, reporting and expenses. The best part about the software is that there are inbuilt templates for reports that you can easily set and customize according to your specifications. It is easy to fill in data to an already prepared template compared to create by yourself. You can take control of your finances. It is a user-friendly software, but it has a learning curve, and you must have some basic accounting knowledge to operate and use this software. To use the software effectively, you must learn and have an in-depth knowledge of the software's essential functions.

2.1.2. The History of QuickBooks

In 1983, two inventors Scott Cook, and Tom Proulx, created the company Intuit. QuickBooks is a product of this company and was first launched in 2003 and targeted to small businesses. Over the years, better and more functional versions of the software have been launched. It remains one of the most widely used financial software for small businesses in the US. Different versions of the software are available in the international markets as well.

1.8. 2.2. QuickBooks Features

QuickBooks is amazing software with multiple features and functions. Here is a list of a few features of the software.

2.2.1. user Friendly

This software is super user-friendly. It is easy to use and navigate. All the financial features needed for a small to medium business are present in this one program. You do not have to record your data in different locations. This single software manages all your data.

2.2.2. Data Migration

This is a wonderful feature. If you want to transfer any data from QuickBooks to the spreadsheet, the transition is smooth. When there is a requirement to present the data on a spreadsheet, you can easily transfer all the software from the software without manually copying it.

2.2.3 Smooth Navigation

To use this software is easy because the navigation is simple. Everything is displayed clearly, and working is smooth. The program interface is clear and simple. However, you will have to learn and get used to the software before you can use it. You need to learn and understand all the financial terms and data entry methods to using this software effectively.

2.2.4. Smooth Transactions

The bank transactions are systematically recorded. Each entry you make is recorded. You can even set up regular transactions like salary payments, commissions, and bills repeated each month or every two weeks. These transactions will be automatically recorded.

2.2.5. Invoices

You can set up the invoices to be generated. The software can even generate invoices from your smartphone or tablet if they are installed with the software. You are not dependent on the computer system or laptop to generate business invoices. This feature is truly per the present requirement where everything can be achieved with a click of a button anytime, anywhere.

2.2.6. Calculate Tax

The feature of tax calculation is included in the software. To do taxes is always a tricky business. With the QuickBooks software, you can easily calculate the taxes quickly, efficiently, and accurately.

2.2.7. Projections

There is an automated feature in the software that will present you with projections. The software can generate all kinds of projections, including profits, expenses, sales etc. Getting the projections makes it easy to make financial decisions.

1.9. 2.3. Set-up QuickBooks

To use QuickBooks, you must have basic accounting knowledge and your own business. To use this software, you must be organized and willing to manage your finances seriously and as a daily feature. Some people install QuickBooks, put in the money, and forget it for months. Some purchase it and never even learn how to use it. QuickBooks does not work in that manner. You must be willing to learn and be consistent. Consistency is the key.

Let us discuss step-by-step guidelines for using QuickBooks.

2.3.1. Start

The first step will be to install the software properly. For installation, you must decide how you are going to use it. When you start the program, you will have two options:

- Network

- Custom Options

You will choose the Custom settings if you use the software on only one computer and use the same computer for installations.

In case more than one computer will use the software, chose the Network setting.

After that, choose the location or folder in your PC where you wish the software to be installed. Add your details, and then set up your company file. After that, click on the QuickBooks icon on the desktop.

2.3.2. setup

As soon as you click on the QuickBooks program, you will see an Easy Setup Wizard to help you set up your company file. By following the simple instructions, you can set up your company file. If you are new to this kind of software, you will be favorable to take help from the wizard. It will make the setup smooth and easy.

2.3.3. Vendor Setup

The next step will be setting up the accounts for your vendors. You will click the Vendor Center in the toolbar placed at the top. Next, select the New Vendor option, and create a vendor account. To add a new transaction, click the New Transaction and fill in the details. You can even bring in details from MS Excel and MS Word.

Add all the vendors similarly if you have more than one.

2.3.4. Setup Employee Accounts

To set up the employee accounts, click the Employee Center. Then click the New Employee button and then add the related information. After the information, you click the button for New Transaction. Add the salary details and any other transaction related to that specific employee. For salary, you must add the date and time for each month. For that, you will click Enter Time and then add the specific time and frequency of salary. Some employers pay per month, and some pay by the week. Put in the information accordingly.

2.3.5. Set Up Customer Account

Like the vendor and employee accounts, add the customer accounts. First, you go to the customer center, then Add Customer and Job. Here you can add it as an income source. Now add the related transaction by clicking New Transaction. Here you will add the information for payments and generation of invoices. There is a link for Excel as well as Word. You can bring the information from Excel and use Word to prepare letters for the customer.

2.3.6. Setup Report Generation

Next, you will go to the Report Center. All the information added by you can be viewed here. You can also customize the kind of report you want to generate. Reports for-profits, payments and expenses can be generated separately.

Add all the employees the same way if you have more than one.

1.10.2.4. Using QuickBooks

After the set up let us try to understand the day-to-day working of the QuickBooks software. What should we expect from the software? How can we manage our finances? What is the essential feature of the software? All these questions will be answered in the following part of this book. Together we will try to understand how the QuickBooks software works.

2.4.1. Chart of Accounts

So, what can you find on the chart of accounts? It will display the company's income, liability, expense accounts, assets, and equity to assign day-to-day transactions. This is what you will find:

- All the financial information about the company. It has the balance sheets, dividend, savings, receivables, and expenses. All this can be seen in the Chart of Accounts as a list.

- All the accounts related to the business, along with the account balances and account numbers. The details of the account holder will also be shared, like the full names and contact numbers. All these accounts will appear when you click the List Menu in the QuickBooks chart of accounts.

2.4.2. Other Lists

These include the list of vendors you deal with. All your regular customers and customer accounts are listed. All the items you deal with and their inventory is listed.

How this is favorable for the QuickBooks user:

- You can manage everything in one place. You do not have to manage multiple lists and settings. All information is compiled in one place. Either it is the product inventory or the vendor; all can be managed in one place.

- When you have all the information in a single space, you can move back and forth with all the lists, account details and information. You can simultaneously manage all your financial situations together. Everything is easy to navigate and extremely user-friendly.

- Another feature is the easy addition ad deletion of details. It is simple to add new accounts, and it is equally simple to delete accounts. Anytime you want to change the existing settings, it is easily done.

- Apart from adding ad deleting details, you can also edit details. Correction and updating details are easy in this software.

2.4.3. The Reports

Report templates are already included in the software so that you can customize them according to your needs. Add the details of your vendors, customers, and items. You must add dates and times as well.

Once you start adding details accordingly and you update daily transactions and activities. The reports will be forming themselves. Anytime you feel like having an overview of your business, you can pull out reports with just one click, and the reports will be generated. These reports will help you make important financial and investment decisions.

2.4.4. payroll

QuickBooks makes it easy to manage payrolls. With the software, you add the information, and the program will itself arrange the payroll process. The software can itself manage the accounts of the employees who have tax exemption. You can customize the settings for other incentives and deductions. If you turn on the setting, the software automatically sends emails, deposits, and receipts.

More than one person can manage the payrolls in this software, the one who has purchased the software has to allow the other users on the network by assigning permission.

1.11.2.5. QuickBooks Versions

QuickBooks is available in different types and versions. Each has a different package and fee. The versions are discussed in detail in the following chapters. Here we will list down the various versions of QuickBooks software:

- QuickBooks Online

- QuickBooks Self Employed

- QuickBooks App

- QuickBooks Desktop Products

    - QuickBooks Pro

    - QuickBooks for Mac

    - QuickBooks Enterprise

    - QuickBooks Premier

Chapter 3. Choosing the Best Version of QuickBooks

With the knowledge you have gained in the previous chapters, you know that QuickBooks is a financial solutions software. It was launched 25 years ago, and it has been the top choice for financial management since 2003. If you look at the company profits, they will show you an upward trend for the last 11 years straight. In addition to that, QuickBooks is used by 80% of small business owners in the US. This information enough should convince you to invest in the software.

Once you have decided to purchase the QuickBooks software, you are faced with yet another dilemma. Which version is for you? As discussed in the previous chapter, various versions of QuickBooks are available.

The QuickBooks family has a product for everyone. Here is a quick assessment of what you may want to purchase.

- If you are self-employed, run your company alone, and are looking to invest in a cloud-based accounting system, you should invest in QuickBooks for Self-Employed.

- If you own a small business and are interested in a cloud-based accounting system, you should invest in QuickBooks Online.

- If you are a small to medium-sized business owner, you must invest in QuickBooks Desktop.

- If you are already using QuickBooks and wish to update to another version, invest in QuickBooks Apps.

One of the deciding factors in any investment is the price range and affordability. This is the approximate price of the QuickBooks Packages available, making it easy for you to decide which product is best for you and is easy on the pocket.

Version	Usage	Price
QuickBooks Online	For businesspersons who want flexible financial access. This is suitable for small to mid-size business owners.	$25 up to $150/month
QuickBooks for Desktop	Suitable for small to medium size business owners in any sector	$399.99 with a one-time payment to $1,213 for one year
QuickBooks for Self- Employed	This is suitable for individual property agents, independent vendors, and Uber workers.	$15/ month

| QuickBooks Mac | This is for small to mid-size businesspersons who have their business set up on MAC | $399.99 paid once |

(Prices of Different Versions of QuickBooks)

1.12.3.1. QuickBooks for Self-Employed

QuickBooks Self Employed is the newest addition to the QuickBooks software versions. This is cloud-based software for financial services. It is specially designed for self-employed business owners and freelance service providers. It is ideal for independent workers like Lyft and Uber drivers. Property agents can also use it.

As this is a cloud-based program, you can access it with any computer or device with the given login.

(QuickBooks Self Employed Interface)

(Display of Reports on QuickBooks Self Employed)

Using this program, you can send data to TurboTax and track personal and business expenses from a single bank account. It also calculates the Quarterly Tax and reminds you of payment.

You will find three types of packages available for QuickBooks for Self-Employed:

3.1.1. QuickBooks Self Employed Package

Investing in this package gives you the following features:

- Users can easily connect to their bank account through QuickBooks Self -Employed

- The users can also connect to their credit cards.

- Users can track the expenses and income from the same account but can be separated into personal and business groups.

- The software calculates taxes quarterly.

3.1.2. QuickBooks for Self-Employed Tax Bundle

This offers all the services provided by the simple package with an addition:

- Users can connect to Intuit Turbo Box that enables them to pay taxes online each quarter.

3.1.3. QuickBooks for Self-Employed Live Tax Bundle

Provides all the services as the packages mentioned above with an addition that:

- Users can consult a CPA all year round.

- The users can get the services of a CPA to review taxes.

3.1.4. Benefit

It can track traveling and Mileage. You can enter trips with dates, reasons, and distance traveled. The system will automatically calculate deductions.

3.1.5. Drawback

Does not provide a service to generate invoices and online payments.

1.13.3.2. QuickBooks Online

QuickBooks Online is also a cloud-based financial solutions software. This had become exceedingly popular after 2014 when it was observed that more business owners preferred the online version over the desktop version. After that, the number of subscribers to the QuickBooks online version has been more than 1 million subscribers. This also tells us about the shift of business owners to a cloud-based system and shows their confidence in solely cloud-based software.

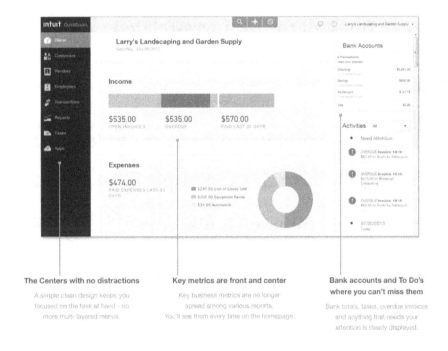

(QuickBooks Online Interface)

3.2.1. Common Features

The common features of QuickBooks Online are:

- Payable and Receivable Accounts:

The program can successfully manage expenses as well as income.

- Invoices and Bills:

It offers recurring or single-time invoices and can pay bills online.

- Management of Expenses:

The software can track all the business-related expenses.

- Reporting:

There are templates of prebuilt reports provided in the software, including the sales and tax reports. Simple Start gives 20 templates, Essentials gives 40 such templates, and gives 60 templates.

The QuickBooks online package does not need to be installed and comes in four packages:

3.2.2. QuickBooks Online Simple Start

The features provided in this package are:

- There is a single-user license.

- You can import your data from the QuickBooks Desktop version or MS Excel.

- You are entitled to consult two accounting professionals (bookkeepers and accountants)

3.2.3. QuickBooks Online Essentials

This version has all the abilities of the above version and, in addition to those capabilities, also has the following capabilities:

- The user is entitled to have 3 user licenses.

- The owner can set up user permissions to determine who is entitled to use the software.

3.2.4. QuickBooks Online Plus

All the capabilities of the Essentials version plus the following added qualities:

- Can set up 5 user licenses.

- The ability to track inventory.

- Users can create and send orders of purchase.

3.2.5. QuickBooks Online Advanced

This includes all the capabilities of the Plus version and the following capabilities:

- Can set up 25 user licenses.

- The ability for automated bill payment.

- The user can set up customized permissions.

3.2.6. Benefits

It is available for iOS, Windows, and Android devices. It can be connected to PayPal and Shopify for transactions.

3.2.7. Drawbacks

All the functions available in the QuickBooks Desktop are not available on QuickBooks Online. This version does not allow the addition of more than one company.

1.14.3.3. QuickBooks Desktop

The QuickBooks Desktop is the most elaborated software version among all three of the versions. Most business owners prefer cloud-based financial services, but if you prefer desktop-oriented software, the QuickBooks Desktop version is for you. This version further has six more variations suitable for different types of small businesses. The six types are briefly explained as follows:

3.3.1. QuickBooks Desktop Pro:

This is good for most small businesses that are not involved in product manufacture.

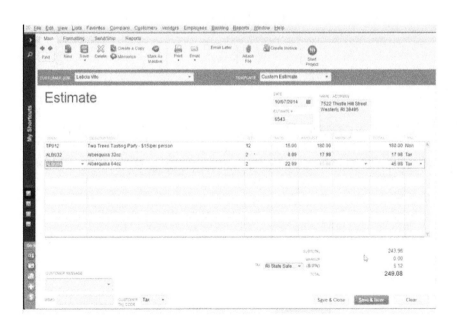

(QuickBooks Desktop Pro)

3.3.2. QuickBooks Desktop Premier:

This version is ideal for businesses involved in manufacturing, retail, and related to charity and non-profit organizations.

(Homepage of QuickBooks Desktop Premier)

3.3.3. QuickBooks Desktop Enterprise:

This is for large companies and enterprises. This version has industry reporting and a custom chart of accounts.

(QuickBooks Desktop Enterprise sales management)

3.3.4. QuickBooks Desktop Plus and QuickBooks Desktop Pro

The QuickBooks Desktop Plus and QuickBooks Desktop pro versions are sold as a yearly subscription rather than a one-time purchase. With these versions, your QuickBooks version is updated yearly, you are entitled to customer support, and your company data will be backed up.

3.3.5. QuickBooks for Mac

This is the only version compatible with Mac. It is like the QuickBooks Desktop Pro version. This is useful for most of the small businesses which are not involved in manufacturing.

1.15.3.4. QuickBooks Apps

QuickBooks Apps are applications that can be used in combination with the QuickBooks software to enhance their features. These are also known as add-on applications. These add-ons can be purchased from the QuickBooks website. Some of the QuickBooks Apps are as follows:

3.4.1. QuickBooks Payments

This can be used as an add-on for the QuickBooks desktop to add some payment functions. This app enables the business to accept payments online as well as through credit cards. This also enables emailing of invoices.

3.4.2. QuickBooks Point of Sale

This is a cloud-based application. It enables the businesses to accept credit cards, track inventory and ring up sales through a point-of-sale dashboard.

3.4.3. QuickBooks Payroll

This app enables businesses to provide salaries to up to 50 employees by cash deposit or check. Two types of versions are available:

- Self-Service Solutions

- Full-Service Solutions

The app can calculate the state, federal, and local taxes automatically.

1.16.3.5. Find the Best Version for You

QuickBooks has been a prominent player in the American market as a financial solution provider. The possibilities are numerous with this software. If you are a new business owner or plan to expand your business, QuickBooks will have a suitable version for you. But how to choose one which best suits your requirements? Here is a list of actions you can take before purchasing QuickBooks software. These activities will clear your dilemma, and the choice can be made easily:

3.5.1. Read Reviews

The best way to get a clear idea about a product is by reading reviews of people who have already used it. See which product is continually rated better. Read about the kind of services the software provides. Sometimes you get more knowledge about a product or service from reading someone's review. Always go through people's reviews and consider the products that most people are buying. Their performance must be the reason for their higher sales.

3.5.2. Take an Online Survey

When you are doing your research online, you may come across some online surveys which ask a few basic questions about your business and earnings. When you have entered your answers, the automated program will suggest the best software for you.

3.5.3. Talk to an Expert.

If you are still confused about which software to buy, try talking to an expert. A professional will be in a better position will suggest you according to your needs.

Chapter 4. The Best Way to Make Money In 2021

The year is all about small businesses and freelance work. In uncertain times everyone is pushing for a side hustle. We often have a misconception that the difficult part is setting up a business; other things follow once that part is covered. We cannot be more wrong in that approach. Though getting an idea, arranging for the finances, resources, place, and the raw material is tough and difficult to obtain, keeping the business afloat once launched is the trickier part. Most businesses come to an end, not because there is a lack of work, but because they could not manage the finances. Not all are indeed good at numbers and finance, and often, help is required.

People have now understood the importance of managing finances and are eager to outsource business financing. Here enters the role of bookkeepers and financial professionals. With the small business boom, there is also a huge demand for financial management. Our focus is on QuickBooks Bookkeeping and how it is the best way to earn money in 2021. In the following chapter, we will see how much a bookkeeper earns in the US. What services you can provide as a QuickBooks Bookkeeper, and which cities are the best for practicing QuickBooks bookkeeping.

1.17.4.1. Salary of Part-Time QuickBooks Bookkeepers

We hear that QuickBooks is a good way to earn money. It is a good side hustle. Be a part-time QuickBooks bookkeeper. No one tells us how much you can make and how much time should be spent to earn a certain amount.

Here we will give you a clear picture of the earnings. A breakdown by weekly, monthly, and yearly earnings.

According to the latest surveys up to 2021, in the United States of America, a QuickBooks bookkeeper's average salary is $50,618 a year. This comes to be around $4,220 per month, around $1000 a week, and about $24 an hour. This sounds very decent for a part-time job. Especially in recent times when we are surrounded by uncertainty, QuickBooks Bookkeeping is a good side hustle.

The figure of $50,618 is the average; it has been reported that you can earn as high as $95,000, and the earnings can even be as low as

$29,000. If you want to look at its percentile wise it will look something like this:

- 90th Percentile earnings $93,500 yearly

- 75th Percentile earnings $ 58,500 yearly

- 25th Percentile earnings $ 36,000 yearly

As the survey is based on all kinds of bookkeepers, from entry-level ones to more professional ones, you see a huge income difference. This also suggests that the more experienced and professional abilities you acquire, the higher you will earn.

The following charts must explain the salaries of part-time QuickBooks bookkeepers in a better way.

- The Yearly Average Income of QuickBooks Bookkeepers

$29,000

National Average

$50,618 /year

$24 /hour

$95,000

- The Average Monthly Income of QuickBooks Bookkeepers

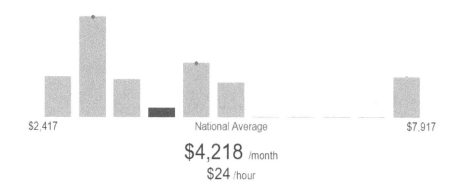

$2,417   National Average $7,917

$4,218 /month

$24 /hour

- The Average Weekly Income of QuickBooks Bookkeepers

$558   National Average $1,827

$973 /week

$24 /hour

- The Hourly Average Income of QuickBooks Bookkeepers

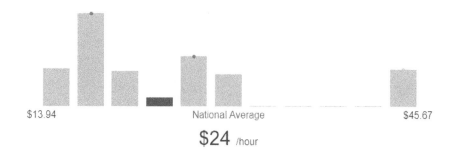

$13.94   National Average $45.67

$24 /hour

The following table will give you a better understanding of the earning possibilities that come with QuickBooks bookkeeping. These are the results of a recent survey. Thus, they also indicate the present trends as well.

	Annual Salary	Monthly Pay	Weekly Pay	Hourly Wage
Top Earners	$93,500	$7,791	$1,798	$45
75th Percentile	$58,500	$4,875	$1,125	$28
Average	$50,618	$4,218	$973	$24
25th Percentile	$36,000	$3,000	$692	$17

1.18.4.2. The Top 10 Highest Paying Cities for Bookkeepers in the USA

The survey also indicated that the pay varies from location to location. Here we have compiled the top ten cities in the US where QuickBooks Bookkeepers' salaries are higher than the national average.

The state that offers the highest salaries to the QuickBooks Bookkeepers is, without any doubt, California. Companies in California employ the highest paying QuickBooks bookkeepers. The top salaries are recorded from San Francisco, CA. San

Francisco's salaries are around $13,636 higher than the national average. That counts for a whopping 26.9% higher average salary than the average. The second highest is Fremont, CA. The third position is held by San Jose, CA, with a $9,337 higher average salary than the national average of $50,618. Following close behind in Oakland, CA, with an $8,668 higher average. After this is Tanana, AK, with an average yearly salary of $ 59,078, number six is Wasilla, AK, with a higher average of $8459 than the national average. Hayward, CA, has an average income of $58,044 for QuickBooks Bookkeepers. At number eight is Sunnyvale, CA, with an average income higher by $7,268 than the national average. The average salary for this part-time job in Jackson, WY, is $57,870. The last of the tip than in Norwalk, CT.

The table will give you a better understanding of the top ten cities for QuickBooks Bookkeeping.

City	Annual Salary	Monthly Pay	Weekly Pay	Hourly Wage
San Francisco, CA	$64,254	$5,355	$1,236	$30.89
Fremont, CA	$61,596	$5,133	$1,185	$29.61
San Jose, CA	$59,956	$4,996	$1,153	$28.82
Oakland, CA	$59,286	$4,940	$1,140	$28.50
Tanaina, AK	$59,078	$4,923	$1,136	$28.40
Wasilla, AK	$59,077	$4,923	$1,136	$28.40
Hayward, CA	$58,044	$4,837	$1,116	$27.91
Sunnyvale, CA	$57,886	$4,824	$1,113	$27.83
Jackson, WY	$57,870	$4,823	$1,113	$27.82
Norwalk, CT	$57,752	$4,813	$1,111	$27.77

Having mentioned all these cities does not mean that the prospects of getting jobs are higher in these places. This is just an overview of the average income you can earn in these states. Other factors should also be considered when you decide to work in a specific location. For example, you see many six cities from the state of California. You might be tempted to search for work there. But according to research, the job market for QuickBooks Bookkeepers is not active in California. The companies might be paying higher, but the job opportunities are less. It is always smarter to work in a place where the prospects of being employed are better. However, you might be earning more if you locate in one of these locations. It all depends upon the service you provide and the requirements of the employer. It would help if you did your survey before deciding to change your location.

Another important consideration when thinking about making a location change as a QuickBooks bookkeeper is the cost of living. San Francisco may be paying the highest, but the basic cost of living is high. You might be earning more but even spending more on necessities like housing, insurance, and food. This might not prove to be a smart move. For a QuickBooks bookkeeper, an important factor in choosing a location might be the salary and a place with a lower cost of living.

1.19.4.3. Best Paying QuickBooks Bookkeeping Jobs in the USA

This is true for any field of practice that your job prospects and earnings increase if you specialize in a specific field. This part will discuss the five types of specialized QuickBooks Bookkeepers who earn higher than the typical part-time QuickBooks bookkeepers. All the jobs discuss earn around $7,683 to $14,935 more than the national average. This makes the values about 14.5% to 29.5% more than a regular QuickBooks bookkeeper's salary. So, it is highly recommended that you try to specialize in a certain domain to improve your higher earnings chances. The five jobs we will be discussing are:

1. CPA Firm Bookkeeper

2. QuickBooks Remote Bookkeeper

3. Telecommute Bookkeeper

4. At home Bookkeeper

5. QuickBooks Consultant

4.3.1. CPA Firm Bookkeeper

The Bookkeeper associated with a CPA firm earns around $65,553 annually. This translates to a $5,463 paycheck each month, roughly $1,261 a week. In this case, you will be charging approximately $31.52 an hour. If you consider it seriously, this is quite a decent earning.

4.3.2. QuickBooks Remote Bookkeeper

This job fetches you a whopping $64,952 annual earning. This is more than $14,300 than the national average. You will be earning $5,413 per month, which is decent.

4.3.3. Telecommute Bookkeeper

According to the survey, the Telecommute Bookkeeper earns $60 795 per year. This is $10,000 higher than the national average. This brings you a decent paycheck of $5,000 per month and weekly earnings of $1,000 plus. Working as a telecommute bookkeeper, you will be charging approximately $30 by the hour.

4.3.4. At Home Bookkeeper

The best thing about this type of bookkeeping is that you can practice it from the comfort of your house, and you will be earning good money. You will be making savings on the commute time, fuel expenses, and outside food expenses, if you practice work from home. Continuing from home, you will still be earning $8,000 more than the national average. You will be earning around $5,000 per month from the comfort of your home.

4.3.5. QuickBooks Consultant

As a QuickBooks consultant, you can earn $57,986 per year. The good part about this is that you can work part-time and take home a paycheck of around $5,000 each month.

This table will give you a better understanding of the benefits of specializing and the financial prospects related to it.

Job Title	Annual Salary	Monthly Pay	Weekly Pay	Hourly Wage
CPA Firm Bookkeeper	$65,553	$5,463	$1,261	$31.52
Quickbooks Remote	$64,952	$5,413	$1,249	$31.23
Telecommute Bookkeeper	$60,795	$5,066	$1,169	$29.23
Work From Home Bookkeeper	$58,536	$4,878	$1,126	$28.14
Quickbooks Consultant	$57,986	$4,832	$1,115	$27.88

Chapter 5. Becoming a QuickBooks Bookkeeper

Now that you have a thorough understanding of bookkeeping and QuickBooks, it must be clear that in present times the knowledge of QuickBooks is essential if you want to work in the US small business community. Sometimes learning the software is not enough. To get the job, you require to show some qualifications and expertise as well. Unfortunately, we are still living in the workplace where showing your qualifications and certificates is essential to acquire a job. But when we talk about QuickBooks, there is no harm in doing a certification. Doing a certification will open many opportunities for you. No one wants to hire an unqualified person. With this Certification, you will be considered qualified for the job. The Certification might teach you the software's basics, but the actual learning is always done practically. Nevertheless, gaining this Certification is beneficial even if it gives you a head start.

Sometimes you have this clear picture in your mind regarding what you want to do but you have no access to proper guidance. Many people want to work as bookkeepers and want to learn further to upgrade their skill set but there is no one to guide them. The information around us is so much that sometimes we are overwhelmed by the excess of information rather than its lack. Sometimes all we need is a plain simple instruction in the right direction. This chapter does just that. It will push you one step further in the right direction.

In this chapter, we will discuss how you can gain this Certification, how much it cost, how long it takes to become certified, the difficulty level of this Certification, the types of certifications available for QuickBooks; all will be discussed in this chapter. In this chapter, we will discuss:

- The type of investment required for Certification.

- Different courses available

- Information about QuickBooks Certification.

- The course fees.

- The duration of the course

1.20.5.1. The Type of Investment Required for Certification

Getting a certification is a big investment. Not only are you investing your money, but you also invest your time and money in such courses as well. In present times, the world is ever-changing and keeping up with the fast-moving times has become mandatory. Otherwise, you will be left behind. Similarly, if you are a bookkeeper, you must upgrade your skillset. You might be employed right now, but what if the employer changes technology and you are no more required to work for him/her, and they hire a person with better qualifications. For such times it is important to be well prepared and keep up with times. Your aim should be to become an asset to the company rather than a liability.

1.21.5.2. The Different Courses Offered

There are three types of courses offered for QuickBooks Certification. Two of them are for the QuickBooks Desktop, and one is for QuickBooks online. Nowadays, most people prefer a cloud-based financial management system, so it would be wise to take the Certification for the online version. The different types of certifications offered are:

- QuickBooks Online Edition: Basic

- QuickBooks Desktop Edition: Basic

- QuickBooks Desktop Edition: Advanced

1.22.5.3. Information About QuickBooks Certification

If you are working as an employee, getting a QuickBooks certificate will reassure your employer of your abilities with the software and convince them that you are an asset to their company. Certification will enhance your credibility. This will equip you with the expertise to deal with any situation that involves QuickBooks. You will be in a better position as a QuickBooks certified employee to tackle tricky situations involving QuickBooks.

When you pass the exam, you will gain the following skills, and your certificate will be proof of your abilities:

- Easily use the main measures of QuickBooks and manage business accounts on the software.

- You can manage all the accounting functions like Payroll, transactions, invoices, and sales smoothly with QuickBooks software.

- Can solve and manage complex scenarios that come up while using QuickBooks.

One thing you should keep in mind, the certifications are not cheap, they cost high prices. But you should consider investing in this Certification as a step towards your better career. You will get profits from this investment very soon.

1.23.5.4. Why Should You Invest

It is a known fact that QuickBooks Certifications do not come cheap. If you are an employer, you might feel that this is a lot of investment, and the courses are time-consuming. If you have many employees, the cost might be an issue for sure. If you are a freelance bookkeeper, the fee might be a big investment. But consider this a useful investment. This is one of the investments you should make. Some business owners consider it an initial investment, and the profits and dividends are gained when the work is done more efficiently and faster.

A lot of groups are offering QuickBooks certification courses. If you are an employer, you can look for bundle package discounts and monthly packages. If you are a freelance service provider, you should look for packages that offer monthly installments as one-time payments are sometimes difficult to pay at once.

You should always look for online courses. Nowadays, many online courses are available, and you can take them from the comfort of your home or office. This can save you the commute expenses and the time which is wasted with the commute. Always look for certifications with live tutoring. These sessions are more interactive, there are live questions and answers sessions, and you learn more this way.

You should be convinced not to take up a QuickBooks certification. If you are still not convinced, maybe this is not for you. But if you want to further your career in bookkeeping, this Certification is essential.

1.24.5.5. The Certification Fee

Most bookkeepers follow the method that they do their training from a tutor and then take the certification exam. Two groups conduct the Certification:

- Intuit, through their ProAdvisor Program

- NBA (National Bookkeepers Association)

Intuit is the maker of QuickBooks, and they conduct the test for free. However, they cover their cost by making you purchase the mandatory membership, which is hundreds of dollars. You will have to become a member to get access to the test.

NBA conducts the other Certification. This is a much affordable option. If you decide to take the test through them, the fee is $150 for the ones who are taking the test for the first time. This fee includes a practice test and the actual test. At successful completion, you get a certificate. The certification must be updated every year. The fee for each subsequent year is around $75.

1.25.5.6. The Length of Courses

There is no specific length for courses. The courses and workshops are carried out by professionals who specialize in QuickBooks software. The Certification is only a 2-to-4-hour program. If you are already familiar with the software, you might just book your test and pass. But for someone, the learning might take from weeks to months. All this depends upon few factors:

- Do you have basic knowledge about the software?

In this case, if you have basic knowledge and take the test straight away, the chances are that you might not be able to gain

Certification. It would be best if you had more than basic knowledge to pass the Certification. You should not take these exams lightly. Since these exams are expensive, you should prepare your best before taking the exam to get greater chances of passing.

- The Certification you might wish to do.

So, there are different certifications offered. In the Desktop version certifications, there is a basic certificate and an advanced certificate. As the name indicates, the advanced certification will be harder and thus require more expertise.

- When you decide to take the test

You must be responsible when you decide the date to take the test. Do not take the test before you are fully prepared. If you decide the test date before proper preparation, the chances are that you might not be able to pass.

Mostly, the tests can be completed in one sitting. The level of the exams is according to the Certification you wish to do. It is recommended to get the basic Certification before you try to obtain an advanced certification.

Chapter 6. Hacks and Tricks for QuickBooks

With every software, you should know about the tricks and tips to make your work more efficient and streamlined. The same is the case with QuickBooks. You can use the experience of others to better your work. You must have heard the term; time is money, and these tips and tricks save your time. And by saving time, they save your money. In present times we are blessed with technology, and we should try to benefit from t as much as possible. The lives we lead in present times are quite stressful, and the work-life balance is frankly off-balance. In such a situation, it is wise to take as much help as possible. That help can be from technology, or you can even benefit from others' experiences and mistakes. Here we will discuss some hacks and tricks the professionals from the field have agreed upon and shared with everyone to benefit from. Here is a list of a few tricks and hacks to make your work quicker and easier.

The trend of 2021 is focused more on cloud-based QuickBooks software. In this chapter, we will discuss the tips and tricks we can apply in QuickBooks Online to gain better results. We have compiled a list of six hacks that you might find helpful:

- Cash receipts should be created.

- Use attachments.

- Use keyboard shortcuts.

- Automate the emails.

- Use QuickBooks Online to track the time.

- Always use the bank rules

1.26.6.1. Cash Receipts Should be Created.

It is always a good idea to organize your working space. The same is the case with finances. If you have your cash receipts created and recorded, you will easily overview all money received at any time. With QuickBooks Online, you can enter the details in the sales center and review the records anytime you want. This is a feature of QuickBooks online, which is easy to use and convenient for financial tracking.

- Usage

How you will create cash receipts is simple, go to the sales transactions and create a file med cash receipts. Next, go to the filter list and go to 'Money Received' and enter the date appropriately.

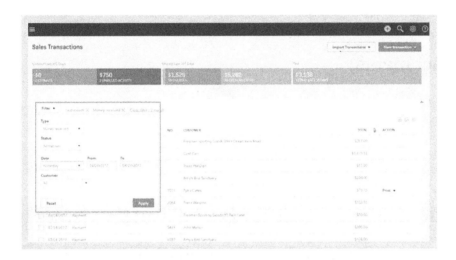

(Cash Receipt Usage)

1.27.6.2. Use Attachments

This is a hack that is overlooked a lot of the time, and most people ignore using it. The hack is to attach all related forms and documents to the vendor accounts to be managed at once. For example, you can attach a W-9 to the vendor's account.

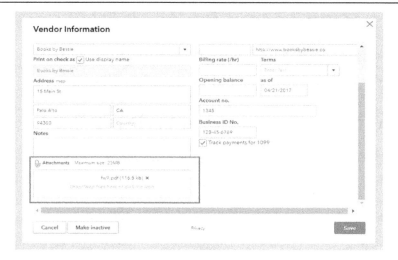

(Using Attachments)

So, when you use attachments, you can also attach the bank accounts' files and the credit card details and statements. When all the documents are attached and compiled in one place, they will be easy to review. Another pro tip will be to use naming conventions. This will make the work more streamlined and easier to track. According to experts, not using attachments wastes time you could be spending on other activities. There is no need to work so hard if you have applications in your software that make your work easier and smoother to operate. If you are using a mobile version of QuickBooks online, you can even take a screenshot of any receipt and attach it to the folder. In the same way, you can even attach the invoices and enter the yearly or monthly estimates. If you have the add-on of QuickBooks Payments, you can even receive payments.

1.28.6.3. Use Keyboard Shortcuts

This is also a huge time saver. When you are working on multiple things, clicking from one program to another makes everything confusing. The same is the case with QuickBooks. When you are managing multiple entities, you need to work fast, and shortcuts are a lifesaver. Following is a summary of all the important shortcuts found within QuickBooks.

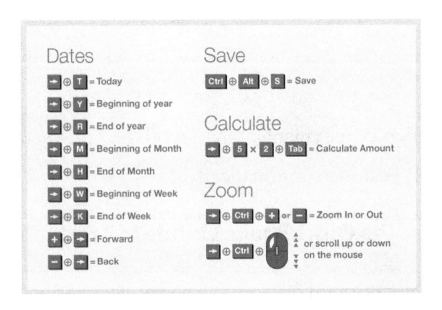

(QuickBooks shortcuts)

1.29.6.4. Automate the emails.

For all the regular payments and receiving, automation is the way to go. You should automate your emails for sales, financial statements, and invoices. You must be thinking about how to go about this? It is easy; you will first set different reports scheduled to email on a specific date. For example, you can set a schedule that emails you your financial statement monthly. You can even get an email for the collection report, and the sales report every week. This will help you keep track of the open invoices.

Apart from this, you can schedule the payments that have to be sent out weekly or monthly. You can arrange for the recurring invoices to be sent automatically by email. Again, if you use the app QuickBooks payments, the received payments can be automatically recorded automatically.

1.30.6.5. Use the QuickBooks Online to Track Time

If time tracking is tough for you, the newer versions of QuickBooks Online will help you. In the older versions of the program, you had to import the T reports to QuickBooks. In the newer versions, you can create the T sheets within QuickBooks online. These are the integrated T sheets. This means that any change, addition, or deletion would apply automatically to the T sheet, and it will be updated by itself. You will not have to manually update the information. This process is carried out in a seamless manner. You can create several employee T sheets and even approve several T sheets simultaneously.

1.31.6.6. Always use the Bank Rules

This is a simple and logical hack. The bank rules are already made, and time tested. If you implement them and set your regular payments to the utilities, vendors, suppliers, etc., on bank rules, the task will become easier. This can save a lot of time for you as well. At the end of the month, all you will need to do is an overview of all the payments carried out in a smooth and streamlined fashion.

These hacks and tips may seem simple but implementing them can save you hours and hours' worth of labor. There will be far fewer things on your mind. It is a one-time setup, and it will be automated from then on. You will easily manage the payments, receiving, employee timesheets, Payroll, and everything else with ease, and you will become less stressed.

Chapter 7. QuickBooks Usage in Small Businesses

Many small businesses use QuickBooks to manage their finances. The software takes care of their bill payments, monitors their cash flow, and manages invoices. QuickBooks is a good software to generated automated monthly financial reports as well as yearly financial reports. Some business owners manage their accounts themselves and are pro users of the software, but most business owners employ professionals to manage their accounts. QuickBooks certified bookkeepers are employed by small to mid-size business owners to manage their accounts.

Small business owners use QuickBooks for several functions and use. Following are the functions for which the small business owners use QuickBooks:

- Make and track invoices.

- Monitor expenses and other bills.

- Generate business and financial statements.

- Manage payroll.

- Do the inventory.

- Simplify taxes.

- Online payments.

- Record Receipts.

- Manage mileage.

1.32.7.1. Make and Track Invoices

The software has the option to create invoices, and you can easily print them or directly send them to your customers. Each invoice generated by the software will be automatically recorded in the system. In this way, you can track all the amount that has already been paid, and the receivables will also be displayed.

1.33.7.2. Monitor Expenses and Other Bills

You have an option to link the QuickBooks software to your accounts and credit cards. This will enable the program to record all payments and bills automatically and keep a record. It will be available for your view whenever you require.

You can enter other bills you receive in the system and take care of the payables. This will help you keep track of your expenses and payables. The software will make sure you do not miss your payments. If you attach the QuickBooks payment app, the payments can even be managed automatically.

1.34.7.3. Generate Business Financial Statements

The software can generate financial statements that will give you an overview of your business performance. The kind of statements you can generate with the QuickBooks software are:

- Cashflow Statement

- Profit and Loss Statement

- Balance Sheets

1.35.7.4. Manage Payroll

The software can manage the Payroll and working hours of each employee automatically. You must create a separate account for each employee, enter each employee's information, and schedule the salary, deductions, schedules, and hours. All can be managed automatically by the software. If you use the software, you can easily manage:

- Payment to the employees can be made by checks or cash.

- The taxes can be deducted automatically, and the tax-exempt employee payments are also managed.

- The software fills tax forms automatically

- The payroll taxes can be managed automatically.

1.36.7.5. Do the Inventory.

The software manages the inventory. It records the quantities and keeps track of the total cost of inventory. The software will indicate when the inventory is getting low, and there is a need to replenish. This all is not done automatically, you will have to enter the amounts manually, but they will be managed and calculated automatically.

1.37.7.6. Simplify Taxes

Taxes is one of the most difficult parts of the business. Most people are fearful of taxes, and in the end, their taxes are piled up. QuickBooks takes care of your taxes. The Tax becomes difficult because your financial statements are not in order. QuickBooks makes the financial statements simplified, and you can easily print them out and let a tax preparer assess the statements and use the required information.

1.38.7.7. Online Payments

The QuickBooks Payments app enables you to accept payments directly from your customers. This app is integrated into the software, so all the payments are recorded in the system automatically.

1.39.7.8. Record Receipts

The QuickBooks app makes it possible for the business owner to upload all the payment and expense receipts to the software, and they can be easily scanned and recorded in the system.

1.40.7.9. Manage Mileage

If you use your vehicle for business purposes, a tax deduction is applied. But to receive the tax deduction, you will have to prove your traveling. You get a deduction of 57.5 cents per mile. To record the miles, you can link QuickBooks Online to your vehicle's GPS, and it will easily record your miles, date, and time

Conclusion

If you have read the whole book, many of your doubts must have been cleared regarding bookkeeping and QuickBooks. This is an amazing opportunity for you to avail yourself if you want to take up bookkeeping as a profession. It is always a better idea to keep up with the current trends and technology because it ensures better job and working opportunities. Therefore, we have mentioned QuickBooks. Being a QuickBooks certified bookkeeper gives you an edge in business. This is because most small to mid-size businesses have installed the QuickBooks software for their financial management. There are different versions of QuickBooks available:

- QuickBooks Self-Employed

- QuickBooks Online

- QuickBooks Desktop

- QuickBooks Apps

QuickBooks is user-friendly and is compatible with other programs like MS Word and MS excel. Different versions are available that are compatible with iOS, android, windows, and Mac operating systems.

It will be a good idea to specialize in cloud-based QuickBooks software because, as of 2014, more and more business owners are interested in keeping their records on the cloud-based package offered by QuickBooks. If you are planning to get your Certification any time soon, the cloud-based product should be your focus. There is a basic course offered in QuickBooks Online; you should consider that.

Another consideration when thinking about QuickBooks bookkeeping seriously is what type of Bookkeeper you are going to be. According to a survey, these five types of part-time QuickBooks bookkeepers are making the highest number of average incomes:

- CPA Firm Bookkeeper

- QuickBooks Remote Bookkeeper

- Telecommute Bookkeeper

- At home Bookkeeper

- QuickBooks Consultant

The next most important point to think about is your location. At different locations in America, bookkeepers make different yearly incomes. The QuickBooks bookkeepers make the highest yearly earnings in San Francisco, California. But before quickly packing your bags towards the sunny state, keep in mind the expenses as well. Before shifting your location, always consider the basic expenses and how you will be managing them. It may be possible that you are earning less in one city, but the cost of living is cheaper, and in another city, you might be making more money, but the expenses are equally higher. In the latter case, you end up losing more money. So, always take a well-thought-out and informed decision.

In all, if you are someone good with numbers and have a consistent work ethic, you can very manage to be a QuickBooks bookkeeper. You can even work as a freelance service provider. Providing services is also generally a risk-free approach. The only investment you make is the training you do and the courses you take. After that, all is gain. In this way, you can set your schedule and take up as much work as you can manage. In present times where the future has become unpredictable, freelancing is the way to go.

CPSIA information can be obtained
at www.ICGtesting.com
Printed in the USA
BVHW051450030621
608732BV00004B/1033